Praise for *The Future of Christian Thec*

"This is, quite simply, a wonderful book. At one level, it is vintage David Ford, in that it contains themes that he has worked on for three decades. At another level, it is all new, and provides an ever deeper integration of themes which is profoundly creative rather than systematic and invites each reader to engage and make fresh connections. At a time when the church is changing so quickly and therefore attentive theology changes also, David Ford more successfully than any other theologian I know bridges the concerns of the academy and those of the worshipping communities. This book contributes massively to that bridge building."

Iain Torrance,
President of Princeton Theological Seminary

"David Ford's *The Future of Christian Theology* is a manifesto for a theology adequate to its new context in the twenty-first century. It is not so much a program for a new theological project as a vision of theology oriented as a search for wisdom, focused on the Spirit, in service to the Church, guided by Scripture construed above all as drama and explicitly read in an inter-religious context, and engaged with the struggles of its host society. It's a bold, powerful and provocative vision."

David H. Kelsey,
Weigle Professor Emeritus of Theology, Yale Divinity School

Blackwell Manifestos

In this new series major critics make timely interventions to address important concepts and subjects, including topics as diverse as, for example: Culture, Race, Religion, History, Society, Geography, Literature, Literary Theory, Shakespeare, Cinema, and Modernism. Written accessibly and with verve and spirit, these books follow no uniform prescription but set out to engage and challenge the broadest range of readers, from undergraduates to postgraduates, university teachers and general readers – all those, in short, interested in ongoing debates and controversies in the humanities and social sciences.

Already Published

The Idea of Culture	Terry Eagleton
The Future of Christianity	Alister E. McGrath
Reading After Theory	Valentine Cunningham
21st-Century Modernism	Marjorie Perloff
The Future of Theory	Jean-Michel Rabaté
True Religion	Graham Ward
Inventing Popular Culture	John Storey
Myths for the Masses	Hanno Hardt
The Future of War	Christopher Coker
The Rhetoric of RHETORIC	Wayne C. Booth
When Faiths Collide	Martin E. Marty
The Future of Environmental Criticism	Lawrence Buell
The Idea of Latin America	Walter D. Mignolo
The Future of Society	William Outhwaite
Provoking Democracy	Caroline Levine
Rescuing the Bible	Roland Boer
Our Victorian Education	Dinah Birch
The Idea of English Ethnicity	Robert Young
Living with Theory	Vincent B. Leitch
Uses of Literature	Rita Felski
Religion and the Human Future	David E. Klemm and William Schweiker
The State of the Novel	Dominic Head
In Defense of Reading	Daniel R. Schwarz
Why Victorian Literature Still Matters	Philip Davis
The Savage Text	Adrian Thatcher
The Myth of Popular Culture	Perry Meisel
Phenomenal Shakespeare	Bruce R. Smith
Why Politics Can't Be Freed From Religion	Ivan Strenski
What Cinema is!	Andrew Dudley

The Future of Christian Theology

David F. Ford

A John Wiley & Sons, Ltd., Publication

This edition first published 2011

Blackwell Publishing was acquired by John Wiley & Sons in February 2007. Blackwell's publishing program has been merged with Wiley's global Scientific, Technical, and Medical business to form Wiley-Blackwell.

Registered Office
John Wiley & Sons Ltd, The Atrium, Southern Gate, Chichester, West Sussex, PO19 8SQ, United Kingdom

Editorial Offices
350 Main Street, Malden, MA 02148-5020, USA
9600 Garsington Road, Oxford, OX4 2DQ, UK
The Atrium, Southern Gate, Chichester, West Sussex, PO19 8SQ, UK

For details of our global editorial offices, for customer services, and for information about how to apply for permission to reuse the copyright material in this book please see our website at www.wiley.com/wiley-blackwell.

Library of Congress Cataloging-in-Publication Data

Ford, David, 1948–
The future of Christian theology / David F. Ford.
p. cm. – (Blackwell manifestos)
Includes bibliographical references and index.
ISBN 978-1-4051-4272-4 (hardcover: alk. paper) – ISBN 978-1-4051-4273-1 (pbk.: alk. paper)
1. Theology–Methodology. I. Title.
BR118.F718 2011
230.01–dc22

2010033793

A catalogue record for this book is available from the British Library.

Set in 11.5/14pt Bembo by SPi Publisher Services, Pondicherry, India
Printed in Singapore by Ho Printing Singapore Pte Ltd

2 2012

For Rebecca, Rachel and Daniel
With joy

Contents

Preface

The question this book tries to answer is: how might Christian theology in the twenty-first century be creative and wise?

The past century has been the most theologically prolific in Christian history. Today more energy than ever is going into theological scholarship and thinking, wisdom-seeking in engagement with God, church, and society, and communicating theology in many modes and media. This book is for anyone who is interested in the future of this global enterprise.

A few parts of the book (especially chapters 8 and 9) might be of special interest to those who have theological scholarship, thought, education, or communication as their jobs, but I have tried even in those chapters to make what is said accessible and relevant to a wider readership. Overall, the hope is that, whatever the careers and commitments of theologically interested readers, this manifesto might stimulate them to seek wisdom about important issues and might help them shape personal and social life in the light of what they discover. I have found doing theology to be extraordinarily gripping, stretching, and surprising, and my deepest desire for this manifesto is that others might be drawn into a similar engagement.

Why a manifesto? I was immediately attracted by this watchword of the series when I received the invitation to contribute to it. It invites to a distillation of thinking and a concentration on what is most important and generative for the future. It is also about going public with a program that one hopes might be taken up by others. One surprise for me in the course of writing it was the extent to which the manifesto requirements made me rethink things. At the beginning I expected it could be written "off the top of my head" and quite quickly; no sooner was it under way than I found myself drawn into all sorts of depths and complexities and was challenged to reconsider a range of categories, judgments, and orientations.

Stretching to meet those challenges took far longer than anticipated, and I thank Wiley-Blackwell, especially Rebecca Harkin, Isobel Bainton, and Lucy Boon, for their patience and encouragement. I have many other debts of gratitude. Simeon Zahl has been a dream research assistant, both on the big issues of theological judgment and on the details of references and the preparation of the final text. Aref Nayed and Steven Kepnes, authors of the forthcoming companion volumes on the future of Islamic and Jewish theology, have been wonderful intellectual companions. Our intensive meeting in Abu Dhabi to discuss all three manifestos was especially fruitful, and it led to extensive revision of mine. The influence of many years of conversation with Aref and Steve, as well as other Muslim and Jewish thinkers, is explicit in chapter 7 on "Inter-Faith Blessing," but it is implicit throughout – they have become part of my life, alongside Christian and secular friends and thinkers. Nicholas Adams' years as Academic Director of the Cambridge Inter-Faith Programme have been especially stimulating, and the Programme's team members (Catriona Laing, Barbara Bennett, Miriam Lorie, and Cheryl Slater) and others associated with it (Mohammed Abdul Latif Jameel, Alison Richard, Leonard Polonsky, Georgette Bennett, Abdullah Al Salmi, Omar Zawawi, Ghazi Bin Muhammad, Abdulrahman Al Salmi, Michael Bos, John Marks, Emilia Mosseri, Edward McCabe, James Kidner, Richard Chartres, Tim Ryan, David and Sharon Rosen, James Marrow, William Salomon, Sarah Coakley, Peter Agar, Graham Allen, Kate Pretty, Debbie Patterson Jones, Jennifer Barnes, Richard Wilson, Stuart and Sibella Laing, Tim Winter, Richard Rex, Fraser Watts, Simon Franklin, Sarah Snyder, Mike Higton, Ahmad Achtar, Diana Lipton, and others) have given vital support. Discussions with graduate students have been continually fruitful. This is, as a result, a Christian manifesto for a complexly religious and secular world, and I hope those of many ages, traditions, and spheres of life will find something of value in it.

Finally, there are other long-term interlocutors who are so much part of my life that they help to shape everything I write. These include the late Daniel Hardy, who was part of the genesis of this manifesto before he died in 2007; Micheal O'Siadhail, first reader of whatever I have written for over four decades; Frances Young; Jean Vanier; Peter Ochs; Tim Jenkins; Ben Quash; Iain Torrance; Robert Gibbs; Annie and Alan Hargrave; Stephen Plant; Susannah Ticciati; Peter Sedgwick; Madeleine O'Callaghan; Angela Tilby; my brother, Alan; my mother, Phyllis Ford; and my wife, Deborah. Since this is a manifesto that above all looks to future generations, it is dedicated with deepest gratitude and love to our children, Rebecca, Rachel, and Daniel.

Source Acknowledgments

Quotations from Dietrich Bonhoeffer in chapter 6 are from the following source: From Ethics: Dietrich Bonhoeffer Works Volume 5 copyright © 2004 Fortress Press. Reproduced by permission of Augsburg Fortress Publishers.

1

A Cry for Wisdom
Theology for the Twenty-first Century

Christian theology is thinking about questions raised by and about Christian faith and practice. That thinking is almost unavoidable in some form by anyone who tries to live a Christian life or who for some other reason is interested in Christianity. Theology by this broad definition is open to all and is part of ordinary life whenever any of a vast range of questions is raised. It is also many other things, but this manifesto is mainly concerned with the quality of theologies that, directly or indirectly, feed the minds and hearts of millions of people and are of interest to many more. That is why its key word for the goal of theology is wisdom, which unites understanding with practice and is concerned to engage with the whole of life.

The search for wisdom is the passion of this manifesto. It leads through the Bible and Christian history; into the depths, heights, and varieties of human life – past, present, and future; into engagement with communities, cultures, academic disciplines, public life, and other faiths besides Christianity; and into the ways a Christian theologian might be formed today. It is driven by questioning and drawn by the desire for God and God's wisdom.

At its core, theological wisdom is about the discernment of cries. In Proverbs, personified wisdom herself cries out:

> Wisdom cries out in the street;
> in the squares she raises her voice.
> At the busiest corner she cries out;
> at the entrance of the city gates she speaks …
> Does not wisdom call,
> and does not understanding raise her voice?
> On the heights, beside the way,
> at the crossroads she takes her stand;
> Beside the gates, in front of the town,
> at the entrance of the portals she cries out:
> "To you, O people, I call,
> and my cry is to all that live …
> Take my instruction instead of silver,
> and knowledge rather than choice gold;
> For wisdom is better than jewels,
> and all that you may desire
> cannot compare with her."
> (Proverbs 1:20–21, 8:1–4, 10–11)

That is a manifesto. Wisdom is often thought of as a rather "cool" concept, associated with slow deliberation and reflective distance. But the poetry of Proverbs shows wisdom's passionate intensity and urgency, represented by a mature, attractive woman. She does not by any means do away with patience, reflection, and deliberation, but opens up the heart of wisdom as a hot, energetic passion for clear discernment, accurate knowledge, good judgment, right living, and far-sighted decision-making. She is also passionately against fools and foolishness. She is wholeheartedly committed to the public realm and the shaping of families, friendships, neighborhoods, and societies, as well as individuals. She wants to attract as many as possible to devote themselves to her:

> "Come, eat of my bread
> and drink of the wine I have mixed.
> Lay aside immaturity, and live,
> and walk in the way of insight."
> (Proverbs 9:5–6)

The cries of wisdom are meant to stimulate us to cry out for her too. If nothing else we desire can compare with her, then we need to relate our desire for wisdom to our other desires. In the midst of all the cries – longings, appeals, and demands that come from within us and from all around us – how are we to shape a wise life? Desiring wisdom means seeking to test and discern the cries, learning how to respond to them. The Bible and life are full of cries: of suffering, joy, wonder, thanks, praise, victory, defeat, fear, faith, despair, hope, remorse, petition, and much else. These are the intensities and urgencies that can call forth a "hot" wisdom. Theology seeks wisdom through this engagement, relating to all that we cry out for – love, food, peace, security, freedom, health, hope, truth, joy, and God.[1]

A classic description of wisdom-seeking in the midst of intense pressure and suffering is the book of Job.[2] It is one of the most perceptive and devastating interrogations of God and of human existence ever. In the first chapter comes the fundamental question of the book: "Does Job fear God for nothing?" (Job 1:9). "Fearing God" is basic to wisdom in the Bible. It is a "right fear," the sort appropriate to a relationship of love and trust, where the main thing to be feared is the damage or loss of the relationship through unwise behavior. But this fear has the further, awesome, dimension of the involvement of God who creates and judges. The quality of Job's fear in relationship to God is tested drastically through the events of the book. Is he in this relationship for the sake of wealth, health, family, reputation, or religious satisfaction? All those are taken from him and he is traumatized. He despairingly faces the evaporation of the meaning of his life, and cries out in anguish again and again. His friends offer traditional, "packaged" theological interpretations, such as that he is somehow to blame for his own situation, or that God runs the world according to a simple rule of repaying good for good, evil for evil. But their wisdom does not discern the key issue in Job's cries: that Job is being tested and searched, and in response he is rightly questioning and searching. The urgency and radicality of his searching is a model for all theology. New, overwhelming challenges require fresh wrestling with God and reality together.

What is at stake is whether Job is relating to God for what he gets out of it or "for nothing,' for the sake of who God is, for God's sake – a typical biblical idiom is "for his name's sake," echoed in the first, embracing petition of the Lord's Prayer: "Hallowed be your name." The Greek translation of "for nothing" is *dorean*, "as a gift." The wisdom Job learnt in the time of his virtuous prosperity was not enough, but he also finds that the most terrible affliction does not have the last word: God does. His eyes are eventually opened to this: "Now my eye sees you!" (Job 42:5). He is proved right over against his friends because he persisted in crying out to God and for God, even when there seemed no point in doing so. He is shown as wanting above all to have God for God's sake.

Who is God? This God is one who lets his name be at stake in the risky openness of life. Why? The most adequate answer for the book of Job, worked out through taking the rest of the Bible into account, seems to be: because of the preciousness to God of the relationship with Job. God does this for the sake of a "for its own sake" relationship. It is beyond manipulation, coercion, self-interest, threat, or retribution, pointing to the deepest wisdom of a relationship of passionate love. And part of this love is a passion for searching out understanding, for questioning beyond the limits of what has been thought so far, for relating all reality to God and God's purposes – that is, a passion for *theological wisdom*. The scope of Job's searching is unlimited: personal and social life; the whole creation; and God.

In the New Testament, perhaps the most influential short passage in the history of Christian theology is the Prologue of the Gospel of John,[3] which has a similar scope to the book of Job. It is daringly innovative in its interpretation of scripture (for John, that meant the Hebrew scriptures or the Greek translation of them, the Septuagint, later called by Christians the Old Testament); in its reconception of creation and of God in relation to Jesus Christ as the Word; in its concern for "all things" and "all people"; in its picture of loving intimacy in God (v.18); and in its weaving together of these themes around the pivotal statement:

> And the Word became flesh and lived among us, and we have seen his glory, the glory as of a father's only son, full of grace and truth. (John 1:14)

John set a standard for later theology in terms of interpretation of scripture, the whole of creation as horizon, utter involvement in history and the contemporary world, and the centrality of God.

John also sowed the seeds of continual theological creativity through his Gospel's teaching of Jesus about the Holy Spirit. The Holy Spirit is probably the most exciting, disturbing, and uncertain topic in Christian theology. The New Testament announcement that, since Jesus' crucifixion and resurrection, God's own Spirit, the Spirit of Jesus Christ, has been poured out "upon all flesh" (Acts 2:17; Joel 2:28–9) is stupendous – and it may be early days yet for adequate realization of its implications. Throughout Christian history, the Holy Spirit (and such closely related topics as holiness, grace, gifts, freedom, power, authority, inspiration, blessing, and all sorts of innovations) has time and again been an occasion for movements that have expanded and renewed Christian communities, often impelling them into internal and external conflict or confrontation. It is as if all efforts to domesticate the Spirit fail, and the wild imagery of fire and wind is actualized in events. It happened in Paul's churches in the first century CE, in the Montanist movement, in Augustine's controversies over grace, in the great schism between the Eastern and Western Christian churches at the end of the first millennium, in many medieval movements, in the Reformation and its radical offshoots, in Quakerism, Methodism, and popular "awakenings" and "revivals." But the twentieth century saw the most amazing development of all. In 1906, in Azusa Street, Los Angeles, the worldwide Pentecostal and Charismatic movement began. This became probably the fastest-growing religious movement in world history, with perhaps as many as 300 hundred million people involved within a century. Its main appeal was to signs of the pouring out of the Holy Spirit. It now has numerous educational institutions, scholars, and thinkers, and one of the most important things to look for in the present century is how they work out their theological wisdom. It is vital to recognize how deeply the Spirit is related to the seeking of theological wisdom. The cry, "Come, Holy Spirit!" is a daily precondition for thinking theologically. But the Spirit also needs to be thought about and appreciated more fully if theology is to be lively and true. John draws together and interprets much in the other Gospels and the early Church. It is one of the first theological syntheses. Here the Spirit is given not in wind and fire but quietly, through the risen Jesus communicating it to his disciples face to face, by breathing on them (John 20:22).

Earlier in the Gospel he had already interpreted what this meant, the most important statement for future theology being: "I still have many things to say to you, but you cannot bear them now. When the Spirit of truth comes, he will guide you into all the truth" (John 16:13). That is a promise that John himself sought to enter into in his innovative Prologue and throughout his Gospel. It is the core challenge to Christian theology down the centuries: can theologians be guided with others into "all the truth," both the wisdom that has already been learned by others and the fresh wisdom needed to discern the distinctive cries of the present time? Job's friends could only offer the wisdom of the past, but failed to discern the meaning of the cries they were hearing. Job too knew and practiced the wisdom of his tradition: "There is no one like him on the earth, a blameless and upright man who fears God and turns away from evil" (Job 1:8). But he was also willing to search for fresh wisdom, inseparable from wrestling with God in a new situation.

The new situation John found himself in was that of trying to make sense of the life, death, and resurrection of Jesus Christ. In order to do so, he practiced what might be called "wise and creative theology," as in his Prologue – trying to do justice to scripture and tradition while also exploring new ways of conceiving the truth. In every generation and situation since then theology has had to come to terms with its past in fresh situations, trying to discern how best to be faithful, loving, and hopeful, and praying for the Holy Spirit as it does so. To cry out for the Spirit is to seek wisdom for God's sake and to be open to following both trodden and untrodden ways.

So twenty-first century Christian theology inherits vast riches from the past but can never simply repeat them. What, then, are the key elements in wise and creative theology? I will try to answer that question by reflections that draw heavily on the experience of editing a textbook on twentieth-century Christian theology, *The Modern Theologians*,[4] now in its third edition.

From the Twentieth to the Twenty-first Century: Theological Abundance and Variety

Was the twentieth century the most theologically productive and creative in Christian history? There is a strong case to be made for this.

It was certainly productive, in two main ways: there was the sheer abundance of it; and there was the generation of new varieties. Each of these has important consequences for the twenty-first century. There are two main reasons for the amount of theology produced in the twentieth century.

The first was the global spread of Christianity. This had accelerated during the nineteenth century and in the twentieth century was massively boosted by Pentecostalism and various forms of Evangelicalism, while Roman Catholicism, Orthodoxy, and Anglican and Protestant churches also grew.[5] This increased demand for what one might call ordinary, basic theology. In general, this meant two things: education for the teachers, preachers, pastors, priests, catechists, writers, broadcasters, and other communicators; and, largely through them, more widespread popular Christian teaching.

The second factor was the spread of education at all levels. There was an explosion of primary, secondary, and tertiary educational institutions all over the world, and a vast expansion of publishing and other communications media. By the end of the century it was normal to talk of the "information age," "knowledge economy," and "learning societies." The synergies of all this with the global spread of Christianity helped to generate large quantities of theology.

Twentieth-century theology was unprecedented not only in quantity, but also in variety. German-language theology, both Protestant and Catholic, was for much of the century the leading academic tradition, and five of the six individuals[6] who might, from the standpoint of the early twenty-first century, be seen as "classics," were formed within that. It is a tradition shaped through commitments both to a range of academic disciplines and to church life (often in some tension with each other), and tested through the century's political and other traumas. Above all, it faced the challenges of Western modernity, producing a range of Christian responses to it. The thoroughness with which these were grounded,[7] thought through, and debated means that classics from this tradition must be on the curriculum of any theologian who does not wish to reinvent the wheel. It is not clear yet what promise this tradition holds for fresh twenty-first century theology – it may be that its most creative successors will not be in its homelands of Germany and Switzerland.

In the rest of Europe and America, most leading theologians and movements were in continuity or continuous dialogue with German theology, but there were also other strands not so indebted to that – Anglican, Protestant, Catholic, Evangelical, revisionist, and liberal theologies, and a range of philosophical theologies and philosophies of religion more influenced by Anglo-American or French philosophers than by Germans. There was also a blossoming of other types: postmodern theologies; an array of "theology and ..." (race and ethnicity; the physical, biological, and social sciences; literature; the visual arts; music; film; spirituality; etc.); and, above all, feminist, womanist, and other gender-related theologies. Of these, the one that most profoundly affected theological consciousness was feminism. In retrospect, this is likely to be seen as a fundamental shift in the twentieth century, as the theological voices of half the world's Christians began to be heard in new ways. In historical perspective, we are also probably still in the early days of theological thinking on gender, and the same goes for the other types mentioned, especially the "theology and ..." list. The implication for twenty-first century theology is clear: this work must be taken much further.

The presence of women's voices in theology is, like many of the new twentieth-century developments, a global matter. The same is true of the theologies of the global churches and communions (Catholic, Orthodox, Anglican, Lutheran, Methodist, Reformed), and of movements such as Evangelicalism and Pentecostalism. All of these have been increasingly shaped by theological thinking from beyond Europe and North America. The grip of certain sorts of American theology on Evangelicals and Pentecostals elsewhere in the world (partly enabled by the Americans' capacity to fund those they agree with) now seems to be loosening due to a double pressure. On the one hand, within America there is a blossoming of new theologies within these churches; on the other hand, there is a new theological confidence elsewhere, especially in Asia, Africa, and South America.

Some of the other churches have also been trying to think together in new ways. The Christian ecumenical movement is unique in world history in having led many religious bodies from situations of confrontation and even conflict to conversation and collaboration with each other. It is mostly a twentieth-century phenomenon. Explicitly ecumenical theology, and the agreed documents emerging from ecumenical dialogues, are only the tip of the iceberg of its influence on theology. As with feminism, there has been a profound shift in consciousness in many churches, opening them to fellow-Christians in ways unimaginable in 1900. Yet, unlike gender-related theologies, ecumenism and its associated theology have not flourished in the years surrounding the turn of the second millennium. One hopeful sign is the birth of "receptive ecumenism," a theological program determined to make the most of ecumenical progress so far and to deepen and enrich the churches through learning from each other in many spheres.[8] This is a minimal requirement for Christian churches this century if they are not to lose the momentum of what has been one of the most healing and transformative movements in Christian history.

The global character of twentieth-century theology lay not just in types that had a global reach and participation, but also in the range of theologies that were often highly specific in their orientation or local in context. In the third edition of *The Modern Theologians* some of these are labeled "Particularizing Theologies," including black theology of liberation; Latin American liberation theology; African, South Asian, and East Asian theologies; and postcolonial biblical interpretation. The list could have gone on almost indefinitely, and new types are constantly arising. Indeed, one safe prediction for the coming century is that such particularizing theologies will multiply as more and more "niches" in the complex religious, cultural, and environmental ecosystem of our world discover the desirability of theological wisdom. There is also a feedback effect on other theologies that might not have seen themselves as "particularist." Just as feminist critiques made us aware how masculine much theology is, so classic German and other European and American theologians now seem far more a part of their own time, place, and tradition.

In a sense, we are all particularist now, encouraged to be more aware of what has shaped us, such as origins, contexts, interests, perspectives, and limitations. This is a common postmodern or late modern emphasis, whose danger is fragmentation, as particulars disconnected from each other develop their identities and put their cases. A tempting response is to attempt a new "modern" integration or overview, or to absolutize a particular identity. In our century at present religion is the favorite candidate for this, but one can see others – Americans and Chinese, for example, who are tempted by global hegemony, complexly combining elements of ideology (religious and secular), politics, economics, and civilization. This manifesto takes particulars with radical seriousness, as seen especially in the retrieval of religious traditions without syncretism or denial of their universal claims. Its response to the terrible dangers is not a new totality, integration, or hegemony, but a diverse ecology of wisdom-seeking, in which the connections are not maintained by conformity within one overview but by partnerships of difference.[9]

Within theology, this is found in the best practices of ecumenical theology – the "receptive ecumenism" just mentioned is a form of hospitable wisdom-seeking in engagement with other churches than one's own. It is also well exemplified in many varieties of "theology and …'These often draw together people with diverse theological convictions into conversation around a common concern. As suggested above, many of the growing points of Christian theology this century come under this broad heading. I would especially highlight four.

First, "theology and poetry" is a matter of deep concern to theology as it tries to shape its language more richly, imaginatively, and effectively. Poetry is "maximal speech," the most condensed and intense use of language in premodernity, modernity, and today. It not only draws listeners and readers into the depths of the Bible and of Christian liturgy, poetry, hymns, and culture; it also gives access to analogous depths in other faiths, civilizations, and cultures, including secular ones. Second, "theology and the sciences," both human and natural, offers a critical set of test cases for the engagement of theology with modernity (whether early, middle, or late), as well as understandings vital for discerning how to shape twenty-first century education and living. Third, "theology and public life" has become of increasing importance in dealing with the fresh prominence of religions in the public sphere, both internationally and in many particular zones of conflict. Fourth, "theology and the religions" is perhaps the most comprehensive challenge of our century. It will be the subject of a case study in chapter 8 of this volume, but some remarks now are relevant.

The reason why other religions are such a comprehensive challenge is that they are analogous to Christianity in their particularity and universality. They are irrevocably particular in that they shape a whole way of life and thought, and one cannot simultaneously participate fully in more than one. They are universal in the scope of their horizons, affirmations, and questions.

Christian thinking about other religious traditions goes back to its origins, but the late twentieth and early twenty-first centuries have given it a new impetus. As the great secular ideologies of the past century either faded as credible contenders for hegemony (fascism, communism), or lost much of their attractiveness in the face of failures, inadequacies, and crises (socialism, capitalism), religions re-emerged in the public sphere. This has been highly ambivalent, accompanied by much violence and other bad news. It has also been a realization of something that in the secular twentieth century had been a largely unrecognized fact (especially among Western media and educated people): that perhaps four to five billion of the world's population are directly involved with one or other of the major religions.

The religions' new prominence has not only highlighted their problems and pathologies, but has also stimulated them to engage afresh with each other. Can they be partners in difference? Do they have the resources to serve the common good together? What about all the conflicts, bad histories, missionary aggression, passionate rejections, contradictory convictions, and other incompatibilities? The present century not only unavoidably presents those sharp questions to the religions; it is also already testing the resources and qualities of each faith as the questions are ignored, rejected, or tackled. Inter-faith theology is perhaps the analogy to feminism and ecumenism in the twentieth century, inviting Christians into a change of consciousness regarding many millions of their fellow human beings.

So Christian theology of the past century has been both abundant and diverse, and some of its varieties are likely to be of special significance for the coming century. But what about theological quality?

Four Elements of Wise Creativity

The case for the unprecedented creativity of twentieth-century theology is more speculative than for its quantity and variety. It is difficult to compare instances of creativity (however defined) in general terms. As Patrick Kavanagh said about recognizing good poetry, "... but I know the beast when I see it." I will use four categories to consider the matter, while acknowledging that judgments of quality within each of them are highly contestable. For brevity's sake, my examples will mostly be from six "classic" twentieth-century theologians in the continental European tradition: Barth, Bonhoeffer, Tillich, de Lubac, Rahner, and von Balthasar.[10] The main aim of the exercise is not just to help in identifying wisdom and creativity, but also to offer an exemplary pattern to those inspired to attempt it.

1. *Wise and creative retrieval*

Christian theology must deal with the past, discerning how best to relate to it so as to resource the present and future. It is what French Roman Catholic theology of the early twentieth century called *ressourcement*, a return to sources that can nourish theology and life now, and the term became a watchword of the Second Vatican Council (1962–5) in its renewal of Catholicism.

Some of its leading exponents were French, such as Henri de Lubac. The variety and historical breadth and depth of his retrievals were remarkable. He was especially perceptive in showing how vital earlier meanings can be lost, impoverished, or distorted with serious consequences, and how their recovery can involve radical change in the present. He did this not only with key figures in the tradition, such as Origen, Augustine, Aquinas, and Nicholas of Cusa, and with core practices such as Eucharistic worship, the exercise of authority in the church, and patristic and medieval exegesis of scripture; he also discerned Archimedean points of leverage in the tradition centered on fundamental terms and concepts, including "the supernatural," "nature and grace," "the vision of God," "the body of Christ," and "the senses of scripture." His retrievals (for which he endured a good deal of official opposition) contributed substantially to the transformation of Roman Catholic sensibility that made the Second Vatican Council possible and influenced its deliberations and documents.

What is the secret of such creative retrieval? There is no formula for genius, and the only adequate way to appreciate it is to follow carefully how he actually does it. But his mixture of ingredients is instructive. There is intensive attention to texts as well as to contexts and historical events, amounting to an ability to inhabit the past in a scholarly yet imaginative way. There is the discernment of pivotal moments, especially of loss or change of meaning. There is also a comparable effort to discern what is most significant in the present – de Lubac wrote on evolution and other scientific topics, on atheistic humanism, on art and literature, and on Buddhism. He is fully involved with the past for the sake of the present and future, with the result that the Christian tradition becomes habitable in a fresh, relevant, and challenging way. In theological terms it might be described as an achievement of prophetic wisdom.

Yet this very prophetic dimension also runs great risks. De Lubac can be accused of distorting the past in order to make his case, and of reading present concerns into earlier periods. Any creative retrieval will open up such debates. For a theology that wants to be genuinely connected with the past it is not an option to avoid the problems that de Lubac faced: the challenge is, if possible, to do better.

A generation after de Lubac's death, his own work too requires the labor of retrieval and renewed reception. One of those who interpreted him in his lifetime was another classic thinker, Hans Urs von Balthasar, whose own efforts of retrieval are on an even larger scale than de Lubac's, and include far more on the direct interpretation of scripture – the task that might be seen as the core of all Christian retrieval. Von Balthasar learnt much from his older Protestant contemporary, Karl Barth, whose major work, the six million-word *Church Dogmatics*,[11] is pervaded with excursuses on one after another past thinker, topic, or debate. The Bible is his prime focus, as it is that of Dietrich Bonhoeffer, in contrast with the concerns of Karl Rahner and Paul Tillich, who in very different ways concentrate more on past theological and philosophical ideas. So the modes of retrieval practiced by such thinkers vary, and are one of the principal indicators of their theological interests, passions, and strategies.

Looking at others, alongside continental European theologians, it is also clear how formative have been discernments about where the focus on retrieval should be. These have ranged through colonial history and missions; the pervasiveness of patriarchal structures and practices; specific denominational, regional, racial, or ethnic histories; or some formative period (the favorites being New Testament, early church, Middle Ages, Reformation, and the nineteenth century). Such judgments on the significance and relevance of the past will continue to be essential to substantial theological wisdom and creativity.

2. Wise and creative engagement with God, church, and world

Alongside *ressourcement*, the other main watchword of the Second Vatican Council was *aggiornamento* – "bringing up to date." It nicely expresses the most essential accompaniment of retrieval: engagement with the present. The double immersion in past and present for the sake of the future is a mark of wise and creative theologians.

The first, incomparable, present engagement is with God. This pervades all other engagements but is above all "for God's sake" – the great commandment is to love God with all one's heart, mind, soul, and strength (Deut. 6:5; Matt. 22:37; Mark 12:30; Luke 10:27). Our six classic theologians all sought to follow that, practicing prayer and worship in diverse ways. The Catholics were Jesuits (De Lubac, Rahner, Von Balthasar for a while before founding a lay institute), the Protestants were Reformed (Barth) and Lutheran (Bonhoeffer, Tillich). Each in his own way offers a theocentric theology that attempts to engage with God and with everything else in relation to God.

Each was also deeply involved with both the church and the world. De Lubac not only wrote on contemporary science and other topics of current interest but was wounded in the First World War, was active in resistance to French Nazi sympathizers in church and state during the Second World War, and for long periods was the subject of controversy in the Catholic Church. Rahner's and von Balthasar's involvements were mostly intellectual, cultural, and ecclesial. Barth was a far more public prophetic figure both in the church and in politics, championing workers' rights, denouncing European domestication and compromising of Christianity, insistently opposing the Nazis, and challenging the American public theologian Reinhold Niebuhr over his support of the Cold War between the Soviet Union and the West. Tillich had to leave Nazi Germany where he had been very active politically; in America he taught in a leading seminary, and eventually appeared on the cover of *Time* magazine as one of the most influential public intellectuals in the United States.

Bonhoeffer is a prime example of engaged theology. His retrievals ranged widely, the main concentration being on the Bible, the early church, the Reformation, and modernity, and the many volumes of his collected works[12] show the depth and range of his theological writings. But throughout his adult life till his execution by the Nazis in 1945 at the age of thirty-nine he was passionately engaged in many spheres of life. As an academic in the University of Berlin he rallied anti-Nazi students and taught confirmation classes in working-class Berlin, while also being active in the international ecumenical movement. With Hitler in power, he helped to found the Confessing Church in opposition to the German Christians who supported the Nazis, and then headed their seminary until the Gestapo shut it down. When he was writing his *Ethics*[13] he took part in a network of resistance that eventually made a failed attempt on Hitler's life. The *Letters and Papers from Prison*[14] that he wrote after his arrest became a theological classic, and display an intense concern simultaneously for Christian faith and secular reality. In the decades after his death Bonhoeffer was to be an inspiration for theology marked by political resistance, especially in West and East Germany, other Eastern European Communist countries, and South Africa.

That theme which preoccupied Bonhoeffer during his months in prison, is another way of describing a most significant engagement of nineteenth- and twentieth-century Christian theology that continues into the present century: facing the challenges posed by the broad array of developments in all spheres of life that might be summed up as "modernity." In the present century the agenda is changing, so much so that some describe our situation as postmodern. This term is acceptable as long as its emphasis on the discontinuities is accompanied by the recognition of so many continuities that it is also justifiable to call our period "late modern." There is considerable wisdom to be gained from retrieving and developing twentieth-century theological engagements with modernity. This manifesto places alongside those the huge importance for our century of theological engagements with other religions. What are the forms of Christian theology that can respond wisely and creatively to both the secular and religious realities of our world, while being true to the depths of Christian faith? That is perhaps the most important question for a contemporary theology.

3. Wise and creative thinking

Thinking goes on in all four aspects of theological wisdom-seeking and creativity. Some of it is what might be termed basic intellectual good practice: asking appropriate questions, thinking logically, using experience and evidence appropriately, ordering arguments clearly, seeking and testing insights, recognizing the variety of ways in which different discourses can be developed, and acknowledging who are the models of good practice to whom appeal can be made. In relation to each of those practices there are debates and conflicting positions, and these lead into large questions of ontology (dealing with the basic character of reality), epistemology (questions to do with knowing that reality), aesthetics (on perception and beauty), and ethics (dealing with appropriate decision-making and right action).

Later chapters will discuss the role of philosophy (which is the discipline where such issues are most fully studied) in theology, concluding that the main aim should be to be sure-footed: it is wise for theologians to have their minds trained in such practices and to be aware of the issues that need to be faced in them, but they do not necessarily need to be able to contribute to technical philosophical discussions of them. Our six classic twentieth-century theologians are highly diverse in their relations to philosophy. Barth was well educated in it but deeply suspicious of its tendencies to dictate inappropriately to theology – above all, by offering a framework of understanding within which God's existence or character could be known. Bonhoeffer was sympathetic to Barth but much more fully immersed in dialogue with philosophy and sociology, and his *Act and Being* is a *tour de force* of thinking through basic concepts in thorough engagement with both philosophy and theology. Tillich and Rahner are perhaps the most technically philosophical throughout their work, while von Balthasar attempts a massive synthesis of logic, ontology, epistemology, and aesthetics.

What of their creativity? This might be seen as what is sometimes named "abduction."[15] It is the imaginative and inventive side of reasoning that conceives new possibilities. Coleridge connects this with people being led to God by God (abduction comes from the Latin: *ab* – by; and *ductus/ducta* – led). We are being attracted to God, "drawn toward the true center,"[16] through particularity (Jesus Christ) and its relating universally (Holy Spirit).[17] Christian theology can be led into the truth (John 16:13), which means stretching the mind and imagination – and often the will too, since some truth is only known through action, above all through loving. It is as theologians open themselves to the attraction of theological truth, in thought that is inseparable from prayer, that their creativity is given.

This can take many forms. In Barth, one thinks of his deep dissatisfaction with classic Christian teaching that God predestines some to salvation and many to damnation. His proposal does not give up God's power, freedom, and foreknowledge in choosing (election), and it also affirms the reality of rejection by God. But he identifies Jesus Christ as the one (and the only one of whom we actually know) who is both rejected and elected. In his crucifixion he is rejected on behalf of all; in his resurrection, his election on behalf of all is shown.[18] In von Balthasar there is an original exploration of the same dilemma by thinking through the meaning of Holy Saturday, the day (between Good Friday and Easter Sunday) when Jesus Christ was dead.[19]

It is not surprising that some of the most creative theological thought is about how human and divine freedom and action might be related to each other. De Lubac wrestled with this through interpreting a range of thinkers on nature and grace, culminating in his conception of the vision of God. Tillich and Rahner drew on different conceptualities to arrive at what Tillich called "theonomy,"[20] and Rahner called the direct, not inverse, ratio of human to divine freedom – in other words, there is no competition between them, but human freedom flourishes and increases the more it is involved with the God who created it.[21] Bonhoeffer in his *Ethics* attempts to resolve this issue, which had been less satisfactorily dealt with in his previous works, by transposing it into temporal terms with his concept of the penultimate and ultimate. The penultimate (nature, human action inspired by God) can prepare for, and can be oriented toward, the gift of the divine ultimate, but does not bring it about or necessitate it.[22]

The many forms of theological creativity include reinterpretation of scripture; conceptual innovation and improvisation; fresh and persuasive arguments; critique of where other theologies have gone wrong; bringing theology into fruitful dialogue with other disciplines, cultures, religions, events, and experiences; and the production of liturgies, prayers, hymns, novels, dramas, films, paintings, and other works of art. "Thinking" is a vague term for the different ways minds are engaged in such creativity in conjunction with many human capacities. We will return to creative thinking (along with the other three elements) in later chapters, but for now it is worth noting the challenge of what might be termed the "architectonics" of theology.

Every theologian takes decisions about the form in which his or her theology is presented. Different periods and traditions in theology tend to favor particular forms, though some, such as commentary on scripture, sermons, catechesis, letters, polemics, and liturgies, tend to be more popular and widespread. Some theologians are content to use conventional forms without much innovation – Rahner mostly uses theological essays; Bonhoeffer after his two academic dissertations wrote scriptural commentary, sermons, letters, and much else, including various types of literature (see below), but was well aware of not attempting a major systematic work; de Lubac mostly uses usual scholarly and theological forms. But Tillich, von Balthasar, and Barth undertake major works that are structured in original ways. Perhaps the most original is Barth's incomplete *Church Dogmatics*, conceived as five volumes on the Word of God, God, Creation, Reconciliation, and Redemption, and including within it the architectonic *coup* of the first three parts of Volume IV on Reconciliation. There he achieves an integration of several doctrines – on Christ, sin, salvation, Church, and faith/love/hope – treated from three different angles in the course of three movements that correlate with God as Father, Son, and Spirit. It is a structure that manages to communicate key theological messages through its pattern and juxtapositions, and also, by its irreducible threefoldness, resists any systematic overview of its subject matter. The form is one appropriate to a mystery that one needs to approach afresh repeatedly, always drawn further into the depths of each part and into its dynamic interrelations with other parts.

4. Wise and creative expression

Theology often does not read well. This does not disqualify it as creative theology by the other three criteria, but yet its purpose is not fulfilled unless it is made as accessible as possible. For this, appropriate genres, structures, and forms are needed, together with attractive language. Many academic theologians are not gifted in this respect, and very few are good at more than one or two of the wide range of arts ideally required to communicate theology as widely and effectively as possible. This calls for writers, artists, composers, program-makers, film-makers, and others. Even within academic theology, wider dissemination than within a small circle of specialists is often better achieved by collaboration with a colleague who is a better writer.

Whether with a colleague, or with someone more fully engaged in communication, finding the right words for ideas is not just about appropriate verbal packaging for concepts separable from the wrapping. Form and content are far more complexly interrelated than that. Whether within one person, or between collaborators, bringing something to its best expression is not just a one-way process of moving from ideas or images to words. The ideas and images are already enmeshed in language, and writing is itself a creative task, in which fresh theological insights can occur. So good theology can become better theology through being expressed better.

In the light of that, it is no surprise that even among the six classic theologians who are our main points of reference in this chapter the quality of expression varies. De Lubac's French is both meticulous and heavily rhetorical, and not easy to translate into the customarily sparser English theological style.[23] Rahner is perhaps the most conceptually dense and difficult, and the majority of his constructive theology is contained in essays, which leave it to readers to interconnect them within a larger coherence. Tillich has a fairly heavy style in German and English, though his sermons and shorter works can move lightly and communicate vividly. Barth and von Balthasar allow an instructive comparison. Despite writing a great deal about beauty and aesthetics, von Balthasar is rather verbose and loose in the structuring of his writing. Barth, who writes far less about aesthetics, won an Erasmus prize for the quality of his prose.

Bonhoeffer is probably the most diverse and effective communicator of all, and in several genres. His two doctoral dissertations (especially the second, *Act and Being*[24]) are comparable in density and difficulty to anything in the other five thinkers. The more popular books published during his lifetime, *Life Together*[25] and *The Cost of Discipleship*,[26] are eloquent and accessible, and the felicitous union of form and content in *Life Together* has helped make it the best-selling of all his works. He left his *Ethics*[27] in unedited fragments, yet its vigorous, concise directness has enabled a wide impact. Finally, there is his *Letters and Papers from Prison*,[28] mostly made up of short papers, poems, and pieces of fiction, together with letters to his friend Eberhard Bethge. It is a feast of genres and of energetic, passionate writing. It retrieves and offers insights into a wide range of texts and thinkers. It is utterly involved with his contemporary world and with looking beyond it to the post-war situation. It is also shot through with seminal creative thinking that continues to inspire theologians and others. In short, it exemplifies all the elements of theological creativity. And in its range of genres it points to their importance, especially of poetry, drama, and fiction, for theological thinking.

Conclusion

The quantity, variety, and creativity of twentieth-century theology has been seen to offer lessons and inspiration for Christian theology of the future. This theology above all desires wisdom, primarily for God's sake. It is a wisdom that is sought in many ways, especially through the discernment of cries – the cries of God to humanity, and of humanity and the rest of creation to God and to each other. The cries are set within the complex, many-stranded drama of God's involvement with creation for its good. The next two chapters set the search for theological wisdom within that drama and describe its basic character in terms of core cries and responses.

2

Drama in Bible, Theology, and Life

Drama has proved to be a remarkably fruitful way of conceiving Christian theology in recent decades. It is closely related to the popularity of narrative, with which it shares many elements. Drama, like life, unfolds over time. It can have plots and sub-plots; major and minor characters and events; clashes of people, ideas, and perspectives that may or may not be resolved; loose ends and mysteries; intensive dialogues, soliloquies, and cries; prose, poetry, and song; wisdom and foolishness; tragedy and comedy. It is able to convey the dynamic particularity of human existence, with its physicality, surprises, initiatives, contingencies, necessities, tensions, and multi-leveled complexity. It may present large overviews of life or delve into the intimate interiority of one character, but its core perspective is that of characters and events in interaction, irreducibly social. As it unfolds, a drama invites us to become engaged, to inhabit its world, and to look toward its as yet open ending.

Looking at this manifesto, drama can be seen as an integrator of many of its concerns. Good drama performs the elements of creativity explored in the previous chapter: it is creative expression that offers rich thought (think of all those quotations from Shakespeare; but, even more, of his dramatic conceptions, conveyed by the ways his plots are constructed and his characters develop), and in the way the mode of dramatic engagement shows the past in interplay with the present. The next chapter employs drama as its core concept in trying to describe what is most essential to Christian theology across the centuries. Furthermore, the fivefold sensibility described in chapter 4 is the least required to do justice to the richness of drama. Drama in itself includes assertions and imperatives, questions, explorations, and desires, and it stimulates all those and more in its audience, as it takes them up into its future-oriented action. It is a helpful category through which to understand the Bible, which in its various genres displays dramatic features, including all those noted above. A mind, heart, and body exercised in performing or following a drama will have had a helpful formation for reading the Bible and participating in Christian worship. Drama is also a powerful way of portraying the complexity of human belonging (chapter 5), allowing for identities and conflicts that change over time and are subject to much negotiation and debate. It is not surprising that wisdom distilled from drama has been so generative.

The Bible: More Dramatic than Epic or Lyric

God is the most distinctive "character" in the Christian drama. "Theodrama" (God-drama) is the term for this drama that was brought into widespread usage by Hans Urs von Balthasar.[1] He argues at length that the way God's involvement with the world is presented in the Bible is appropriately described in dramatic terms, though without excluding other modes.

The Christian theodrama has an Author who is also the leading character. The plot begins with creation, moves through the story of Israel to the later prophets, and has its climax in the Gospel story of the life, death, and resurrection of Jesus Christ. The next act is the era of the church, and the New Testament also looks forward to a final act, a God-centered future. That overarching story, from creation to the culmination of history, has been the main framework of Christian understanding and identity for two millennia. It is embedded in worship and liturgy, in the church year, and in hymns, art, architecture, literature, and other forms in many cultures influenced by Christian faith. It has also provided the principal focal points for theological teaching: the main doctrines of the church correlate with its stages – God, creation, sin, providence, Jesus Christ, salvation, Holy Spirit, church (including worship, ministry, and sacraments), ethics, and eschatology. So it is extraordinarily important for Christian faith and practice. It is not surprising that something so central should be open to very different interpretations, to serious distortion and misuse, and also to radical challenge.

Von Balthasar draws on Hegel's distinction between drama, epic, and lyric in order to show that, while each has a role, drama is the leading, embracing category. The three are also useful in showing how the dramatic character of the theodrama can be lost – if Christian faith becomes too "epic" or too "lyric" there can be serious consequences. Drama, epic, and lyric are helpful categories for describing different sorts of faith and theology, so it is worth stating clearly what is meant by them (in which I follow the perceptive discussion by Quash).[2] They are to be taken as "ideal types," which are not likely to fit any actual theology or position precisely but yet illuminate important tendencies.

Epic, as a theological mode, tells in a monologue, as objectively as possible, about people, events, and ideas. It speaks of God in the third person as "He," and tries to get the facts right and to complete the narrative without the intrusion of personal viewpoints or other forms of subjectivity. Individuals are subordinated to the plot, which moves toward a necessary conclusion. The epic mindset likes clarity, completeness, and objectivity, systems, overviews, and comprehensive structures. It is impatient of ambiguity, indirectness, irony, multi-leveled meaning, and multiple perspectives, and of characters, ideas, or events that do not seem to fit the movement toward a final resolution.

Lyric theology is subjective, concerned with inwardness, self-expression, and the present moment. God is "thou/you," addressed by an "I," and the relationship can be intense, with ups and downs, messiness, and loose ends. In this existential engagement important things happen, and third-person narratives cannot do justice to them. An "epic" account may get the facts right but fail to capture the subjective truth. Significant past events cry out to be entered into imaginatively and with feeling, and the diverse testimonies to them may not come together smoothly into an epic monologue. The more one delves into the particularities of individual perspectives, conscious and subconscious motivations, rational and irrational responses, diverse worldviews, conditioning factors, hopes, fears, suspicions, doubts and desires, the less it seems that human reality can be done justice through an epic mindset. Yet should one give up on a coherent plot, an overarching meaning? Does not belief in God require us to assume there is one, and does not belief in revelation require us to assume we can know it – at least at the eschaton?

At its best, drama is able to embrace the objective and the subjective, to maintain a sense of plot and purpose without suppressing individuality, diversity, and the complexity of levels, perspectives, motivations, and ideas. It can have epic detachment and lyric intensity, and enable a sense of coherence without assuming one overview. Because its primary concern is with characters and events in interaction, it can resist absorption either into the lyric interiority of one subjective consciousness or into an epic overview that assumes a standpoint far above the contingency and untidiness of life.

The greatest theatrical dramas in Western culture, those of the Greek tragedians (Aeschylus, Sophocles, Euripides) and of Shakespeare, are prime examples of this. They can portray the epic mindset (the Greek tragic chorus often does this, as do some Shakespearean characters, and even show what happens when it is dominant (Creon in *Antigone*, Lear in *King Lear*); they can also sound the depths of subjectivity (Euripides' *Medea*, Hamlet's soliloquies) and leave us still in the grip of radical, unresolved conflicts (the endings of *Antigone*, *Oedipus Rex*, *Hamlet*, or *King Lear*); and by holding both epic and lyric within the drama they do more than either can. Good drama gives a sense that the dramatist is neither in authoritarian control (and just describing what has been predetermined in advance) nor simply chronicling a set of diverse subjectivities.

But what of God and the Bible? Surely God ought to be in control of the divine epic moving toward its predestined end?

Or, if God's involvement with people is deeply subjective and located primarily in our interiority, ought we to despair of any form of objectifying description and revel in the variety of subjective testimonies, allowing their lyrical intensity to evoke our own existential responses? The problem is that the Bible does not fit easily within either description. It testifies to a real drama of love and freedom, and the most serious matters are at stake in the interactions of God, humanity, and creation. There is a sense neither of inevitability nor of purposelessness. There is no contradiction between divine purpose and initiative, on the one hand, and human freedom and responsibility, on the other. *Human freedom is fulfilled in involvement with God and God's purposes, and this means constant discernment of vocation and responsibility within an unfolding drama whose central act is the life, death, and resurrection of Jesus Christ.* This is an ongoing, irreducibly dramatic reality, and living within it requires alertness to God, other people, oneself, creation, and whatever is happening now, always looking toward the future God is promising. Baptism gives an identity immersed in this God-centered drama, and Christian living is daily participation in it. There are epic and lyric aspects, but drama is a less inadequate primary category.

Gospel of John – Epic, Lyric, and above all Dramatic

A good test case of the importance and fruitfulness of the theological use of these categories is the Gospel of John. It could be seen as simultaneously the most epic, most lyric, and most dramatic of the four Gospels, and so especially helpful in thinking about the interrelation of these aspects. It is also the biblical book that has probably been most influential on Christian theology, and, as discussed in the previous chapter, offers a charter for theological creativity through the leading of the Holy Spirit "into all the truth" (John 16:13).

John's Prologue (1:1–18) introduces and integrates the three in its own way. The opening four verses might be read as an epic framework:

> In the beginning was the Word, and the Word was with God, and the Word was God. He was in the beginning with God. All things came into being through him, and without him not one thing came into being. What has come into being in him was life, and the life was the light of all people. (John 1:1–4)

That is an uncompromising affirmation of the initiative of God through the Word, later identified with Jesus Christ. All things, all life, all people are encompassed by this, and the light might suggest a universal overview.

It is easy to see how such statements, with corresponding passages elsewhere on the initiative, sovereignty, and overarching knowledge, authority, and power of God, could be used to support a theology of complete divine foreknowledge and control. The overall tendency of much classical Christian theology is toward this epic mode. The logic of God's sovereignty and power seem to press unavoidably toward it. So concepts of divine omnipotence, omniscience, and omnipresence were worked out to show, for example, that God's divinity is at stake in predetermining the destinies of all people and things.

The Prologue also emphatically affirms the importance of human response to the Word in faith: "so that all might believe" (1:7); "his own people did not accept him. But to all who received him, who believed in his name …" (1:11–12); "we have seen his glory" (1:14); "From his fullness we have all received, grace upon grace" (1:16). How to think this active receptivity together with divine initiative has been a perennial issue for Christian theology down the centuries (under such headings as human and divine freedom, nature and grace, Holy Spirit and human spirit, faith and works, primary and secondary causality), and the very persistence of the problem points to its insolubility within an epic framework.

Might it be solved in a more "lyric" way? That is how one of the most powerful commentaries on John's Gospel in the twentieth century could be described. Rudolf Bultmann offers a radically existentialist interpretation of the Gospel and sees this clearly indicated in the "overture" of the Prologue.[3] The epic framework is seen as a mythological terminology used to convey a message aimed at the transformation of the reader's subjectivity. The message is a revelation, the Word in person, who poses a decision between two possibilities: a new self-understanding (light, life, grace, truth) through receptivity in faith; or losing oneself irrevocably through rejecting it (darkness, death, failure to receive or to trust). "The event of the revelation is a question, is an offence. This and nothing else is what is meant by 'The Word became flesh.'"[4] This offence, the paradox of "glory in flesh," questions us radically, and our response determines our existential participation in "light" or "darkness." God is not an object of knowledge ("No one has ever seen God" – 1:18), and it is pointless to try to solve questions such as the relation of divine and human freedom or to explore the meaning of divine attributes such as omniscience or omnipotence: the point is to actualize the possibility of subjective transformation through a new self-knowledge in faith.

In complementarity with epic objectivity (emphasizing overview and actuality) and lyric subjectivity (emphasizing interiority and possibility) is the many-personed drama that is introduced in the Prologue (John sent by God; the Word, Jesus Christ – rejected by his own people, living "among us" and "close to the Father's heart") and is central in the rest of the Gospel. The author carefully crafts his dramas and accompanying dialogues. There are stories of calling disciples and of the healings, debates, clashes, and plotting that led eventually to his death; there are "set pieces" such as the wedding at Cana, the conversations with Nicodemus and with the Samaritan woman, the feeding of the crowd, and the raising of Lazarus; and there is the culminating three-part drama of farewell discourses, crucifixion, and resurrection (the latter in two parts, each thoroughly dramatic). The many voices, actions, individuals, and groups cannot be adequately presented or conceptualized in epic or systematic terms. The light shines between people, in encounters, conversations, dense symbols, and multi-leveled events. The meanings can be explored in many "moods" (see chapter 4 of this volume) and from many angles, but cannot be summarized, wrapped up, or packaged satisfactorily in non-dramatic forms.

The drama has to be followed, entered into, and meditated upon as it unfolds. Its purpose is not just to give factual knowledge (though some is given) or enable a new self-understanding (though Bultmann is right in affirming that), but above all to enable the continuation of the drama in a life of faith that acts out the direction of Jesus: "As the Father has sent me, so I send you" (John 20:21). The sending of God creates drama, above all the drama of love and friendship in human existence in interplay with God, and potentially with "all things" and with "all people."

John's Gospel might be seen as pedagogy for those who desire to take part in the theodrama more fully and with deepening understanding and love. It probably was written with a good deal of knowledge of the other Gospels (or at least of the main traditions of testimony on which they drew) and assumes much of that knowledge in its readers. It is sometimes called the "most theological" of the Gospels, which is unfair to the others if it implies that they are not thoroughly theological (i.e., thinking about God and everything else in relation to God and God's purposes) in telling their stories. Yet it is differently theological, teaching far more explicitly and deliberately what it means to go on doing theology generation after generation.

One option the author would have had was to try to tell the most complete story of Jesus, drawing on the Synoptics and other sources, and giving definitive meanings grounded in appeal to the eyewitness authority of the "beloved disciple." Instead, there is a very different thrust. In place of any claim to completeness there is testimony to a superabundance that can never be done justice to, culminating in the final verse: "But there are also many other things that Jesus did; if every one of them were written down, I suppose that the world itself could not contain the books that would be written" (John 21:24). In place of definitive meaning there is, again, superabundance. It is there within the Gospel, often expressed in simple language that is almost infinitely rich – the Prologue is one example of very many, itself perhaps matched by the farewell discourses climaxing in chapter 17. There is also an imaginative, symbolic depth in the great words and images – just in the first four verses are "beginning," "word," "all," "life," "light," "darkness" – and these in turn feed into endless further meanings as the drama unfolds. There is also an extraordinary density of intertextuality as John in his text quotes, resonates with, indwells, and improvises upon his own scriptures (probably read by him in both Hebrew and Greek), the Synoptic traditions, and other texts (about which scholars speculate). Further back than Abraham and Genesis, John's horizon extends to before all creation, and is ultimately grounded in the divine "I am."

Above all, John acknowledges his own incompleteness. In Jesus' farewell discourses on the Holy Spirit he opens the way for further overflows of activity, meaning, and truth. The Spirit will inspire doing "greater things" in the future and will guide further into "all the truth." In terms of the future of theological thinking this is the strongest conceivable encouragement to get on with it – praying for the Spirit, utterly steeped in John and other scriptures, attentive to all things and all people, and especially following Jesus in the way of love. The encouragement extends far beyond theology, to whatever might contribute to glorifying the God who loves the world like this. It is a theology that has a definite center, the "I am" of the One who is the Word, who is "close to the Father's heart," and who sends the Spirit; it also has an open, ever-widening circumference.

John's recognition that there is more and more truth to be received is part of a life of faith whose character is suggested by his key term *menein* – dwelling, abiding, remaining, lasting, inhabiting, "living in." The life of faith involves the whole self, not just trusting and believing but also knowing, working, belonging, loving, imagining, worshiping, and more. *Menein* gathers all that together, and can refer to ordinary physical living in a house or place (1:39, 40), the Spirit remaining permanently on Jesus (1:32, 33), the indwelling word (5:38), the ongoing nourishment given by Jesus, leading to the mutual indwelling of Jesus and the one living in faith (6:27, 56), dwelling in the word of Jesus (8:31), eternal life with Jesus (8:35), not living in darkness (12:46), the mutual indwelling of the Father and the Son (14:10), the dwelling of the Spirit of truth for ever with and in those who receive him, involving the mutual indwelling in love of Jesus and the Father, and of disciples and Jesus (14:15–21), and disciples living in Jesus and his love with joy as branches in the vine (15:1–11).

This is "ordinary" Christian living, involving nothing less than daily living in intimacy with God, minds and hearts being stretched, active in love, alert to whatever is required to glorify God, to "bear much fruit," and to be learners (15:8). Its quietly dramatic character is summed up in John's account of the giving of the Holy Spirit (20:19–23) referred to above. Jesus suddenly appears to his fearful disciples, saying "Peace be with you." He shows them his hands and his side, with the marks of his suffering and death, the climax of the dramatic life John has described. The disciples are glad. Jesus again says "Peace be with you," and gives them responsibility for the ongoing drama, described as analogous to what he himself has performed: "As the Father has sent me, so I send you." Then Jesus breathes on them: "Receive the Holy Spirit." His closing words authorize them to forgive and retain sins.

That is a scene with profound implications for continuing the drama. Fear, in individuals and whole groups, is one of the most powerful motives in human life, both personal and political, and Jesus twice repeats his peace blessing to the disciples who are deeply fearful. He himself, in person, is central to the scene, his identity inseparable from his life, death, and, now, resurrection. This is central to the plot of history, its pivotal moment after which there is something permanently new, and he continues as the main character.

The "as … so" of the sending connects the earlier with the later acts of the drama. It authorizes the search for analogies and resonances between the earlier and later. In later periods one of the main ways of seeking a way forward can be the rereading of scriptures and the discernment of lessons from the past. Above all, the "figural" or "typological" reading of scripture can help to shape Christian wisdom that is rooted in past testimonies and patterns yet remains open to the new. This is a common scriptural practice (for example, Isaiah's use of the Exodus to respond to the exile to Babylon) and John shows his mastery of it from the first verse of his

Gospel as he draws Genesis 1:1 into his identification of Jesus Christ. Types can be used to try to subsume every event into a fixed epic pattern that excludes ongoing drama. But the giving of the Spirit encourages not identical repetition, but rather improvisation on the biblical patterns in order to do justice to new people and events, and this has remained one of the principal Christian ways of making sense of ongoing history in dramatic mode.

The giving of the Spirit is also simultaneously a reminder that Jesus Christ remains the main character and that he has now decisively shared responsibility and more: he has breathed into them his own Spirit. The whole Gospel has prepared for this moment and it is perhaps the most stupendous assertion of all. Yet there is no hint of the spectacularly dramatic wind and fire of the Day of Pentecost in Acts chapter 2; rather, there is a sober reminder, by referring to the ongoing need for forgiveness, that things can still go terribly wrong. Indeed, the implication might be that the community which receives this Spirit especially needs means of coping with the endlessly inventive, corrupting, and destructive ways that it can be misused and abused.

John's Gospel concludes with another scene of huge importance to the way Christians take part in the continuing drama. The setting is the Sea of Tiberias, with Peter and other disciples returning to work as fishermen. Jesus guides them to an abundant catch, and after sharing breakfast he asks Peter whether he loves him, responding with instructions to "Feed my sheep" (21:17). Jesus then predicts Peter's future suffering and death and says: "Follow me" (21:19). So far the message seems to be about the significance of everyday life, love, building up the Christian community, and faithful discipleship, together with readiness for intense pressures and even martyrdom. It reads like a summary of what it might be like to be sent "as" Jesus was sent, with the ordinary and extraordinary woven together into the drama's next act.

Then Peter asks about another disciple, "whom Jesus loved" (21:20), and the response and author's comment are an important pointer to how Christians might see themselves in the years and even centuries following this:

> Jesus said to him, "If it is my will that he remain (*menein*) until I come, what is that to you? Follow me!" So the rumor spread in the community that this disciple would not die. Yet Jesus did not say to him that he would not die, but "If it is my will that he remain (*menein*) until I come, what is that to you?" (21:22–3)

The key word, *menein*, has by this stage in the Gospel gathered the rich meanings discussed above, suggesting the many aspects of ongoing Christian living. In the Synoptic Gospels there are vivid apocalyptic scenarios of the future, but in John, probably the last Gospel to be written, those are not included. Instead, the return of Jesus is quietly taken for granted, and the culmination of history, whenever it takes place, is definitely centered on him; but everything else is left vague, and curiosity about precise details is discouraged with a rhetorical question twice repeated. The positive emphasis is on "Follow me!" – drawing attention to the immediate, dramatic future, and again centering on Jesus.

This is the final, decisive example of the dramatic perspective. It undermines confidence in any "epic" overview of history that speculates, or claims to know, how or when it will end. It is not focused on the "lyric" subjectivity of the disciples but on their relationship with Jesus and their "dramatic" vocation of following him. And in its insistence on remaining open to various possibilities, while concentrating on dedicated involvement in the continuing drama, it encourages a responsible, alert faith that can develop in its multidimensional *menein*, continually shaped and deepened through indwelling the message of this Gospel. John's Gospel may be the richest single textual resource for participants in the theodrama.

Intensity and Extensity in the Ongoing Drama

What has happened to theology in the centuries since John wrote, and what about its contribution to participation in the theodrama in the twenty-first century?

John, the fourth and culminating Gospel, might be seen as the purest example of a twofold wisdom of Christian faith that continues to be replicated generation after generation with many variations, somewhat like the theodrama's genetic code (see the next chapter for an exploration of this metaphor).

First, there is a wisdom of intensity and reserve.[5] John focuses on what he sees as the core identity of Christian faith, leaving out a great deal in the Synoptic tradition (which is itself the product of much selection and distillation), and reshaping much else so as to indicate certain utterly basic matters. Chief among these is his concentration on the person of Jesus, above all his "I am" incarnating the "I am" of God. Similarly, he emphasizes faith and word, love, glory, Abraham, Moses ... the Holy Spirit, crucifixion, resurrection. The early church continued seeking this wisdom, distilling its faith into a range of key elements: a scriptural canon that included John; baptismal formulae "in the name of the Father, Son and Holy Spirit," around which formed concise creeds to act as a "rule of faith"; patterns of Eucharistic liturgy; core elements of catechesis covering faith and practice; a "church year" and lectionary of selected scriptural readings that represented key events and characters of the theodrama; and doctrinal definitions, especially regarding Jesus Christ. It was a complex process accompanied by much prayer, debate, and controversy. At its heart was a sense of the value of underdetermined texts and practices in which all could participate with something of the multi-dimensional *menein*, indwelling, discussed above. At its wisest, it was content not to over-define a reality inexhaustibly rich, not to be over-prescriptive regarding a single normative understanding, and to leave plenty of room for fresh interpretation and improvisation. It allowed for a God-centered intensity while recognizing the mystery of God and God's purposes.

Second, there was a complementary wisdom of extensity and ramification.[6] In John, this is seen right from the start in the Prologue's leading term for Jesus, *ho logos*, the Word, and his association with all creation. By using a key term of the Jewish scriptures, which was also a key term of Greek civilization, John underwrites the endless task of seeking fruitful connections and insights beyond the Bible. Christianity has only rarely attempted to restrict its theology to what is explicitly in scripture, because it sees scripture as authorizing going beyond scripture to engage thoughtfully with whatever is found in creation and culture. John firmly makes the identity of Jesus inseparable from his relevance to all things and all people. His culminating affirmation of the open-ended ramification of Christian truth, in line with his recognition of the incompleteness of truth (even about what Jesus did) in his own Gospel, is in Jesus' teaching on the Holy Spirit "leading into all the truth," as discussed above. It is a theology of superabundance taken up in varying degrees by the early church, as exemplified vividly by Origen, Augustine, and the Syriac poet-theologians Aphrahat and Ephrem. The abundant exploration, improvisation, and application around core themes and practices of faith are vividly seen in commentaries, teachings, philosophies, sermons, prayers, hymns, letters, martyrologies, hagiographies, histories, confessions, and other genres, besides being represented in poetry, art, architecture, music, and other artistic forms.

How are these two wisdoms interrelated? One approach (rooted in the prudent wisdom of reserve) is to seek normative criteria for the correspondence of one with the other, asking whether the ramifications are in line with the identity expressed in canon, creed, and other core expressions of the faith. This quest to define orthodoxy has been a major issue in theology over the centuries and still is today. It must be possible for a community of faith to say whether or not a particular expression is within the boundaries of what it considers Christian. Every church does this somehow, though their ways of deciding vary greatly, as do the consequences of their decisions for those judged unorthodox. The most common situation is for a controversial statement, action, practice, work of art, or whatever to provoke debate which sometimes leads to a definitive community verdict of acceptance or rejection. Communities differ enormously in the amount of debate, diversity, and dissent they can accommodate, yet they all need to cope with it as wisely as possible.

So there is needed a wisdom of argument, dispute, deliberation, and decision – a wisdom that is, of course, inseparable from taking decisions about the contents of both the distillations and the ramifications. Many chapters in the history of polemical dispute in

Christian theology are appalling in their bitterness, misrepresentation, and lack of gentleness and generosity. Appropriately, the main area of recent theology in which a gentler and more generous wisdom of dispute can be found is ecumenical theology, which tries to deal with the consequences of past disputes that led to church divisions. Yet within particular Christian churches, although they frequently owe their survival without division to those who have learned the wisdom of dispute, this is rarely explicitly discussed or taught. My own church, the Anglican Communion, has been driven by recent divisions to reflect on this more than most, and it is possible that out of its anguish there may emerge a more explicit, matured wisdom of dispute about Christian identity from which others can learn.

Yet there is another, more adventurous, dimension of Christian wisdom that is vital to the constructive interrelation of the wisdoms of reserve and ramification and, like the wisdom of dispute, intrinsic to both of them.[7] It has been mentioned above as the theological practice most obviously in line with Jesus' giving of the Holy Spirit after saying: "As the Father has sent me, so I send you" (20:21). The "as … so" deeply connects the earlier and later acts of the theodrama and invites theology into many modes of interpreting "in the Spirit" both scripture and ongoing history. Above all, this needs to be sensitive to the dramatic quality of the divine involvement in history, as is classically attempted in typological or figural interpretation of scripture.

The New Testament's interpretation of the Old Testament is the basic example of this, and is the main model for continuing interpretation, theological teaching, liturgical expression, and ethical, ecclesial, and political discernment. The basic "language" of the New Testament accounts of Jesus Christ and the first churches is that of the Old Testament. There is a thriving scholarly industry that continually finds more echoes, common terms, analogies, patterns, structures, tropes, and other traces of the Old in the New, besides abundant obvious references to texts, stories, characters, and images. Just within John's first chapter, in addition to explicit reference to creation, God, children of God, Moses, the law, Messiah,

Elijah, "the prophet," Isaiah, Holy Spirit, Son of God, Lamb of God, King of Israel, and Son of Man, there are key terms whose first context of interpretation should probably be the Old Testament (word, life, light, believe, darkness, sent, witness, know, people, power, will, flesh, glory, fullness, grace, truth, Jerusalem, wilderness, water, sin, Heaven, disciples, and angels) and clear traces of patriarchal stories (especially Jacob), wisdom literature, psalms, and various prophets. As the New Testament is steeped in the Old, so it is desirable, in line with the "... so I send you" for Christian understanding of later history and of all spheres of life to be steeped in both Old and New.

There is a vast variety of ways in which this happens, from study, catechesis, and memorizing to worship, preaching, and art, but the two most substantial theological approaches are, on the one hand, typological or (more comprehensively) figural interpretation and, on the other, doctrines or (more comprehensively) teachings which focus on one or more aspects of the theodrama with a view to current understanding and practice. These are inseparably related.

Figural interpretation recognizes the ongoing dramatic character of Christian living. So the most essential move in understanding and living within any particular period is to be as discerning as possible in making significant connections between it and the biblical drama. This is a risky venture, and Christian history is full of examples of mistaken, ill-judged, or even disastrous identifications with biblical characters and events – sometimes by whole churches or peoples. "The corruption of the best is the worst" has frequently been borne out in this regard, but it remains at the center of most Christians' identity to identify with the death and resurrection of Jesus in baptism and Eucharist, and somehow to figure oneself and one's community into a biblical understanding of the present age.

Doing this as thoughtfully as possible has opened up a range of fundamental questions correlating with aspects and events of the theodrama. These range from, "Who is God?," and, "How is creation to be related to current scientific understanding?," to, "What is salvation?," and, "What might we hope for?" Classically, these have been gathered together under the category of "doctrines" or *loci* ("places") of theology, which some thinkers have ordered as systematically as possible (sometimes the field is called "systematic theology"), but which have generally allowed for a wide variety of configurations and interrelations. Three basic points need to be made about these theological teachings.

First, their setting within the theodrama and in the service of continuing participation in it needs to be remembered. It has at times been tempting to think of theology as ahistorical truth. This is one aspect of the larger point that it needs to be continually rethought in fresh engagement with scripture, tradition, and contemporary life and thought.

Second, a benefit of trying to think systematically about any one major teaching or *locus* is the discovery that each needs to be related to all the others. Further, to rethink one teaching means drawing it through consideration of the others and being open to rethinking them too. So, a development in one's doctrine of God is likely to affect one's understanding of creation, providence, Jesus Christ, salvation, and so on. That in turn means that the different stages of the biblical drama are being thought through in relation to each other and that they are also being related to the ongoing drama today. This indicates from another angle the fundamental importance of figural interpretation. Working out specific teachings on, for example, the presence of Jesus Christ, the mission of the Church, or the Kingdom of God in history, is the hard intellectual work inseparable from recognizing one's role in the theodrama today.

Third, that intellectual work needs to be resourced as richly as possible, especially by the range of intellectual disciplines. The next chapter will take up this point, but for now it is worth highlighting one discipline, philosophy (which for many centuries embraced many of the other disciplines which have since become autonomous). The relation of Christian theology to philosophy has long been a contested matter.[8] From the standpoint of the present chapter's concern with theodrama, the fruitfulness of philosophy for theology is not through offering an overall systematic understanding of reality through and within which the drama can be understood and intellectually justified. On the contrary, the identification of God and God's purposes through the biblical testimony is not assimilable within any other framework, though it might be importantly questioned and illuminated.

There is today a very wide range of conversations going on between different theologies and philosophies, with many models of their relationship. For this manifesto, the most helpful map of that complex field is that of Hans Frei.[9] It is of special relevance in this chapter because the distinctive feature by which he characterizes mainstream Christian identity is the Gospel story understood as a realistic narrative testifying to Jesus Christ – in my terms, the climactic act of the theodrama. His typology gives primacy to the narrative/dramatic. The types that are most congenial to my manifesto for the future of theology (though in fact, as for Frei, all have their contribution) are those that allow the biblical drama to be the primary source for identifying who God is and what God's purposes are, while also thoughtfully engaging with many other sources.[10]

The recent theological work that perhaps best exemplifies this type, and is explicitly in line with Frei, is David Kelsey's *Eccentric Existence: A Theological Anthropology*.[11] Kelsey gives primacy to identifying God with reference to Jesus Christ and to "the narrative logic of canonical [biblical] accounts of how God relates to all that is not God."[12] He resists any totalizing epic tendency by differentiating three basic ways God relates in creating, in consummating, and in reconciling, and he criticizes most Christian theology for its tendencies to allow one or two of these to be absorbed and lose its distinctiveness.[13] In my terms, the theodrama is primary, while being rethought and having its traditional interpretations critically assessed. Kelsey is also "systematically unsystematic."[14] He is rigorous in conceptualizing doctrines and their interrelations, and showing how they are warranted by scripture and responsive to cultural and intellectual questions and developments. Yet he also recognizes, with Kierkegaard, that existence is not a system, and that there can appropriately be many theological loose ends. He draws on various philosophies without allowing any to dictate what he argues are the non-negotiable elements in a Christian understanding of humanity. These essentials are the implications of human existence being centered in God (therefore centered outside itself, so "eccentric"), who creates it, draws it to eschatological consummation, and overcomes whatever hinders that consummation. Kelsey's narrative and conceptual approach sometimes risks losing the sense of drama, but that sense is repeatedly renewed by his focus on the "quotidian" – the everyday, public world of ordinary human practices where faith, hope, and love are realized or not.

Conclusion: Drama, Wise Theological Creativity, and an Unanswered Question

The vision that is emerging from this drama-centered discussion, about how to try to do wise and creative theology in the future in line with the Bible and the best in the tradition, might be seen as a refinement and enrichment of the four elements introduced in the previous chapter.

Retrieval needs to be especially alert to the ways in which, in the Bible and previous periods, the wisdoms of reserve and ramification have maintained a primary focus on the dramatic character of God's involvement with the world. They have sought to remain faithful to the Gospel and self-critical of Christian ways of responding to it, while daring to respond creatively to new problems and situations.

Theological engagement with God, church, and world needs to conceive of itself as playing a responsible role in the theodrama, especially practicing figural reading of the Bible, rethinking and improvising upon classic teachings (all the *loci* from God to eschatology) in primarily dramatic categories for the twenty-first century, and being wary of the many attractions of overly epic or lyric approaches. Its primary perspective is not the grand overview or the self's interiority, but the ongoing, open drama of people and events in interaction in church and society amidst the ups and downs of human history.

Theological thought that figures itself into the theodrama will return again and again to scripture, as this chapter has attempted in a little way to reread the Gospel of John, in order to renew as wisely and creatively as possible the intensity and extensity of its thinking. Encouraged by scripture, it will also look to many other sources, including philosophy and the other disciplines to be discussed in the next chapter. It will be as conscious as possible of its own historicity – its use of concepts that have been historically shaped and the contribution that fresh thought might make in the present "act" of the drama.

Theological expression will not only be sensitive to the lyric, epic, and dramatic elements in its communication but will also be aware that its own discourse, spoken and written, is itself an event in the ongoing drama. Words have effects, and how, where, when, and by whom they are spoken or written matters greatly.

Finally, there is a major unanswered question about the theodrama as so far discussed. Frei's typology is especially concerned with European and, in particular, German-language academic theology since the early nineteenth century, as it grappled with the impact of Western modernity. It might be seen as a study of the main theological strategies that were developed during that period in response to what has probably been the most comprehensive challenge that the classic Christian theodrama has faced. It is the challenge of what Charles Taylor has called "A Secular Age,"[15] and that will be the starting point for the next chapter, whose accompanying theme of theology's relationship with the arts, sciences, and humanities is one way of exploring how that challenge can be met.

3

A Dramatic Code for Twenty-first Century Theology

How do we describe the epoch we are now living in? Is it modern, late modern, "chastened modern," postmodern, "a secular age," post-secular, religious and secular, or none of these? For an epic mindset, as described in the previous chapter, this can be a serious problem as it tries to identify the unifying features of our period and its relation to what preceded it. Epic accounts have been very influential in the past few hundred years. In the twentieth century vast forces were mobilized to promote and impose various epics – the Nazi thousand-year Reich, Communist revolution leading to the classless society, and capitalist competition leading to a wealthier world. Of those three, the Fascist focus on race and the Communist focus on class had largely lost their impetus as expansive ideologies by the end of the century. This left the capitalist focus on economic life and money in a dominant position, though confidence in that has since been affected by crises relating to debt, credit, and banking.

In the early twenty-first century money continues as a primary focus, often associated with the epic economic rise or decline of major economic "empires," especially the United States, Japan, the European Union, China, India, Russia, and Brazil. Other epic options include a scientific "metanarrative" drawing on Darwinian evolution, an apocalyptic scenario of the world headed for ecological disaster, and various predictions of a world dominated by one religion (usually Islam or Christianity) – for worse or for better.

At the opposite extreme are the many "lyric" possibilities. Religion has for many become a largely private, individual matter, with a vast variety of choices in values, spiritualities, and practices. There are many new religions, and within most traditional religions there is a wide range of options, with thousands of new groups springing up. Beyond what is labeled "religion" is a plethora of lifestyles, quasi-religious or secular. Faced with almost unlimited possibilities, individuals can put together portfolios of jobs, interests, activities, relationships, and pastimes, with frequent changes according to preference, and all the while their minds and imaginations can be variously entertained by many media available while they are at home, traveling, or just stopping for coffee.

So, as the grand epics lose plausibility or relevance for many, there is fragmentation, individualism, and a riot of pluralism. That may seem a negative summary, but it could just as well be described as opening up the development of rich and diverse subjectivities, allowing for imaginative and committed engagements in many spheres of life, and enabling responsible planning, persuasion, and decision-making in communication with a wide variety of stakeholders.

I would suggest that "drama," as understood in the previous chapter, is a helpful category for coping with this dynamic polarity, for describing what has been best about Western modernity, and for helping to shape a vision of the sort of theology that is most desirable in the present century. The "dramatic code" (the distant yet suggestive analogy is with a genetic code) with which this chapter culminates is an attempt to identify key normative intensities for current theology. It is a double set of "cries," seven to be heard and seven to be uttered. They are a code for thinking in line with the Christian theodrama, alert to its forms in scripture and down the centuries to the present, and for fruitful engagement with God, church, and world today. First, however, it is necessary to put the case for a dramatic alternative to the epic narrative that has been most influential in Western modernity's account of religion.

Modern Secularity and the Health of the Public Sphere

A common story begins by saying that around five hundred years ago (though the starting point can be earlier or later) Western society was religious. Then came developments that are summarized under the heading of modernity, such as Renaissance and Reformation, colonization of the Americas, Enlightenment, American and French Revolutions, nationalism, Industrial Revolution, natural and social sciences, scientific medicine and technologies, modern bureaucracy, democracy, policing and surveillance, new forms of warfare, transport and communication, mass education and new movements in the arts, culture, and philosophy. The result has been the decline of religion in the public sphere and the decline of religious belief, especially among the better educated. There is therefore an epic of modernity in which a religious society turns into a secular society. The latter, on this account, may still have forms of religion but they do not play a significant role in public life and progressively disappear as educational levels rise.

This epic correlation of modernity with secularization was, as regards religion, largely adopted by other influential epics of the twentieth century. Fascism, Communism, capitalism, and ideologized versions of Darwinian evolution had each virtually written religion out of its scenario of the future, seeing itself as part of a linear movement from a religious to a secular world. In recent decades this scenario has become less persuasive. Empirically, religion has made something of a comeback in the public sphere in various forms – Christian, Muslim, Jewish, Hindu, Buddhist – in different parts of the world, and statistics seem to indicate more not fewer adherents. What is arguably the most modern nation, the United States, has never exemplified the thesis that modernity leads to religious decline, and the current evidence from Africa, South America, Russia, and Asia seems to be more in line with the US. Indeed, Europe seems the exception rather than the rule, and those who developed the epic appear to have been generalizing from their own untypical case.[1] It may even be that Europe is changing in this regard: a historian writing on Christianity and Islam in contemporary Europe predicts a thriving future for both of them.[2]

The increasing implausibility of the dominant epic has led to alternatives, especially claiming that we have now entered a "post-secular" age. Yet the evidence that made the one-way secularization epic plausible is still there. I suggest that, rather than replacing one epic with another, a better way is to think in terms of an open-ended drama. This has the general advantage that it is more suited to a situation in which the forces that are the "heroes" of epics, such as Communism, Fascism, capitalist democracy, science-based ideologies, and religions, are in conflict with each other. Unless one completely aligns oneself with a single epic it is difficult to tell the story of modernity as if one has an overview of it, and the interaction of the forces invites a dramatic narrative form.

This allows acknowledgment of the beneficial role of the secular dimension of modernity in enabling societies to be genuinely dramatic in ethos, while at the same time critiquing its tendencies toward one-sided dominance in epic or lyric modes. In response to lethal and devastating religious conflict in Europe, above all in the Thirty Years War (1618–48), many religious people as well as skeptics and atheists (then few in number and influence) saw the sense in what might be called a minimal secular framework. This aimed to allow those with different religious commitments to live in peace. "Toleration" was one of its watchwords. Within states it provided minorities with the right to practice their religion, which in turn could develop into full citizenship. Between states it removed religion as a cause for war. There were complex histories in different European countries, with varying degrees of toleration and varying rates at which it was granted, and what was put in place in the United States of America after its War of Independence was different from any of the European frameworks. But the main, beneficial thrust of minimal secularism, wherever it was practiced, was toward peaceful accommodation of religious differences. Religiously identified forces had fought bitterly without any one gaining overall victory; peace could not be on the terms of one religion only; minimal rules and values that might be called "secular" allowed a conception of the public good that was not constantly threatened by religious conflict.

In my terms, what was happening was that epic conceptions of religion were learning through the bitter lessons of history how to be part of something more like a drama in which there could be genuine engagement around some common aims and values. This happened most successfully within nations. It was complexly interwoven with the growth of modern constitutional democracy, which at its best is the most thoroughly dramatic polity: it creates a stage on which deep differences can engage with each other according to rules and customs, where no one party can claim the right to long-term power, and where individual and corporate agency (e.g., legislature, judiciary, civil service, corporations, trusts, and institutions of civil society such as religious bodies, charities, trades unions, professional associations, and universities) is not simply subsumed under an "epic" state or ideology.

Between nations the epic mindset proved harder to modify. It tended to migrate from religion and come to animate nationalisms and imperialisms, and it was only after the Second World War (1939–45) that European nations began to shape the theater for their international interplay that grew into the European Union. That developed with widespread religious and secular support. On the wider global scene, the success of attempts to create analogous frameworks for peaceful dramatic interaction and resolution of conflicts has been far more sporadic.

The development of pluralist states and peaceful relations between states according to constitutions and other arrangements that do not assume a particular religious commitment, and in which all can participate fully whether they belong to a religious body or not, is a massive achievement of secularism. But, as with most achievements, it has been accompanied by temptations. One has been to forget its largely religious origins and to underestimate the extent to which those roots are still needed to nourish it. The most serious (closely related) temptation has been to attempt to replace religion in the public realm by secularism in a comparably epic mode. The French Revolution, various imperialisms and nationalisms, Communism, and Nazism have been the most obvious forms of anti-religious or non-religious epic dominance, and within democracies there have been various secularist bids for overarching power. The latter can be seen in attempts to exclude religious bodies from state-recognized education, refuse them state funding for charitable activities carried out according to their own principles, and impose secularist or "religion-blind" norms in matters of gender, marriage, family life, adoption, abortion, dress, food, calendar, display of religious symbols, observance of religious obligations, chaplaincy, and much else. Inseparable from such bids is the effort to win the high ground in the clash of world-views and public perception.

The situation now, in the early twenty-first century, is that militant forms of religion and secularism have sharpened debates and conflicts. One response to that is to side with an epic solution and work for its victory. The one suggested here is to renew and develop further the minimal secular framework so painfully worked out in Europe and North America in the centuries after the Thirty Years War. None of the traditional "settlements" (whose main variations are seen in Britain, France, Germany, Holland, Scandinavia, Switzerland, the United States, and Canada) is working without problems, caused partly by the presence of major new religious players (especially Muslims) but also by transformations in cultures, politics, and economics. New settlements would need to take seriously the particular convictions and practices of the various groups, while also being clear about the importance of the public, common good and how that is to be negotiated and sustained. There has to be the potential for religious and other groups to contribute to the common good from their own resources – spiritual, intellectual, ethical, organizational, and material.

The ideal is for each major group player, and as many as possible individuals, to see themselves in dramatic terms. They have roles in a drama that has other players with whom one needs to have dialogue, negotiation, and collaboration for the sake of the flourishing of the whole society. Players can have very varied rationales for their public engagements, and can draw on diverse sources in their own traditions in order to enrich society beyond their own groups.[3] No one group has sole control of the plot – it is worked out through various realms of engagement, involving not only democratic politics but also media, law, education, business, and every other sphere of life and work. There will, of course, be limit situations in which individuals or groups who opt out of the drama and its minimal secular rules need to be restrained or even coerced – those who choose violence in pursuit of their aims are the obvious examples. But fear of such elements should not be allowed to suspend the drama in favor of a state that has systemic control, rationalized by an epic overview and supported by modern techniques of surveillance and coercion.

The opposite danger to the health of the democratic and pluralist drama comes from what I have called the "lyric" side. Whereas the epic at its extreme strives for too much coherence and control, the lyric threatens disintegration and fragmentation so that there is no coherence or possibility of conversation and collaboration in support of the common good. Its extreme, as discussed above, is radical individualism with no sense of responsibility toward any tradition, group, or common enterprise. This can be one reaction to epic impositions, and its prevalence can in turn increase the attractiveness of epic solutions. The dramatic way vitally depends on the health of the various intermediate groups, networks, organizations, parties, and institutions in between the state and the individual. In the public sphere these are the main players, and individuals are largely effective through being identified with them. The societal drama therefore relies on individuals whose identity includes participation in such groups and a sense of responsibility toward the flourishing of the whole society. This in turn requires formation and education that shape people in the understandings and habits of living in a pluralist drama, and these need to be developed as wisely and rigorously as possible by each group. The last part of the present chapter and all of the following chapter (on seeking wisdom with those of other faiths) attempts to think through a Christian way of doing so.

What about the present state of groups and individuals with a secular worldview within this drama-centered perspective? They generally mirror the range of options on the religious side. There are strong attractions toward the extremes of the epic and the lyric that pull on both the religious and the secular, and also on those many who attempt some sort of hybrid of the religious and secular. Yet there are also many on the more secular side who resist the temptations and maintain aspects of the epic and lyric within a dramatic framework. I suspect that the flourishing of societies in the present century will depend to a considerable extent on how well those working within a generally dramatic perspective will be able to converse and collaborate across the boundaries of traditions and commitments. The history of the secular option in modernity (which will be a major concern in the next section) might in this regard be seen as moving from a modest brokering of peace among religious groups, enabling them to shift into seeing themselves as actors in a public drama, through a "heroic" period of epic ambition to take over from an epic religion, to today's widespread disillusionment with secular epics. Many follow what is here advocated as the wiser way: they see the construction of a purely secular worldview (what Taylor labels "exclusive humanism" – see further below) as a new possibility that has many parallels with religious positions and that needs to work out ways of engaging with them for the common good. The vision is of a complexly secular and religious society[4] with a healthy intensity of dramatic engagement in public life and all areas of ordinary life and work. Great things are at stake in this, but the flourishing of societies can only be achieved if there are limits on how any group can seek to get its own way.

A Drama-centered Account of Modernity

The main focus so far has been limited to the shaping of a secular and religious public sphere in a dramatic perspective. Now I will extend the scope by offering a drama-centered take on one of the most recent and ambitious accounts of Western modernity, that of

Charles Taylor in *A Secular Age*,[5] as the extended horizon within which the intensity of the "dramatic code" which follows can be understood. I will take much of what Taylor says in his vast work to be true enough for the purposes of this chapter, while pressing his account further in the direction of the dramatic, since a more dramatic understanding of modernity and of Christian faith seems to be in line with his best insights.

Taylor's helpful master concept about the secular is what he calls "Secularity 3." Secularity 1 is about the reduced significance of religion in the public sphere of common institutions and practices. Secularity 2 is about the falling off of religious belief and practices such as churchgoing. Secularity 3 is about the conditions for belief. In Europe, in 1500, God was intrinsic to the meaning of life and human flourishing, the nature of society and the natural world. Today, faith in the Christian God is still possible, but the conditions within which it occurs are radically different. It is held as one option among others and in many situations is not the norm and is difficult to embrace and sustain, so that faith as a lived experience is transformed. "Secularity in this sense is a matter of the whole context of understanding in which our moral, spiritual or religious experience and search takes place."[6] The difference is seen above all in the fact that atheist "exclusive humanism" is now taken for granted by millions of people, and it is normal to find those whose conception of a full human life is fully immanent, without reference to God or anything transcending the world or going beyond death.

In my terms, Taylor is describing how the context in which Christian faith is held has become far more thoroughly and comprehensively dramatic. In 1500, of course, faith could be practiced in such a way as to give primacy to the dramatic perspective of people and events in interplay over time. But today believers are unavoidably in encounter with worldviews and individuals whose whole ethos and conception of reality questions and contradicts theirs. So to hold and practice their faith involves continual awareness of alternatives and frequent conversation and argument with them. This dialogue may be with people we know, with written or media representations, and internalized in thought and feeling.

It also requires faith-inspired action (from prayer and worship to ethical and political witness) in often unsympathetic or even hostile settings. So a lively faith requires many forms of dramatic performance. It also requires something of the epic mindset in trying to make overall sense of history and cosmos (yet without claiming too much, as the epic mindset by itself tends to); and it cries out for nourishment of its subjectivity (mind, desire, imagination, and will) in order to have the "lyric" depth and resilience for faith to flourish under difficult conditions (yet without giving in to the lyric temptation to disengage from the ongoing drama).

This account of the present situation is inseparable from Taylor's story of how it came about. His main polemic is against what might be seen as the classic epic account of secularity, what he calls the "subtraction theory": that it emerged as the natural outcome of superfluous layers of religion and superstition being stripped away by growing scientific understanding. He shows persuasively how the emergence was more zigzag than linear, that it was not at all an inevitable result of scientific understanding, and that exclusive humanism is a creative, contingent achievement.

Taylor's account of how the transformation from 1500 to Secularity 3 came about has a central storyline, the "Reform Master Narrative." It tells how Latin Christianity generated a reforming energy directed initially at purifying the faith and making Christian society more fully Christian. It began in the late Middle Ages and its most comprehensive achievement was the Reformation, followed by the Counter-Reformation. The energy was channeled into secular as well as Christian reforms, and Taylor is alert to the ways in which these often took on characteristics I have been calling "epic." So there was a concern for uniformity, order, codes, rules, and the disciplining of whole churches and societies. There was the "iron cage" constructed by the disenchanted rationality of bureaucrats, and the incarceration and punishment of the marginal and deviant. The public sense of time became linear and homogenized. A critical opening for the development of atheist, exclusive humanism was given by deism, which made way for conceptions of the world as autonomous and impersonal. God was an architect or watchmaker, not active in history and so not dramatic. For those who dispensed with God, this rational world was enough.

Taylor also tells of new forms of subjectivity, the shaping of senses of self, some in line with the epic elements (disciplined, "buffered,"[7] autonomous, rational, disembedded,[8] egalitarian, benevolent); some in partial or full revolt against it (the Romantics, Nietzsche, Freud). He sees the culmination of modern subjectivity in a post-1950 cultural revolution in the North Atlantic world, with its "expressive individualism" on a mass scale, a new consumer culture, an ethos of authenticity and personal fulfillment, gender equality and sexual pleasure, emphases on creativity, feeling, imagination, choice, individual responsibility, and accompanying spiritualities beyond religious institutions.[9]

Taylor's main points tend to be subsumed under what I call the epic and the lyric, together with the dialectic between them, yet he would probably not object to his master narrative being called a drama in my sense. His danger is that he presents a fragmented picture, culminating in "galloping pluralism," and finally gropes for an epic coherence.[10] Yet there are also rich dramatic resources in his constructive proposals that help set the scene for the "dramatic code" to be presented below. These are primarily in his understanding of time, the pedagogy of God, and ordinary life.

On time, Taylor perceptively analyses the modern dissolution of the public temporal framework of the Christian liturgical year, with its "high times" and ordinary times connected with the Christian narrative, in favor of the homogeneous, empty linear time of a vast, impersonal universe. Yet he also resists taking this as the last word. It is possible to interpret and be formed in faith by the Bible in a Galilean and Darwinian universe, just as it was within a Ptolemaic and Aristotelian one, and there are even "new loci of mystery" that can be fruitful for belief as well as for unbelief.[11] The "gathered time" of Augustine, "the gathering together of past into present to project a future,"[12] can have its contemporary versions in forms of history, narration, commemoration, celebration, ritual, and responses to death.[13] Taylor's overall message is clear: while today's atheist interpretations of time make sense in terms of his story (his hermeneutic of generosity in relation to those with whose conclusions he disagrees is an attractive feature of his work), so too does a contemporary Christian understanding of "gathered time." In other words, the Christian theodrama can be plausibly affirmed and inhabited today.

Taylor is thoroughly and orthodoxly incarnational in his own conception of Christianity.[14] His Christianity is no static essence and can learn the lessons of history through multiple events and transformations. Its dramatic struggles in the present he describes as a three-cornered battle between secular humanists, anti-humanist neo-Nietzscheans, and "those who acknowledge some good beyond life."[15] He then significantly differentiates the third into two very different approaches: those who want to return to an earlier understanding of reality, and those, such as himself, who owe a great deal to modernity, including its unbelief. Later, facing the problem of violence (the seriousness with which he takes this is a good index of his dramatic sensibility), he proposes a theology of the pedagogy of God: "God is slowly educating mankind, slowly turning it, transforming it from within … But at the same time, the pedagogy is being stolen, has been misappropriated, and misapplied; the education is occurring in this field of resistance."[16] It is a slow pedagogy that can also include leaps and breaks with some earlier forms. "We might see God as the supreme tennis player, who responds to our bad moves with new ways of countering them."[17] This is a conception of providence that (whatever we make of its tennis metaphor) encourages a drama-centered theology.

What Taylor is most grateful for in modernity is its emphasis (both in Christian and secular versions) on ordinary life. "The practical primacy of life has been a great gain for human kind."[18] Human flourishing in everyday life might be seen as the core concern of his philosophy and his love-centered Christian theology. It is the perspective that the previous chapter discovered in the Gospel of John, and it is in line not only with the narratives of Old and New Testaments but also with other biblical genres such as law, prophecy, psalms, wisdom, and letters to young churches.

These three elements of temporal framework, historical pedagogy, and ordinary human flourishing in love can be understood as converging on a dramatic conception of contemporary life and thought. They encourage an attempt to encapsulate the dramatic shape of future Christian theology in a "dramatic code" that tries to encourage wise creativity in retrieval, thought, and expression while being deeply engaged with God, church, and world.

A Dramatic Code for Theology Today

What follows is an experimental exercise in what the previous chapter called a wisdom of intensification or reserve, together with indicators of an accompanying wisdom of ramification or extensity. The imagery (which should not be pressed too literally) is from genetics: a double helix of cries that has the potential to generate new theological life that allows for both continuity and mutative innovation. Above all, the intention is to be true to the primary dramatic focus of this and the previous chapter, while also recognizing the importance of the epic and lyric. The cry[19] is seen as a form of primary utterance in scripture and in life, a sign of intensity and importance, in itself a dramatic event that calls for wise discernment and response.

Here is a suggested set of primary cries. They are in pairs, the first being in each case a cry that, from a Christian standpoint, is primarily to be heard, the second a cry that is primarily to be uttered; though all are, of course, both heard and uttered.

The Lord is God!	Alleluia!
Christ has died! Christ is risen! Christ will come again!	Come, Lord Jesus!
Receive the Holy Spirit!	Come, Holy Spirit!
Beloved, let us love one another!	Let everyone who is thirsty come!
[The cries of the world]	Your Kingdom come!

Hear instruction and be wise!	But where shall wisdom be found?
[The call to each by name]	Here I am!

A brief theological rationale for these particular cries is as follows.

1. The Lord is God! – Alleluia!

"*The Lord is God!*" is at the heart of Jewish and Christian worship, repeated with many variations in scriptures and liturgies. It is rooted in fulfilling the primary command of *torah*:

> "Hear, O Israel: The Lord is our God, the Lord alone. You shall love the Lord your God with all your heart, and with all your soul, and with all your might." (Deuteronomy 6:4–5)

In line with this are the responsive cries to God of praise, adoration, blessing, rejoicing, thanks, hallowing, lament, protest, and repentance, led by the Psalmist's repeated:

"*Alleluia!*" – Praise the Lord.

The theodrama is centrally between God and God's creation, and the most concentrated expression of it is in the poetry of scripture, supremely in the Psalms, which are almost pure cry. They affirm the epic scope and completeness of God's glory and involvement with creation, and pour out lyric expressions of subjectivity in all its moods and passions, but above all they articulate the drama of engagement with God in history and in ordinary life. Perhaps the most comprehensive cry, pervading so many liturgies and prayers, is: "Lord, have mercy!"

To discern the meaning and implications of these primary cries, theology needs to think through not only the doctrine of God but also all reality in relation to God, from within the dynamic of praise and thanks,[20] and from knowledge of grief, suffering, and forgiveness. This also especially leads into the theology and spirituality of prayer, worship, and liturgy.[21]

2. Christ has died! Christ is risen! Christ will come again! – Come, Lord Jesus!

Christ has died! Christ is risen! Christ will come again! is a climactic cry in many liturgies of Eucharist or Holy Communion. It points to the central events of the Christian drama, which are also fundamental to Christian identity in baptism. This cry reaches forward to the culmination of history and figurally back to creation and fall (Jesus' resurrection being seen as a new creation, and the cross as healing the sin of Adam and reversing his death), so there is an epic and mythic scope, together with the primacy of drama. The other figural resonances of Jesus with Old Testament events, figures, and images are almost inexhaustible. Above all, the focus is on the person of Jesus Christ as the central character of the drama. All roles are played in his presence, before his face, and Christian subjectivity consists in living with this face shining, and this voice sounding, in the heart.[22] His cries are to be attended to constantly, among them: "The Kingdom of God is at hand: repent and believe the Gospel!," "Follow me!," "Blessed are the poor, the merciful, the pure in heart, the peacemakers," "Love your enemies!," "Do not be afraid!," "Come to me, all who labour and are weighed down," "Let anyone who is thirsty come to me," "Take, eat, this is my body," "My God, my God, why have you forsaken me?," "I am with you always."

Come, Lord Jesus! is the final cry of the Bible (Revelation 22:20). What to hope for and expect is centered on who is hoped for and expected. The content of Christian orientation to the future (eschatology) has been highly controversial from the time of the first disciples and is still deeply divisive among churches around the world today. This manifesto is Johannine in advocating a wisdom of reserve and intensification that concentrates on ongoing participation in the theodrama of love, with a minimum of epic prediction or speculation (as discussed above in chapter 2 in relation to the ending of the Gospel of John).

The theological discernment called for by these cries relates to the whole theodrama from the standpoint of Christology, soteriology, and eschatology,[23] with a special concern for the theology of baptism and Eucharist.[24]

3. Receive the Holy Spirit! – Come, Holy Spirit!

Receive the Holy Spirit! is the quiet exclamation of Jesus breathing the Holy Spirit on his disciples in the Gospel of John (John 20:22 – see above, chapter 2). The more spectacular events on the day of Pentecost, told in the Acts of the Apostles (chapter 2), are accompanied by speaking in various tongues and Peter's interpretation of the event as fulfilling the prophecy of Joel:

> "In the last days it will be, God declares,
> That I will pour out my Spirit upon all flesh."
> (Acts 2:17)

That combination of Johannine intimacy with Petrine publicity, the face to face with the global horizon,[25] is vital to the continuation of the theodrama so as to do justice both to the lyric transformation of selves (God is, as Augustine says, more intimate to us than we are to ourselves[26]) and to the epic scale of the Gospel's significance.

Come, Holy Spirit! is a basic, comprehensive Christian prayer. It trusts that God is more willing to give than we are to receive, and that the supreme gift, renewed daily and inexhaustibly abundant, is the Holy Spirit. The giving of the Spirit of God, the Spirit of Jesus Christ, energizes and inspires all that is desired by God for us and for "all flesh," and all that might fulfill our deepest desires. Within the theodrama, the Spirit hovers over the face of the waters before creation (Genesis 1:2[27]), initiates the ultimate cry of "Come!,"[28] and in the meanwhile inspires children of God to "cry, 'Abba! Father!'" and "helps us in our weakness; for we do not know how to pray as we ought, but that very Spirit intercedes with sighs too deep for words" (Romans 8:15, 26).

Yet the Spirit is normatively seen in the drama of Jesus. The Spirit rests on him in his baptism, the opening act of his ministry.

Jesus claims to be fulfilling the words of Isaiah in his first public statement in his home town of Nazareth:

> "The Spirit of the Lord is upon me,
> Because he has anointed me
> to bring good news to the poor.
> He has sent me to proclaim release to the captives
> and recovery of sight to the blind,
> to let the oppressed go free,
> To proclaim the year of the Lord's favor."
> (Luke 4:18–19)

That is a manifesto of the inauguration of the Kingdom of God as historical drama, and it also initiates the dramatic provocation and confrontation that were to lead to Jesus' death: "They got up, drove him out of the town" (Luke 4:29). The Spirit leads Jesus the way of the cross, and that is the dramatic model for Christian baptism and discipleship.

The theological challenges posed by the coming of the Spirit again encompass the whole theodrama, now from a third angle. Its special concerns include some of the most contentious issues among Christians and between Christians and other people. What is "baptism in the Spirit"? How and by whom might claims to "have the Holy Spirit" be decided? What is it to be "holy," and how might holiness be acquired, sustained, and increased? What about the "gifts of the Spirit"[29] and "fruits of the Spirit"?[30] How are biblical inspiration and authority to be understood? How are "word" and "Spirit" related? How does the Spirit relate to church authority and succession? Is the Spirit given in other religions and beyond religions? How might Christian evangelism and mission best be understood and practiced? In answering such questions, the way theologians balance the epic, lyric, and dramatic is a critical dimension of the overall wisdom and creativity of their retrieval, their engagement with God, church and world, their thinking, and their communication.

These first three are the core Christian cries, focusing on God, Jesus Christ, the Holy Spirit. Yet attending and responding to these is a place where other cries are heard and uttered too. The dramatic code's double helix is longer.

4. Beloved, let us love one another! – Let everyone who is thirsty come!

Beloved, let us love one another! (1 John 4:7). This is the quiet cry, indicating on what the health of the church and its mission depends: love. As the context makes clear, this is rooted in God's initiating love revealed in Jesus, which in turn is grounded in the ultimate affirmation: "God is love, and those who abide in love abide in God, and God abides in them" (1 John 4:16 – on the key word "abide," *menein*, see above, chapter 2). The church is an attempt to abide in God's love. As the letter of John shows, this is not primarily about feelings, interiority, and experiences (important though these are), but about behavior in the drama of ordinary life: "How does God's love abide in anyone who has the world's goods and sees a brother or sister in need yet refuses help? … Those who love God must love their brothers and sisters also" (1 John 3:17, 4:21).

A drama-centered practice of love should have no difficulty with seeing the appropriateness of organizations, institutions, and structures of many sorts. Essential to the church is the capacity to organize worship, build up forms of community life, teach and witness to the faith, and engage in discernment, service, and mission. There are, of course, on the lyric side, temptations to be overly preoccupied with their members' demands for various personal satisfactions unrelated to love and service; there are also the attractions of a seeking to play a heroic role in history and society, and to offer people a confident overview, a prescriptive certainty, and a sense of superiority that turn the drama into a triumphalist epic.

"*Let everyone who is thirsty come!* Let anyone who wishes take the water of life as a gift" (Revelation 22:17) is the final biblical form of the utterly open invitation given by Jesus Christ. It resonates with the cry at the end of Second Isaiah:

> Ho, everyone who thirsts, come to the waters;
> and you that have no money, come, buy and eat!
> Come, buy wine and milk without money and without price.
> Why do you spend your money for that which is not bread,
> and your labour for that which does not satisfy?
> Listen carefully to me, and eat what is good,
> and delight yourselves in rich food.
> Incline your ear, and come to me;
> listen, so that you may live.
> I will make with you an everlasting covenant,
> my steadfast, sure love for David.
> See, I made him a witness to the peoples,
> a leader and commander for the peoples.
> See, you shall call nations that you do not know,
> and nations that you do not know shall run to you,
> because of the Lord your God, the Holy One of Israel,
> for he has glorified you.
>
> (Isaiah 55:1–5)

The book of Isaiah has with justification been called "the fifth Gospel," and seminal forms of all the cries in this dramatic code might be found there. Here, in the imagery of thirst, feasting, satisfaction, and delight, the life-giving generosity of God is opened up. It is intrinsically attractive and open to all, and part of the covenantal drama of God's "steadfast, sure love for David." This is in line with Jesus' proclamation of the Kingdom of God as a feast (Matthew 22:1–14); with his cry "Let anyone who is thirsty come to me, and let the one who believes in me drink" (John 7:37–8); and with the celebration of the Eucharist: "Take, eat … Drink from it, all of you" (Matt. 26:26–7).

This fourth pair of cries points to fundamental theological and practical challenges for Christians. How are we to witness to the overwhelming generosity of God's love in a world where much seems to contradict it, and where others give conflicting witness?[31] How can the church in its various forms be a positive sign of that love rather than, as often, a negative one? How can we delight in what we have received from God and invite others to share it in appropriate ways without violating the spirit of that love by being insensitive, disrespectful, manipulative, or coercive? Trying to answer such questions leads into many doctrines,[32] and especially into all aspects of the theology of the church (ecclesiology). In classic, creedal terms, these questions call for constant rethinking of the meaning of the church as one, holy, catholic (or universal), and apostolic, alert to new developments within and beyond the church. In ordinary church life, they involve practical and pastoral theology, catechesis and homiletics, spiritual accompaniment, organization, and fundraising. They require sensitive use of all the "moods" of theology (see the next chapter) and recognition of the church as a school and theater of drama-centered wisdom.

5. [The cries of the world] – Your Kingdom come!

The cries of the world express suffering, joy, wonder, protest, longing, fear, hatred, love, and much else. God is often said to hear cries, and to be in God's image is to be an attentive listener to cries. Jesus frequently responded to cries of, or on behalf of, the blind, sick, hungry, possessed, guilty, and bereaved. There is something like a biblical economy of cries, especially involving God, victims of suffering and injustice, and those with the ability to relieve suffering and injustice.

> If you close your ear to the cry of the poor,
> you will cry out and not be heard.
> (Proverbs 21:13)

> You shall pay them their wages daily before sunset, because they are poor and their livelihood depends on them; otherwise they might cry to the Lord against you, and you would incur guilt. (Deut. 24:15; cf. 15:9)

> Shout out, do not hold back!
> Lift up your voice like a trumpet!...
> Is not this the fast I choose:
> to loose the bonds of injustice,

to undo the thongs of the yoke,
to let the oppressed go free,
and to break every yoke?
Is it not to share your bread with the hungry,
and bring the homeless poor into your house;
when you see the naked, to cover them,
and not to hide yourself from your own kin?
Then your light shall break forth like the dawn,
and your healing shall spring up quickly;
your vindicator shall go before you,
the glory of the Lord shall be your rear guard.
Then you shall call, and the Lord will answer;
you shall cry for help, and he will say, Here I am.
(Isaiah 58:1–9)

Attending to cries leads straight into ethics, economics, politics, law, medicine, science, technology, the media, education, human rights, national and international security, and, in the limit cases, questions about the use of force, the justification of revolution, and the legitimacy of war. We are inundated by an overwhelming volume of important and often urgent cries, made more immediate by modern communications.

Your Kingdom come! is the first response: a cry in prayer to God for a world in which God's will of love, wisdom, justice, health, peace, and the overall flourishing of human beings and creation is fulfilled, in line with Isaiah 58 and related texts. The perspective is again primarily dramatic, the "appeal in the face of the other"[33] being the central concern and criterion, for all the importance of subjective interiority and systemic analysis and transformation.

The prayer, if it is not hypocritical, carries with it a commitment to theological discernment and to action. The theology of the Kingdom of God relates the theology of the church and its mission to all that can be discerned through ethics, economics, politics, and the other spheres of understanding and engagement listed above. That is a massive set of tasks, and it is in trying to do justice to these that Christian theology is perhaps most obviously inadequate today. In attempting to do better, its response to the sixth pair of cries is vital.

6. Hear instruction and be wise! – But where shall wisdom be found?

Hear instruction and be wise! (Proverbs 8:33) is part of Wisdom's first-person cry which imagines the intimate companionship of Wisdom with God in creation:

> Then I was beside him, like a master worker;
> and I was daily his delight,
> rejoicing before him always,
> rejoicing in his inhabited world
> and delighting in the human race.
>
> (Proverbs 8:30–3)

It is a charter for wisdom-seeking in all areas of knowledge and understanding, and an invitation into the delights as well as the labors of learning. This manifesto attempts to take up and extend the invitation.

But where shall wisdom be found? (Job 28:12[34]). Wisdom can be found in the discernment that responds to each of the cries, and the agenda outlined so far is quite substantial. Yet it is only with the fifth pair of cries that explicit mention has been made of the dimensions of theological wisdom to be found in exploring other academic disciplines. This has arisen at several points in previous chapters, and is implicit more broadly. "Theology and ..." has been seen as one of the most important and attractive areas for twenty-first century theology to develop, and, given the remit of theology to think about God and everything else in relation to God, no discipline can be ignored. So the agenda includes relevant engagement with the natural and human sciences, arts and humanities, medicine, technologies, and applied disciplines. There is no general formula for how to go about this: each field has its own methods, demands, and possibilities.

One discipline that, as in the previous chapter, requires special mention is philosophy. Whether as logic, epistemology, ethics, or metaphysics, philosophy is relevant to theology's learning from all other disciplines. Sometimes, specialist philosophical skills are called for; usually, knowledge of the history of philosophy and of leading philosophers is helpful; above all, a theology (I deliberately do not say "a theologian" because very often in interdisciplinary matters the best work is collaborative) needs to be philosophically "sure-footed."[35] This means being alert to possible philosophical contributions and pitfalls and, where the questions require more specialist help, asking for it.

Some disciplines seek an epic scale of scientific knowledge in cosmology, geology, evolution, or (at the micro level) subatomic physics; others explore human subjectivity through a variety of methods (neurology, genetics, psychology, psychiatry, psychoanalysis, psychotherapy, some types of literature); others have a more obvious dramatic focus, whether in the human sciences, literature, history, or some types of psychology and psychotherapy. Yet the main significance of the priority of the dramatic is not in the object of study but in the community of those who pursue the study. Each field, and each relationship across fields, is an ongoing disciplined conversation. Its drama is in the intensity of engagement between colleagues and between them and students. Whatever the object of study, whether quasars, childhood trauma, or social life in seventeenth-century Italy, it figures within the interpersonal drama of a particular quest for knowledge and understanding: that gives it its human scale and primary context as human knowledge.

7. [Call to each by name] – Here I am!

> When the Lord saw that he had turned aside to see, God called to him out of the bush, "Moses, Moses!" And he said "Here I am." (Exodus 3:4)

One element in the rich, foundational story of the Burning Bush is the call of Moses by name. It has many analogies elsewhere in the Bible,[36] and helps to make a vital point: God not only relates personally to those in the theodrama but calls them by name to play roles in it. How God relates to each person is in many ways mysterious, both in our own case and even more in that of others – "If it is my will ... what is that to you?" (John 21:22, 23). The essential is the "Here I am" in response to the "Follow me!" (John 21:22). It is dramatized for every Christian in his or her baptism, where their naming is accompanied by the sign of the cross and the making of promises.

"Disciple" means "learner." Baptism includes commitment to loving God with all one's heart, soul, mind, and strength, and so calls every Christian to be something of a theological thinker. What this might mean for those who are drawn to study theology academically will be the subject of chapter 9 of this volume. For now, the point is simply that without many responses of "Here I am" there can be no twenty-first century Christian theology. In the transmission of the dramatic code this cry is the essential lyric moment.

Conclusion: Within and Beyond the Drama

Drama has, I hope, been a helpful category through which to understand not only the Bible, theology, and life (chapter 2), but also the relationship of the religious and the secular in the public sphere and the development and significance of Western modernity (this chapter). This has culminated in an attempt to distill a double helix of cries as a generative "dramatic code" for this century's theological thinking. Attending to these cries and discerning how to begin to do justice to them leads into the main questions of theology.

But these cries also continually open onto realms that reveal the limitations of the category of drama. This is most acute in discourse about God. The God of Jesus Christ is utterly involved in the drama of history to the point of incarnation. Yet, even at the point in the New Testament where this is most explicit, there are simultaneously clear indications of utter transcendence. The theological rationale of the Prologue of the Gospel of John has been one of the deepest questions of Christian theology for nearly two thousand years. Its most concise form is to ask how the following statements go together:

> The Word was God ... And the Word became flesh and lived among us, and we have seen his glory, the glory as of a father's only son, full of grace and truth ... From his fullness we have all received, grace upon grace ... No one has ever seen God. It is God the only Son, who is close to the Father's heart, who has made him known. (John 1:1, 14, 18)

To answer that question, the category of drama as developed in this and the previous chapter is useful but not sufficient. The Prologue itself suggests terms such as word, light, life, name, power, glory, grace, truth, and fullness. These are vital to describing and improvising upon what goes on in the theodrama, but they also transcend both it and the categories of lyric and epic. One key term, that of blessing, will be taken as the lead concept in discussing inter-faith engagement in chapter 8 of this volume. But now a different enrichment and expansion of the category of drama will be opened up through exploring the "moods" of theology.

4

Desire Above All

One caricature of theology is as a neat, unquestioning package of dogma in which there are affirmations that say "Believe this!" and commands that say "Do this!" That is theology in what grammarians call the indicative and imperative moods. These are in fact the dominant moods of a great deal of theology, and they are as vital to theology as they are to life. A man and woman getting married are right to exchange basic affirmations: "I do," "I will." A fire-fighter at a blaze is right to order: "Clear the building!" But affirmations and commands by themselves do not make for good theology any more than they do for good living. Before the marriage comes the mutual questioning, the exploration of whether it is the right move, and above all the discernment of whether the desires of each are sufficiently in harmony. After marriage there are (one hopes) years of living out the promises, with a great deal of further questioning, experimental trial and error, and the further shaping and education of desires. The fire-fighter's order is not arbitrary, but comes from years of training, practice drills, and experience, learning to ask the relevant questions and to take decisions after assessing situations in line with the overarching goal of saving lives.

Likewise in Christian theology: there are endless questions to be asked as minds and hearts are stretched in trying to do justice to the wonder of God and God's relationship to all creation – past, present, and future. There is an overarching desire for God and the purposes of God. Between the questioning and the desiring, and weaving into them in fascinating, ever-new ways, are the experiments with possibilities, the affirmations of truths and commitments, and the imperatives that guide judgments and decisions.

A Balanced Dynamic of Theological Moods

This is the dynamic ecology of theological thinking. It is dynamic because it is not a formula (which would reduce it to a simple imperative guideline) but lists essential elements that need to be sensitively combined according to topics and situations. Theological wisdom lies in getting the balance right in a given case. Job's friends came with packaged answers when they should have joined in Job's questioning and longing for God; and good pastors know that in counseling the bereaved there is a time when one simply stays with the agonized, unanswerable cries of grief. The Gospels are primarily testimony to Jesus Christ, and so are largely indicative; but all the other moods – interrogative, imperative, subjunctive (the "may be, might be" mood of experiment and possibility), and optative (the "if only ..." mood of desire and longing) are there too (see below). One blight on the theological tradition has been the attempt to assert overall theological conformity through systematic statements and allied imperatives. These often assume that modes of theology which specialize in the indicative and imperative, such as certain sorts of dogmatic or systematic theology and theological ethics, should be seen as more comprehensive and authoritative than those which (at their best) integrate other moods more fully, such as biblical commentary, theological hermeneutics, philosophical theology, spirituality, pastoral theology, liturgy, hymns, and poetry. One of the advantages of "wisdom," as the key term for what theology is seeking, is that it can accommodate the latter as well as the former genres.

Between Closed Religion and Wide Open Religion

The importance of a wise balance of questions, explorations, affirmations, commands, and desires goes far beyond the writing of theology. Whole communities and traditions can be characterized according to their habitual balances between them. What in our time is often rightly labeled "bad religion" or "dangerous religion" tends to be based on packaged theologies with a heavy investment in telling members exactly what to believe and what to do, and in limiting any scope for questioning and exploring. Such packages have enormous attraction, especially in times of insecurity, pluralism, and rapid change. They appear in all the religions today and also in secular forms of dogmatism. Within many Christian denominations and local congregations there are ongoing battles over the soul and spirit of the faith, and over the boundaries of the community, in which packaged certainties fight it out with more balanced ecologies. Unwise theology has serious practical effects.

There is an opposite pole: forms of religion that are so wide open, fluid, vague, or fragmented that they seem to lack the capacity to make definite affirmations or give any clear guidance for living. "Mix-and-match" temporary blends of experimental beliefs and practices, satisfying the desire for self-fulfillment, would be an extreme version of this, but the mindset represented by these is common in consumer societies and therefore within many religious communities. Often these are not much concerned with theology, but the tendencies contribute to a caricature of theology that is common among those whose own theology is more packaged.

This is the caricature of "liberal" theologies as endlessly interrogative and experimental without ever being able to come to conclusions or to offer nourishing theological food for ordinary people. They are so alert to the array of possibilities, to the suspicions and critiques that can undermine all positions, and to the dangers of exercising authority by supporting doctrinal and ethical instruction (think of all those fundamentalist extremists!), that they cannot say anything definite at all. So there is a dissipation of intellectual energy, and despair at finding a habitable faith. Kierkegaard brilliantly analyzed this extreme as the despair of possibility, over against the opposite, inflexible tendency, as the despair of necessity.[1]

This manifesto's conception of a healthy future for Christian theology rejects the extremes but is hospitable to the moods they represent. There are very high stakes here, both for the church internally and for its ways of relating to other religions and to the rest of society. To advocate a balance of moods that constantly tries to discern what the right blend is for a particular topic, situation, or genre is not only to require continual debate and deliberation but also to invite attack from those many positions that want to eliminate or minimize one or more of the moods. This means that the balanced position must be theologically supported – mostly in the indicative mood!

Theological Moods in Bible and Tradition

It is especially important that the ecology of moods be theologically justified with reference to the Bible. The deadening lack of recognition of the complex interplay of moods across a range of biblical books opens the way for both neat packages and amorphous fragmentations. What follows is only a brief sampling to show how the Bible inspires a theological wisdom that continually seeks to shape faith in many moods, and it will be accompanied by even briefer indications of how the Christian theological tradition at its liveliest has been true to the Bible in this regard.[2]

Indicative testimony and promise

Narrative is the most common biblical genre and, for Christians, the central one. It is the primary mode in which testimony to God is given and the main human characters and history portrayed. Without being able to affirm a good deal on the basis of scriptural testimony Christian faith would not persist. Judging just what can be affirmed is a major task, and the subject of endless scholarly and theological debate. These narratives, largely in the indicative mood, often include inquiry, exploration of possibilities, commands, and hopes. More complexly, they can generate further affirmations, as well as questioning, experimental thinking, imperatives, and desires. Narrative hosts all the moods, and the interplay between them is critical for the shape and thrust of a theology.

The biblical theodrama, from creation to the "last things," with the Christian climax coming in the story of Jesus Christ, shows why the indicative cannot be the embracing mood of Christian theology. This is an unfinished story; final affirmations cannot be made yet; all are provisional until the consummation. The promises embedded in biblical testimonies kindle the desire for God's future, and this openness is reflected in a theology led by this desire and alert for possibilities and surprises. So the optative of desire and longing repeatedly challenges both the neat packages, which already have past, present, and future wrapped up, and the opposite tendencies toward lack of definiteness and direction.

The most central affirmation of all is the naming of God, "I am who I am" (Exodus 3:14), set in the context of the foundational story of the Exodus. God's self-identification includes a narrative of the past – "I am the God of your father, the God of Abraham, the God of Isaac, and the God of Jacob" (3:6); response to the immediate suffering of the people in slavery – "I have heard their cry" (3:7); and promise of future presence – "I will be with you" (3:12). This is not an affirmation that wraps God up; on the contrary, it is more like a riddle, a refusal to offer a self-definition, and an encouragement to question, explore, and find out more as one lives in line with the promise.

The name can also mean: "I will be who I will be." There will be more history, with surprises at least as great as in the past. God is free to be God in new ways. The God of Isaiah in the trauma of exile renews and expands the message: "I am the Lord, your Holy one … I am about to do a new thing; now it springs forth, do you not perceive it?" (Isaiah 43:15, 19). The God of Jesus Christ raises him from the dead and pours out the Holy Spirit "on all flesh"

(Acts 2:17, cf. Joel 2:28), the sign of a "new creation." Witnessing to Jesus Christ "in the Spirit" (the mode of affirmation that is most distinctive of Christian faith) generates a new, unpredictable history with glorious and terrible possibilities. Theology, as it feeds and tests Christian witness in worship, community living, and engagement with the world, needs a wisdom of affirmation that is alive to all the moods of faith.

Imperative law and teaching

"Law" is in English an inadequate translation of the Hebrew "torah." This is perhaps best appreciated by reading (or, better, singing) the longest chapter in the Bible, Psalm 119. It is certainly about imperatives, above all to keep God's decrees, precepts, statutes, commandments, ordinances: in short, God's law. But the spirit of it is not what we usually associate with keeping the law. The psalm is about happiness coming from walking in "the law of the Lord" (Ps. 119:1), passionate pursuit of God and God's ways (v.10 and throughout), "delight in the way of your decrees" (v.14 and throughout), meditation on precepts (v.15 and throughout), understanding being enlarged (v.32), longing for God's precepts (v.40 and throughout), "trust in your word" (v.42 and throughout), love of the commandments (v.47 and throughout), hope in the word of God (v.49), the blessing of keeping the law (v.56 and throughout), good judgment and knowledge (v.66 and throughout), and life, mercy, fear, faithfulness, steadfast love, wisdom, sweetness, light, praise, joy, salvation, justice, cries, promises, truth, and memory. The imperatives are connected in the liveliest ways with all the other moods in the dynamic of living in response to the word of God, with the leading mood being the optative of passionate desire.

Something similar happens in Jesus' Sermon on the Mount. In Matthew's version, there is a strong insistence that "until heaven and earth pass away, not one letter, not one stroke of a letter, will pass from the law until all is accomplished" (Matt. 5:18). So there is no neglect of the imperatives, and Jesus goes on to intensify some of them – not only do not murder, but do not be angry or insult others; not only no adultery, but no lustful looking; not only no "eye for an eye" in retaliation, but non-resistance, turning the other cheek, and giving more than is being extorted or begged; not only love of neighbor but love of enemy too.

It is not possible to come to terms with such commands without radical questioning of oneself and one's whole way of life, including habits of thought, imagination, and action. Sometimes, indeed, the effect of a command can be simply to reveal the truth of our troubling inability to keep it. The questions also inevitably lead to "what if …" exploratory thinking. But above all they lead us to question where our heart is, what we really desire. That is the point of the opening of the sermon, the Beatitudes. They combine affirmations and promises:

> Blessed are the poor in spirit, for theirs is the kingdom of heaven. Blessed are those who mourn, for they will be comforted. Blessed are the meek, for they will inherit the earth. Blessed are those who hunger and thirst for righteousness, for they will be filled. Blessed are the merciful, for they will receive mercy. Blessed are the pure in heart, for they will see God. Blessed are the peacemakers, for they will be called the children of God. (5:3–9)

This amounts to a re-education of desire. The word for blessed, *makarios*, suggests what fulfills our longings, what is most deeply satisfying and complete (it was applied to Cyprus as the island that was considered to have everything). Later, the sermon imperatively orients desire toward the ultimate in blessedness: "Be perfect, therefore, as your heavenly Father is perfect" (5:48). The sermon concludes with a parable about the wise man who built his house on rock by acting on what Jesus taught, and the foolish man who built his house on sand (7:24–7). Command and obedience are central in Jesus' own life and teaching and in that of his followers, including theologians. But it is only wise if it is part of an ecology of other moods, with desire for God and the Kingdom of God above all.

Interrogative prophecy and lament

Questions are scattered throughout the Bible and intrinsic to its message. The word of God sometimes comes in questions, and may be far less welcome that way, since there can be no straightforward reception. How do you obey a question? You are stretched and searched through trying to answer, and cannot know for sure whether your answer is right.

Prophecy is a complex phenomenon, employing all the moods, the interrogative perhaps most poignantly, to articulate the cry of God to his people and their cry in return. "Why do you continue to rebel?" asks God (Isaiah 1:5). "Who among you will give heed to this, who will attend and listen for the time to come?" (Isaiah 42:23) "What wrong did your ancestors find in me that they went far from me and went after worthless things, and became worthless themselves?" … "How can I pardon you? … Shall I not punish them for these things? … I will now refine and test them, for what else can I do with my sinful people?" (Jeremiah 2:4; 5:7, 9; 9:7). The questions of Second Isaiah (chapters 40–55) set the rebellion and salvation of Israel within the largest possible theological horizon. "To whom then will you compare me, or who is my equal? says the Holy One. Lift up your eyes on high and see: Who created these?" … "Is my hand shortened that I cannot redeem? Or have I no power to deliver?" (40:25, 26; 50:2).

The questions in the mouth of God are only one side of a vigorous mutual interrogation that often imitates the form of a trial in court. The people can direct daring questions to God. "Why, O Lord, do you make us stray from your ways and harden our heart, so that we do not fear you?" … "After all this, will you restrain yourself, O Lord? Will you keep silent, and punish us so severely?" (Isaiah 63:17; 64:12). The anguished questioning reaches its greatest intensity in Jeremiah. "Is the Lord not in Zion? Is her King not in her?" … "Have you completely rejected Judah? Does your heart loathe Zion? Why have you struck us down so that there is no healing for us?" (Jeremiah 8:19; 14:19). The personal climax is some of the most bitter lament in the Bible, comparable to Job: "Cursed be the day on which I was born! The day when my mother bore me, let it not be blessed! ... Why did I come forth from the womb to see toil and sorrow, and spend my days in shame?" (Jeremiah 20:18).

Job (see further below) might be seen as the climax of the biblical wisdom tradition's interrogation of God. The Psalms have established such lament at the heart of Jewish and Christian worship, and with them a tradition of questioning God and theological teachings that refuses to see doubt, protest, and even despair as simply opposed to faith in God.

Jesus is one of the sharpest questioners in the Bible. Luke describes him as a twelve-year-old "in the temple, sitting among the teachers, listening to them and asking them questions," and then responding to his anxious parents: "Did you not know that I must be in my Father's house?" (Luke 2:46. 49). At the point of death he cries out (in the words of Psalm 22): "My God! My God! Why have you forsaken me?" (Mark 15:34), and after his resurrection his final encounters with his disciples are laced with questions: "Was it not necessary that the Messiah should suffer these things and then enter into his glory?" "Why are you frightened and why do doubts arise in your hearts?" "Have you anything here to eat?" "Woman, why are you weeping?" "Have you believed because you have seen me?" "Simon, son of John, do you love me?" "If it is my will that he remain until I come, what is that to you?" (Luke 24:26, 38, 41; John 20:13, 29; 21:15, 16, 17, 22)

So Jesus' life is framed by questions, and his ministry was likewise thoroughly interrogative, with him questioning and being questioned on numerous occasions. It was a prophetic ministry whose words and actions challenged religious and political authorities to the extent of leading to his execution. Above all, his message of the Kingdom of God stood as a question to all other conceptions of God and God's purposes, and was conveyed in teaching (such as the Sermon on the Mount) and parables (see below) that were designed to provoke puzzlement and arouse profound questioning. It is neither closed and packaged nor indefinite, but draws the hearer into a searching relationship where he or she can face the ultimate claim of God: "For those who want to save their life will lose it, and those who lose their life for my sake and for the sake of the Gospel will lose it. For what will it profit them to gain the whole world and forfeit their life? Indeed, what can they give in return for their life?" (Mark 8:35–7).

A theology engaged with the prophets, the wisdom writings, the Psalms, and the Gospels will value questioning. One thinks of the medieval scholastic insistence on the *quaestio* and the dialectic of argument that culminated in the theology of Thomas Aquinas – a new tradition inculcating rigorous debate. Modern thinkers have often directed hostile questioning of extreme suspicion and skepticism against Christian faith from the outside, but it may be the insiders who have asked the most disturbing questions – Martin Luther, Søren Kierkegaard, or Donald MacKinnon. Few Christians who have access to the best thinkers on both sides tend to find themselves convinced by the arguments of anti-Christians – there are usually rebuttals by Christians who are at least as intelligent, educated, and rationally persuasive as their opponents. But to be interrogated by a Kierkegaard is to find oneself realizing the inadequacy of one's life before God and of one's Christian faith and practice, and having to choose between despair and more wholehearted discipleship. God's questioning, as in the prophets, Job, and Jesus, turns out to be more dangerous than any of those who try to explain God away, and it by no means excludes terrible doubt and wrestling with God. The wisdom of interrogation and dispute that is so vital to Christian theological existence includes dispute about and with God.

Subjunctive wisdom and parable

Job has just been used as an example of theological questioning. It would also be possible to argue that the embracing mood of Job is optative, seen in Job's sustained desire for God and God's justice despite massive difficulties. Yet it is just as persuasive to see the whole book written, metaphorically, as an experiment in the subjunctive mood.

Using the device of a conversation in heaven between God and Satan, the author sets up the experiment in chapter 1. God asks Satan whether he has considered Job: "There is no one like him on earth, a blameless and upright man who fears God and turns away from evil" (Job 1:8). Satan responds with the question that gives the criterion for the outcome of the experiment: "Does Job fear God for nothing?" (v.9). The rest of the book tests Job in his relationship to God.[3] From the standpoint of God and Satan, Job may or may not be shown to fear God "as a gift," for God's sake, rather than for the sake of whatever he gains from God. For readers, this sets up the same possibilities. Our lives too may or may not be lived for God's sake. And for theology too this is the ultimate criterion: is our theology done for God's sake?

As soon as ideas of experiment, testing, and possibility are brought into interpretation of the Bible, the stranglehold of indicatives and imperatives is broken. The fundamental misunderstanding of Job's friends is that they do not realize (how could they?) the drama of possibilities within which Job is acting. Their confident dogmatism about what is happening and how Job ought to respond misses the main theological point. What is at stake is the ultimate wisdom. Job is portrayed by God as the wisest person on earth, and then his wisdom is tested in its most vital element: his relationship with God and, through God, with everyone and everything else.

Jesus in the Gospels is also part of such a drama of possibilities. He is tested by Satan in his temptations, and wrestles in the Garden of Gethsemane with the possibility of turning away from his suffering and death. There are deep issues here about the relationship of the necessity of his death to the possibility of him refusing it; but, however they are resolved, the narrative presents an obedience that has been confronted by real, momentous, alternatives.

Jesus' teaching also presents such alternatives to his listeners, as in the parable above of the wise and foolish men building on rock or sand. There is no sense of mechanical determinism: people are faced with possibilities and their decisions really matter. Otherwise, why bother teaching, preaching, and appealing to them? These possibilities need to be presented as imaginatively and forcefully as possible. Within Jesus' teaching, the Sermon on the Mount is one way he does this; he also does it though his many parables. They try to arouse desire for the possibility of sharing in the feast of the Kingdom of God; or to make it imaginatively obvious that, when offered the magnificent pearl of the Kingdom, the sensible choice is to sell everything else for it (Matthew 13:45).

In the preaching of Paul and of the early church, Jesus himself, in his life, death, and resurrection, is the message of possibility, the challenge to follow, for God's sake, this way of paradoxical, cross-centered wisdom. In the Christian tradition, perhaps no one explored the theology of possibility and paradox more profoundly than Søren Kierkegaard. His philosophy and theology is a prophetic protest against the ways in which affirmations and imperatives of conventional Christianity have missed this challenge. He sees the whole life and death of Jesus as presenting people with a decision that tests them to the core. He writes from many angles and under many pseudonyms in order to confront readers with the questions that will probe them most deeply. He practices subjunctive biblical interpretation – most famously, in his several retellings of the story of Abraham and Isaac in "what if …?" mode[4] – in order to draw readers into what is at stake for them. His wisdom of theological experiment and possibility continues to serve as a devastating critique of the many successors to Job's friends.

Subjunctive theology can be less existentialist and more systematic than Kierkegaard. Indeed, David Kelsey characterizes his massive work *Eccentric Existence* as an invitation to experimental thinking "in the hypothetical mode":

> I consider this entire project in theological anthropology to be in the mode of making theological proposals so that it repeatedly has the form: Here is an important theological question; try looking at it this way. In that fashion, this project seeks to promote and provoke further exploration of the issues and further discussion, rather than assert conversation-stopper pronouncements of what Christians must say on a given topic.[5]

Optative praise and apocalyptic

There are times when one mood rather than another is the theological mood of the moment and needs to take priority, a discernment for which there is no formula. Yet, in ordinary Christian living, the usual situation is that the lead is best taken by the optative mood of desire. The psalms, which daily prompt the spirits of so many Jews and Christians, embrace all moods in the longing for God and the desire to praise, thank, and petition God.

> As a deer longs for flowing streams,
> So my soul longs for you, O God.
> My soul thirsts for God
> For the living God.
> When shall I come and behold the face of God?
> (Psalm 42:1–2)

> Let everything that breathes praise the Lord!
> Praise the Lord!
> (Psalm 150:6)

St Augustine is one of the greatest theologians of desire, often inspired by the Psalms. "Seek ye God, and your soul shall live" (Psalm 69:32). "It is because He is hidden that he must be sought in order to be found; and being found He must still be sought in order to be found; and being found He must still be sought because of his immensity … For he satisfies the seeker in the measure of his capacity and He makes the finder to have greater capacity so that he may again seek to be filled when his ability to receive has grown."[6] "And truly this is the sense of 'Seek his face evermore' (Psalm 105:4), meaning that finding should not end that seeking by which love is testified, but with the increase of love the seeking of the found One should increase."[7]

That gives the main reason why desire is the leading mood of theology: because of the immensity of God, who is endlessly rich in love, wisdom, and all perfections, and therefore our desire too can be endless. God's goodness "is both sought that it may be found the more sweetly, and found that it may be sought the more eagerly."[8]

The other main reason for the priority of desire is because we are still journeying toward our goal, and before we reach it we "see in a mirror, dimly, but then we will see face to face" (1 Cors. 13:12). The problem with theologies dominated by clear indicatives and imperatives is that they tend to ignore the "dimly."

The most vivid reminder of the "not yet" stage in which we live now is apocalyptic, the genre which presents God's future in terms of dramatic, interruptive revelation. Interpreting it, not least the apocalypse in the book of Revelation that concludes the New Testament, is a difficult and often risky task. But one thing at least is clear: in the midst of suffering and persecution, it offers a vision of what is utterly desirable:

> And I heard a loud voice from the throne saying:
> "See, the home of God is among mortals.
> He will dwell with them as their God;
> They will be his peoples,
> And God himself will be with them;
> He will wipe every tear from their eyes.
> Death will be no more;
> Mourning and crying and pain will be no more,
> For the first things have passed away."
> And the One who was seated on the throne said, "See, I am making all things new."
>
> (Rev. 21:3–5)

> "Let anyone who wishes take the water of life as a gift."
>
> (Rev. 22:17)

The book of Revelation offers a taste of the worship of heaven at full strength, thunderously performed in line with the psalmist's wisdom of desire and adoration, resonating with the joy of a perfect marriage:

> Then I heard what seemed to be the voice of a great multitude, like the sound of many waters and like the sound of mighty thunder-peals, crying out,
>
> "Hallelujah!
> For the Lord our God
> The Almighty reigns.
> Let us rejoice and exult
> And give him the glory,
> For the marriage of the Lamb has come,
> And his bride has made herself ready …"
>
> (Rev. 19:6–7)

Such cries of praise before God give occasion for theological discernment that, as Augustine says, intensifies yet further the desire for God, while at the same time expanding our capacity for it.

God-centered Moods: The Divine Passive

Yet there can be a problem with the discussion of the moods of faith and of theology so far. We have spoken of people affirming, commanding, questioning, experimenting, and desiring in the active voice, and of God as involved in these in various ways. Now all this has to be turned around, not to invalidate what has been said, but to put it in a radically different perspective. The problem – which is more good news than a problem – is God and God's initiative. Theologically, our affirming depends on the divine voice – us being affirmed by God; our commanding and obeying depend on us being commanded by God; our questioning is premised on us being searched and questioned by God; our exploring springs from confidence in the abundance and endless surprises of God; and our desiring is a response to being attracted, desired, and loved by God.

Further, each of our moods can be inspired by all of God's modes of taking the initiative.

There is also the silence of God, perhaps best understood as God's listening.[9] Much thought about revelation one-sidedly emphasizes God's active initiatives. Without compromising the priority and freedom of God, the silent receptivity of divine listening may be seen as a condition for the possibility of God-oriented theological study and expression. The presence of God as listener evokes our speech in all its moods. It is the fuller realization of this presence that draws us into our own ever more attentive listening to the affirmations, commands, questions, possibilities, and desires

5

Belonging
Church, Collegiality, Conversation

Christian theology is never just an individual matter. It is inextricable from relating to other people and to God. Above all, as it engages with the past and present for the sake of God's future, its creativity depends upon many types of belonging. How adequate can the labor of retrieval and description be if it is done by only one scholar? What sense does a lone individual's theological engagement with contemporary life make? Some popular ideas of creative thinking imagine it being done by an isolated genius, but experience suggests the opposite: the best thinkers are usually those who are most deeply engaged with the thought of others, alive and dead, and who have the best teachers and conversation partners.[1] It is perhaps in creative expression that the utter sociability of theology is clearest: the very words and forms used are learnt from others and shared with others; the receiving of tradition is the condition for improvising on it, and any innovation must persuade others of its authenticity if it is not to be seen as just odd or idiosyncratic rather than creative. A fundamental, repeated question for any theologian is: where, and with whom, do I belong?

In theological terms, "creativity" (understood analogously as part of what it means to be created in the image of one's Creator) might be seen as what serves to open people to God and God's future – "the

Kingdom of God." This is at heart a matter of being loved and loving. It should not be sentimentalized: God's love is satisfied with nothing less than all God has created us to be. The "all" includes body, intellect, heart, imagination, and will, energized and inspired by God's Spirit to love God and all God has created and loves. The ultimate invitation is to a face-to-face joy that is spoilt by anything less than wholehearted, understanding love. Given the sort of world we inhabit, with many deep-set resistances to loving and being loved that are embedded in ourselves, others, and whole groups, cultures, institutions, and societies, we desperately need a wisdom of love and we also desperately need other people to share in the drama of loving. Theology is part of that drama, and its goal is to think together the love of God's wisdom and the wisdom of God's love. The way to that goal is in a world that constantly distracts, dispirits, and even traumatizes those committed to wise loving. But it is a way that can hardly be traveled at all without companions in understanding and loving.

The fundamental forms of belonging come together on this path: belonging to God and to each other as fellow-Christians and as fellow-human beings. This is a threefold dynamic, in which each can deepen and intensify the other.

Belonging to God and Each Other through Covenant

At the beginning of each new year, and at other special times, many Methodists take part in the Covenant Service, and it is also regularly used by other Christians around the world.[2] It is a vivid, powerful expression of Christian belonging. The key elements are: the love of God as the embracing reality of belonging; Jesus Christ as the one through whom Christians are "born into the family of God"; the "fellowship (from the Greek *koinonia*, sharing, having in common) of the Holy Spirit"; confession of sins against belonging ("the poverty of our worship, our neglect of fellowship ..."); readings from the books of Jeremiah and Hebrews about covenant; and a radical image of belonging to Jesus Christ from the Gospel of John:

> Abide in me as I abide in you … I am the vine, you are the branches. (John 15:4–5)

Then comes the climax, the renewal of the Covenant, first through singing (a characteristically Methodist note!), and then through a culminating affirmation in prayer that pivots around belonging to God:

Minister: …We are no longer our own but yours.
People: I am no longer my own, but yours … And now, glorious and blessed God, Father Son, and Holy Spirit, you are mine and I am yours.[3]

The Covenant Service concludes with the Lord's Supper, the ongoing Christian celebration of belonging within the "new Covenant."

So covenant is identified as the most basic form of Christian belonging to God and other people. In the Bible, covenant is associated with key people and events: Noah, Abraham, David, many prophets, and above all Moses and the giving of the law at the center of Israel's covenant with God at Sinai. The strongest social imagery is used to express its meaning. Belonging to a people is basic; it is supplemented by the language of marriage, family (especially parent–child), friendship, servant, slave, and ownership of material possessions. Some prophets anticipated a "new Covenant" written on the heart (e.g., Jeremiah 31:31ff), and in Luke's Gospel Jesus took up the phrase to interpret his death at the Last Supper (Luke 22:20; cf. Hebrews 8:8; 12:24)). With the death of Jesus being understood like this, covenant is established at the heart of Christian identity, as enacted initially in baptism and repeatedly in Lord's Supper or Eucharist.

If the identity of the Christian theologian is covenantal in this strong sense, what are the implications for thinking? Belonging to God means that all thinking is within that relationship, trying to be as alert as possible to its significance for all areas of understanding and living. This involves thinking immersed in prayer and worship, which is not just a quantitative matter of time spent. Rather, it is about a fundamental orientation toward God, springing from thankful appreciation of the covenant love of God. Like marriage, it is a state, a commitment, and a way of life that thrives on mutual communication in joy, truth, and love, but that can also plunge into agony of mind and heart.

Paul's wrestling with how the new Covenant relates to Moses, the law, and his fellow Jews who reject his Gospel evoked some of his most profound and controversial theology. "I have great sorrow and unceasing anguish in my heart" (Romans 9:2), he writes as he begins to grapple with it in Romans, chapters 9–11. At issue is his own crisis of belonging as Jew and as Christian. He recapitulates much of the letter up to that point, in which he had presented a concentrated account of his theology, and focuses it on this issue. He works through a string of scriptural passages[4] as he thinks his way to a dramatic conception of God's mercy "to all" (11:32), crowned by a cry of amazed praise: "O the depth of the riches and wisdom and knowledge of God! How unsearchable are his judgments and how inscrutable are his ways!" (11:33).

In 2 Corinthians 3:1–4:6, Paul comes at the problem from a different angle as he defends his "new Covenant" ministry (3:6) against opponents who cause comparable anguish. It is one of the most difficult passages in the New Testament,[5] combining controversial scriptural interpretation, passionate engagement with the Corinthian Christians, and inspired, condensed thought and imagery. He moves toward one culminating statement:

> Now the Lord is the Spirit, and where the Spirit of the Lord is, there is freedom. And all of us, with unveiled faces, seeing the glory of the Lord as though reflected in a mirror, are being transformed into the same image from one degree of glory to another; for this comes from the Lord, the Spirit. (3:17–18)

This is then supplemented by another:

> For it is the God who said, "Let light shine out of darkness," who has shone in our hearts to give the light of the knowledge of the glory of God in the face of Jesus Christ. (4:6)

There is a whole theology latent in these verses,[6] but for now the point is what they suggest about belonging. "All of us"[7] are located in the freedom of the Spirit and the glory of God, within a dynamic of transformation that is rooted in belonging to creation and oriented toward the face of Jesus Christ. Our most intimate selves are marked as belonging to him, as his face shines in our hearts. In this belonging and transformation minds too are fully active: how else can "the light of the knowledge of the glory of God" be received and responded to? The dense thought of the letter offers one such response.[8]

The Gospel of John does not use the language of covenant, but right from the start is part of that thought-world, concerned with belonging, above all, to God: "He came to what was his own, and his own people did not accept him. But to all who received him, who believed in his name, he gave power to become children of God, who were born, not of blood or of the will of the flesh, or of the will of man, but of God" (John 1:11–13). As in Paul, this belonging is set in the context of God's glory: "And the Word become flesh and lived among us, and we have seen his glory, the glory as of a father's only son, full of grace and truth" (John 1:14). And, again, a fundamental concern is for continuity and discontinuity with Moses: "The law indeed was given through Moses; grace and truth came through Jesus Christ" (John 1:17). John goes on to present belonging to God in perhaps the most radically intimate terms in the Bible. This reaches its greatest intensity in the final prayer of Jesus with his disciples:

> They were yours, and you gave them to me, and they have kept your word … They do not belong to the world, just as I do not belong to the world … The glory that you have given me I have given them, so that they may be one, as we are one, I in them and you in me, that they may become completely one … so that the love with which you have loved me may be in them, and I in them. (John 17:6–26)

Such union is the ultimate: belonging not just to God but in God, in love to others. Perhaps the most comprehensive challenge to

Christian thought is to realize what this means, to live in union with God, and to think in ways that correspond to this reality.

Yet John also sharply raises the question of the exclusion of whatever is consigned to the categories of "world" and "unbelief." Paul has a similar dichotomy: "the god of this world has blinded the minds of the unbelievers" (2 Cors. 4:4). Jewish–Christian relations give some of the most vivid examples, century after century, of the terrible consequences of what can be the other side of Christian belonging: exclusion, rejection, and aggressive violence by Christians. Paul and John have both been used in support of this, and the extent of their own responsibility for it is the subject of an ongoing debate.[9] Strong identities tend to require firm boundaries and exclusions. When God is invoked as the source of an identity the problems of exclusivity can multiply. When two or more sides invoke God the dangers can become most acute. Two or more forms of ultimate belonging, each of utmost importance to its members, can lead to terrible conflicts. These can become so bad, as in our century, that for many the very idea of belonging to God is discredited.

How might Christian thinkers respond to the corruptions and pathologies of religious, and especially Christian, belonging? Answering that question leads through the rest of this chapter, envisioning forms of belonging in church and other relationships that are alert to bad as well as good possibilities and that might help to heal the pathologies. The question recurs with special force in two later chapters: when we explore how theology is done in complex contexts (chapter 6); and when the interaction between religions is faced directly (chapter 7). One of the great questions of our century is how people from diverse communities can peacefully live together. Is a pluralist world with partnerships of differences possible? How can different forms of ultimate belonging coexist?

For a Christian attracted, called, and committed to the love of God, giving up on one's ultimate belonging is not an option. Christian belonging has been enacted over the centuries and around the world today in extraordinarily diverse ways, sometimes appalling and tragic. Yet, without forgetting that the corruption of the best can be the worst, it is necessary to try to envisage the best, and that is especially the task of a manifesto such as this.

Paul and John, for all their problems, attempted that in their articulations of what it means to belong to God in covenant. They were seeking, before God and "in Christ," a wisdom of faith, hope, and love. Inseparable from this is the deepest, open secret of their belonging to God: the Holy Spirit. The Spirit, in the passage from Paul quoted above, is at the heart of Christian freedom and of being transformed within Christian community. In John's Gospel, those in the Kingdom of God are "born of the Spirit" (John 3:8); worship of God is to be "in spirit and truth" (John 4:23–4); the promise of the Spirit as *parakletos* (advocate, helper, comforter, encourager) is closely associated with love and truth (John 14:15–17 and throughout John chapters 13–16); and the breathing of the Spirit by Jesus on his disciples is linked by him with the healing of relationships through forgiveness (John 20:23). The Spirit is the bond of belonging in love and truth. Yet, as chapter 1 described, the Spirit has also been at the center of some of the most divisive conflicts within and between churches.

There are resources and lessons here for trying to work out a theology of belonging to God and to each other in the church. It is a theology with a long, controversy-laden agenda, from authority, baptism, and community to mission, pastoral care, and worship. Having outlined a scriptural framework of covenantal belonging capacious and open enough to accommodate most Christians, the concern of this manifesto is not to work through the agenda but to ask about the church dimension of theological creativity.

Theological Creativity in and for the Church

The first point is that the creativity is utterly joint and shared. Christian theology is a collaborative enterprise inseparable from membership of the church. This can allow for a wide variety of relationships with fellow members of the church and its leadership, but its basic concern is for the thinking that is part of ordinary Christian life and worship.

Worship is a particularly good sign of the shared nature of theology.[10] It performs the identity of a church before God, and it embodies in communal form all four elements of theological creativity.

So, worship is about shared retrieval, resourced by the past of scripture and tradition. Even when it is not directly quoting scripture it is often indebted to it, and its language and structure embody the outcomes of centuries of communal experience, debate, and discernment. Without that, for example, the prominence in many liturgies of Trinitarian statements, such as "Glory be to the Father and to the Son and to the Holy Spirit," is unthinkable. The choice of scriptural passages in lectionaries helps form the mind and imagination of a community year after year. A basic pattern of retrieval is embodied in a church's calendar. By taking part in a liturgy, one is sharing in the community's central form of *ressourcement*.

Worship is also a present joint engagement, above all with God. Cries of address and praise, exclamations spoken or sung, and bodily movements – these acknowledge the central, encompassing, shared reality of the presence of God. There is also engagement with church and world. Preaching and teaching are where scripture and tradition are thought through in relation to the present and future. The contents of thanksgivings, intercessions, and petitions are indicators of a community's concerns and involvements.

Worship encodes seminal, creative theological thinking of the past in its uses of scripture, in creeds that distill classic teachings, in the shape of liturgies, and in hymns and songs. It also allows for new thinking in sermons, prayers, and improvisations on habitual forms. *Lex orandi, lex credendi* (the rule for praying is the rule for believing) has long been a commonplace of Christian thought, though not uncontroversial. Its wisdom is in recognizing the deep mutuality of prayer and faith, together with their sociality (taking *lex* as something recognized by a whole community); and thought is intrinsic to both of them.

The twentieth century was perhaps the most creative century in the history of Christian worship. There was an explosion of new music, songs, hymns, chants, ritual, and dance, and revivals of many traditional forms. The Roman Catholic Church radically revised its liturgies and began celebrating them in scores of the world's languages. The liturgies and lectionaries of many other churches were revised, often allowing for wide local variations. It is no accident that the twentieth century was also so creative in theology (see chapter 1 above). Every liturgical development has required theological thinking and discernment, and a vast amount of intellectual and imaginative energy has gone into these transformations of worship. There are also the daily and weekly theological demands on those who organize and lead worship, trying in lively and relevant ways to shape congregational services, baptisms, confirmations, ordinations, weddings, funerals, feast days, and events such as the Methodist Covenant Service. Add to all this the thinking that is stimulated in ordinary worshipers as they pray, sing, listen, discuss, and respond variously to worship (for example, by relating it to the rest of their lives), and it becomes clear that this might be seen as the sphere of maximal and most explicit Christian theological creativity.

Then there is creative expression. The inseparability of creative thought from creative expression is especially important for worship, which offers forms of word and action to hundreds of millions of people week after week. It is not just that every word counts; each genre, juxtaposition, ordering, gesture, article of clothing, musical accompaniment, architectural environment, and cultural setting is also part of the performance and its meaning.

Overall, therefore, worship is something like the genetic code of a Christian community. It condenses core meanings that are transmitted across the generations, and it allows for variations. Theological thinking both helps to shape it and is shaped by it. A fundamental discernment to be made about any theology is whether it rings true with the worship of one or more churches. In other words, does it share the "genetic code" or "grammar of faith" to be found in worship? Deciding this, of course, itself requires theological discussion, and there are times when a community decides to innovate. But few things illustrate the joint, shared character of Christian theology more than the social processes through which worship is shaped.

The lesson from this for theology (whether ordinary or more academic theological thinking) is both that thought needs to be shaped through long-term, faithful immersion in worship with fellow-Christians and that there is a responsibility to join with others in serving the theological health of worship, including wise innovation. Worship is where the code is transmitted, the grammar learnt. It is the performance that, when done well, condenses and communicates formative retrieval, engagement, thought, and expression. To internalize a rich practice of worship is to expand the capacity for fresh creativity. Those who write classics are usually those who are steeped in that language's classics. Like a jazz player whose mastery of instrument and repertoire enables virtuoso improvisations on well-known themes, the theologian who is steeped in worship is more likely to offer discernments and proposals that not only ring true with past and present Christian wisdom but also add to its sum.

Yet worship is still only one of the dimensions of the church with which theology is concerned. The two other principal ones are community life, with its catechesis and education, pastoral care, social activities, organizations, and institutional structures; and mission beyond the Christian community, in evangelism and various forms of dialogue and service to the common good. These go on locally, regionally, nationally, and internationally. Theological thinking needs to happen in each aspect and at each level, and also to think about them together. Again, it is clear that the seeking of wisdom in all these areas has to be conversational and collaborative if it is to be true and fruitful. This is by no means to deny the importance of individual formation and responsibility, but to stress the primacy of belonging.

The conception of the church that emerges from this discussion, in line with earlier chapters is as a "school of wisdom."[11] The wisdom of God and God's purposes is to be learnt with others through worship, community living, and discerning engagement in many spheres of life, and the church is a school for that. Yet it is not the only place where wisdom is sought and where learning and teaching go on. The rest of this chapter describes briefly forms of belonging, some Christian and some mixed with those of other faiths or none, through which Christian wisdom can be pursued.

Learning and Teaching Together: Collegiality

So far, the jointness of theological thinking has been related to primary Christian belonging in the worshiping community, but this can also be focused in forms of collegiality that are centered on learning and teaching theology in a more educational, academic sense. If one were to ask where a church seeks scholarly and theological wisdom as it goes about deciding its forms of worship, the answer is usually: from those teaching in academic institutions. "Collegiality" is a term for the jointness of those places, where theology is taught by a group of colleagues.

If one imagines Christian theological education around the world today as an ecosystem, by far the largest niche is made up of church institutions of many sorts. These range from courses set up by local or regional church bodies, through study groups, Bible colleges, religious orders, distance-learning organizations, and seminaries, to research centers and Christian universities. These are the places where most of the Christians who have the chance to learn any theology do so, and also where most of the vast company of clergy, preachers, teachers, catechists, evangelists, youth leaders, religious broadcasters, writers, and interested lay people are educated. The need for such places for the learning, teaching, and wider communication of Christian faith and practice should be obvious. This manifesto is intended to apply to the theology done there as well as elsewhere. They face many problems and challenges, but in respect of the topic of this chapter they are relatively unproblematic. Belonging to them as a teacher or student is usually in direct continuity with ordinary belonging to a particular church (or, in ecumenical settings, one of a set of churches). There, collegiality raises all the usual issues of theological complexion, curriculum, teaching methods, how to work together, and relations with church authorities and other bodies. But some form of Christian belonging as such is not problematic, however much its varieties may be explored.

There is, however, in the ecosystem of Christian theology another, smaller niche, where Christian theology is done in settings that are not solely Christian. This manifesto sees such mixed settings as a healthy development that is not necessarily in tension or competition with the larger niche. On the contrary, both niches contribute to the flourishing of the whole ecology. Theology learnt and taught in places where there are teachers and students who belong to different religious and non-religious or secular traditions can be of great value in societies that are complexly religious and secular.[12] In society at large, different forms of belonging must try to work out how to get along together; it is therefore deeply appropriate that there be places of education, scholarship, and research where it is possible for those with a range of commitments to tackle the many questions concerning these commitments, including those raised by the religions, between the religions, and about the religions (and not least the questions raised by those who do not belong to them).

The main places where this happens at present are some universities. Most universities in the twentieth century approached religion in what might be called a secularist way. This was partly in reaction against centuries of religious domination of universities, which often involved compulsory commitment to one tradition. Academic suspicion of religion came to be taken for granted, aided by critiques by many leading thinkers (Marx, Feuerbach, Nietzsche, Freud, and a host of later ones) and by the century's dominant ideologies (Fascism, Communism, capitalism, scientific naturalism), tending to write religion out of their scenarios of the future. When religion was studied, it was through a range of disciplines – historical, literary, social scientific, philosophical, psychological – that treated religious faith as an interesting phenomenon but not as a live option for educated contemporaries. There were many who resisted this trend, working out critical and constructive positions that were alert to the critiques and offered intelligent and habitable theologies, but most universities were not hospitable to them. The academic secularist approach to religion reached its clearest expression in some of the ways in which the discipline called "religious studies" was conducted: insisting on a "neutrality" and "objectivity" that had no place for arguing or affirming the truth of a faith, ruling out questions of faith-informed practice, and cutting off academic study of religion from many of the most important debates and concerns of religious and other communities. It was as if economics had concentrated on the history and analysis of economic thought and practice but refused to engage with contemporary issues of how economies should be run or businesses conducted, and even discouraged economists from having anything to do with money.

Yet some universities sustained theological thinking in pluralist settings.[13] It happened in some North American settings and especially in Britain, where there was a slow, complex development of varieties of what is often called "theology and religious studies." Here academics can be of any faith or none, and there is no inhibition (or compulsion) regarding the explicit relating of their commitment to their academic work if it is relevant. So, for example, the doctrine of the Trinity can be explored and debated by Muslims, Jews, atheists, and Christians, and the latter can present, as part of their academic work, an argued, constructive account of the God in whom they believe. Or each can study the key texts of the others without seeing as "un-academic" a Jewish argument in favor of a particular view of forgiveness that is based on Tanakh, Talmud, and current philosophy. Within theology and religious studies, there can still be specifically Christian, Muslim, or other forms of collegiality, but it is set within a larger collegiality that has its own dynamics and possibilities.

This complexly diverse belonging corresponds to the character of our world. This manifesto advocates strongly the importance of the conversations and collaborations that can be enabled by a collegiality that crosses the boundaries of faiths and other positions. These can, of course, occur between those in separate institutions – and given that most theology happens in single-faith settings that will be how most of such interactions occur – but it is of value to the whole ecosystem if there are some niches where it is embodied internally. There the difficulties are multiplied, but so too are the possibilities. For the sake of the common good of the twenty-first century world, these niches should be expanded, without neglecting the less institutionally confined interactions discussed below. Chapter 8 will offer a manifesto within this manifesto, advocating the niche called "new theology and religious studies."

Extended Belonging: Conversations

Conversation is a marvelously (yet somewhat annoyingly) flexible term, ranging from the most casual encounter to a lifetime of intense interaction. The two following sections below say a little about the intense end of the spectrum. Here the intention is simply to note the importance of the middle range of conversations. One can belong to a conversation for an afternoon or a year, participants can multiply or contract, and one can be part of several in a day. Technology has vastly expanded the possibilities for conversations.

Most theological conversations that are more than casual happen within structured environments. In the academic study of theology beyond one's home institution this means conferences, activities of societies for the study of aspects of theology, and increasing numbers of training days, seminars, broadcasts, media events, dialogues, and discussions after lectures. Surrounding all these is a penumbra of informal encounters, emails, telephone conversations, chat rooms, blogs, and occasionally letters.

Essential for the organized events are the organizers, whose theological role is often ignored. Organizational creativity is as precious as other sorts, and requires all four of the elements of retrieval, engagement, imaginative thought, and expression. Good organizers write their theology in fruitful interactions between people. They choose themes and people, shape sequences and schedules, attend to the practical aspects of travel, food, accommodation, and financing, liaise diplomatically, cope with crises, and have a maestro conductor's sense of timing. Unwise judgments and decisions make the event impoverished or even counter-productive. Wise organization is one condition for the possibility of the wonderful conversations, formal and informal, that can happen.

The future health of Christian theology partly depends, therefore, on the discernment and dedication of creative organizers who shape the agendas and environments needed for high-quality face-to-face communication. It is important for the established long-term conversations to continue; it is also vital to discern which recent ones to concentrate on and which new ones to initiate. In Randall Collins's massive sociological study of intellectual creativity in philosophy, over millennia in many cultures, the simple central conclusion is that a critical condition for the best philosophy is intensive conversation.[14] The most influential philosophies have been generated in conversation between contemporaries, and have been sustained and developed by institutions that provided the necessary conditions.

What are the growth points for Christian theological conversation in the present century? It is significant that conversation is of the essence of key topics that have emerged from this manifesto so far, such as inter-faith theology and the range of "theology and ..." (see above, chapter 1). It is a mark of such theological thinking that it is almost impossible (and even undesirable) for one person to be an "expert" in the range of things needed. In relation to the Abrahamic faiths, for example, it is unlikely that one person will have the linguistic competence in the required languages (Hebrew, Arabic, Persian, Greek, Syriac, Latin – just to mention those in which many of the classic texts are written), let alone be a scholar of the whole Bible, the Talmud, the Qur'an, the Hadith, and all periods of the three faiths, including their contemporary expressions around the world. If I were choosing just three, besides inter-faith and science, as having most potential for Christianity at present, they would be conversations around the Bible, around poetry, and around economics. But the utterly joint character of Christian theology means that conversation is intrinsic to all its inquiries, and the topics are not so much a matter of one right agenda as of discerning many cries – for God, and for truth and meaning, joy and beauty, justice and love – and pursuing the varied theological vocations that might address them.

Intensive Belonging: Cohabitations, Collaborations, and Movements

With whom do we live, work, and try to realize God's future for others and ourselves? Conversation is more important than ever in these relationships where communication is complemented by commitment. Some of the most formative theology is stimulated through relationships of cohabitation – meaning not just family life but certain localities, religious orders, retreats, and other places where people live together with some degree of common intention. In terms of religious commitment, these are sometimes very mixed, which is another incentive on the academic side of theology to help resource ordinary life by cultivating the sorts of mixed settings discussed above in relation to universities. Work is the other primary setting for committed relationships in daily life, where Christians likewise often join with others of different faiths and none.

In these contexts of living and working, it becomes clearer why it makes sense for theology to be conceived as wisdom. Theological thinking here tries to make deep and practical connections with Christian faith and experience, and to discern with others, who may not share one's faith, how to shape life and work. There is a vast amount of academic and more popular theology (often labeled as spirituality or ethics) that attempts this.[15] A common weakness is that it fails in one side of its task: either it does not have the theological richness and maturity, or it is not engaged deeply or wisely enough in the particular area of life or work.

Shared living and joint working are the ordinariness of being together, and the theological thinking that accompanies this is distributed widely through all spheres where believers are present. This thinking is often, of course, not labeled "theological," but yet is directly related to the purposes of God in the world. It is perhaps the most pervasive sort of theology, fed by whatever has been learnt through being part of a worshiping community and in other ways. One of the key tasks of theology in educational and academic settings is to inspire and nourish such everyday thinking. This might be seen as part of a broader aim, in conversation and collaboration with those of other faiths and none, to shift our "knowledge society" into a "wisdom society."

There is another, increasingly influential, form of belonging that is more extraordinary than ordinary. In a book about Christianity, Islam, and Europe's current religious crisis, the historian Philip Jenkins makes what to many is the surprising prediction that Europe's hard-pressed Christians have the necessary resources for a Christian revival, with global implications.[16] A key element in his argument is the existence of so many vibrant Christian movements, many of recent origin. These include the Pentecostal and Charismatic movements (the latter a potent force within many churches), the Taize community, Opus Dei, the Focolare, the Neocatechumenate, Sant'Egidio, the Schonstatt movement, the Emmanuel community, Regnum Christi, the Alpha course, L'Arche, the Cursillo movement, and more. Such movements have become a focus of belonging within the church for large numbers of people, and their impact is far wider than their membership, often affecting whole congregations and local communities. They also have their (extremely diverse) theologies, some more explicit and developed than others, and it is often through their thinking that their influence spreads. The intensity of involvement often demanded by movements means that they do not attract mass membership, but they are well suited to a pluralist society in which more embracing bonds of belonging have weakened. They are also another prime case of "the corruption of the best is the worst." Intensity can be bad as well as good, and is a short step away from accusations of "elitism," "extremism," "fanaticism," "exclusivism," or "factionalism." Discerning the cries of powerful movements is a major challenge for contemporary wisdom-seeking theology.

There are also specifically theological movements. The twentieth century was, as chapter 1 showed, a seedbed of new movements in theology, from feminism and liberation theology to ecumenical theology and postliberalism.[17] Most of those continue. If one were risking a guess at which might prove of special importance in the present century's theology and also require most practical collaboration, the list would include movements related to the religions (on the analogy of the intra-Christian ecumenical movement), to the environment, and to lifestyles that are accountable to the weakest, poorest, and most marginalized. There is also immense scope for creative retrievals along the lines of the twentieth century's new interpretations and applications of theologies of the past, such as those of Gregory of Nyssa, Maximus the Confessor, Augustine, Thomas Aquinas, Martin Luther, John Calvin, Ignatius Loyola, Richard Hooker, and Jonathan Edwards. Without ignoring those, it may be time to hear more about Origen, Aphrahat and Ephrem, Bonaventure, Dante, Erasmus, Traherne, Milton, Coleridge, and Christoph Blumhardt.

Intimate Belonging: Friendships

A founder member of the ecumenical movement once summed up to me what he thought was one of the main secrets of whatever it had achieved: friendships. He named some deep one-to-one friendships, often initiated and sustained with considerable courage, that were at the heart of the strong bonding, creative thinking, practical initiatives, and seminal statements that went into the ecumenical movement. My study and experience confirm this. In the ecosystem of Christian theology today, I have not found lively creative wisdom apart from intensive conversation rooted in long-term, loving friendships. Some elements of creativity can, of course, come about without this, but, for all four to come together in a way that rings true with the best in the Bible and the tradition, somewhere there needs to be the niche of friendship.

Friendship comes in the climactic discourse of the most theologically rich Gospel. Jesus, on the night before he dies, says to his disciples:

> This is my commandment, that you love one another as I have loved you. No one has greater love than this, to lay down one's life for one's friends. You are my friends if you do what I command you. I do not call you servants any longer, because the servant does not know what the master is doing; but I have called you friends, because I have made known to you everything that I have heard from my Father. (John 15:12–15)

At the center of this friendship is costly and truthful sharing. It links friendship to the core dynamic of God's love, and the logic is clear: to be friends of Jesus involves loving one another as friends too. The Quakers have summed this up in their official name: Society of Friends.

Yet there is another aspect of the friendship of Jesus. In the Synoptic Gospels Jesus is accused of being "a friend of tax collectors and sinners" (Matthew 11:19; Luke 7:34), in other words, a friend of those most despised and marginalized. Christian friendship is primarily with Jesus, who simultaneously is friends with those who are in closest mutual relationship with him and each other, and also with those on the edges of conventional society. The Quakers have often exemplified this combination. Again, the logic is clear: the community of Christian friends will be healthiest, and truest to its Lord as friend, when at its center are those whom society in general finds it least easy to include, respect, and love. My own most vivid experiences of this have been through living in an inner-city parish in Birmingham, and through getting to know some of the L'Arche communities for those with and without severe learning difficulties.[18]

In the Gospels of Matthew and Luke the statement of Jesus in which he accepts the description by his enemies of his friendships is followed by variations on the same thought: "Yet wisdom is vindicated by her deeds" (Matthew 11:19); "Nevertheless, wisdom is vindicated by all her children" (Luke 7:35). To belong to wisdom's family is to risk forming unlikely friendships. The deepest theological wisdom of the coming century is likely to be discovered here.

Conclusion: Complex Belonging

Putting together in one life the various forms of belonging to God and to each other through covenant, conversation, living together, working together, and participation in movements and friendships is a complex task even before taking into account belonging to different classes, races, genders, cultures, nations, and diverse subgroups. Each form of belonging can be conceived as a summons, even a cry, to give of oneself. In helping to judge what are the priorities and interrelationships among these cries, theology faces a fundamental challenge to its wisdom. Grappling with the complexity of belonging requires a comparable complexity of faith and theology. The next chapter explores one aspect of this complexity.

6

Church and Society

The Christian church began nearly two thousand years ago as a Jewish group within the Roman Empire who later welcomed non-Jews and developed a separate identity. In the early centuries, it was often persecuted and excluded from power and influence in the empire. Its acceptance as the religion of the Roman Empire was a major development; but both within and beyond that empire (even before its official recognition) it had many different ways of relating to the societies of which it was a part. Since then that diversity has multiplied further as it has come into contact with cultures in all parts of the world. But "it" has not been one thing: the church itself has been multiple in form across time and space; diverse even within officially united denominations (some of which see their diversity as required by their faith).

The twenty-first century promises even greater variety. An internet search calls up around 270 million results for "church," and any hope for neat categories is overwhelmed by browsing through them. In more scholarly mode, a survey of the most impressive publication to deal with the history of the church in recent decades, *The Cambridge History of Christianity*, demonstrates that any theory about how the church habitually relates to society dies the death of a thousand exceptions, and even typologies seem rigid and inadequate when faced with the range of actual instances. This is even more evident when, as in that history, an attempt is made to do justice to the burgeoning forms of popular Christianity.

It is perhaps in social anthropology that the societal particularities of Christianity, as it is actually being lived in the twenty-first century, are most thoroughly described and analyzed. It is a curious fact that (for whatever reasons[1]) Christianity was for most of the twentieth century a neglected field in the social anthropology of religion. That is now being redressed, and ethnographic studies of local Christianities in many societies are multiplying. Yet these reinforce the lesson drawn from *The Cambridge History of Christianity*: that any generalization is dangerous, especially if used to conclude anything normative. It is not only the riot of specific forms of life that Christianity exhibits in different settings, appreciation of which is enhanced by each new ethnography; there is also the sheer number of methodological frameworks that the anthropological tradition is bringing to bear on Christianity,[2] and the difficulty of the questions it raises.[3] As Lambek concludes:

> While outsiders look to anthropology for generalizations, anthropologists themselves, some notable exceptions aside, remain happier exhibiting differences, exploring particularities, following connections, tracing patterns, elaborating context, demonstrating complexity, illuminating paradoxes, or simply poking holes in the universalizing theories of other disciplines. Our craft is one of recognizing incommensurabilities and their limits; hence we remain more comfortable with raising questions than with answering them.[4]

That will not do for a manifesto such as this. The aim here is, while being as alert as possible to that variety of phenomena, frameworks, and questions, to offer a constructive Christian position for readers to think with. Like the next chapter, which will do its Christian inter-faith theology mainly in dialogue with two leading initiatives in the field, this chapter will take two relevant specific case studies and reflect on them. The context being assumed is that of contemporary Western democracies where the main churches, especially Protestant and Catholic, have long traditions of wrestling with the relationship of church to society. It is hoped that those in different contexts and in different traditions of Christianity will yet find something worthwhile in the discussion – it can be as fruitful to think with differences as with similarities.

In relation to previous chapters, one advantage in having noted the difficulty of generalization is that the inappropriateness of what was called the "epic" mode, ordering and integrating the variety of phenomena into a single overview, is reinforced. The pressure is rather toward "lyric" particularity, but this is contained by the focus on social units and their interplay. The most congenial category is therefore that of a "drama" in which the actors are groups and institutions, as well as individuals.

First Case Study: Dietrich Bonhoeffer

The first case study on church and society concerns a theologian in one of the darkest periods of the last century's history. Thinking through a case study of Dietrich Bonhoeffer (1906–45) opens a way into some of the most profound issues facing churches of many sorts in their relations with their societies in the twenty-first century. Why might he be an appropriate case to study?

Bonhoeffer has already been discussed in previous chapters as a classic Christian thinker of the twentieth century who more than satisfactorily meets the criteria suggested for theological wisdom and creativity (see above, chapter 1), so this is an exercise in theological inquiry in the company of a master. He combined academic theology across a broad range of topics and disciplines (historical and systematic theology, biblical interpretation, philosophical theology, ethics, sociology) with deep engagement in the contemporary church (both his own Lutheran Church and the ecumenical movement) and in his society. In relation to Germany, he was not only passionately involved in resistance to Hitler but was also concerned at the same time to think beyond Hitler. His value is as someone who gives an example of doing responsible and creative theology on church and society, both for an extreme situation and for ordinary civilized life.

We take up his story between 1940 and 1943 when Bonhoeffer was writing his *Ethics*, while also working for the *Abwehr* (German Military Counter-Intelligence) and secretly taking part in a plot to assassinate Hitler. A double motivation can be seen in this work. He was thinking theologically and ethically about his experience of Nazi Germany and in particular about his decision to support an attempted assassination and coup. But, even more importantly, he was looking ahead beyond the war, trying to discern an ethic to live by in times of peace. Vital to this was the relation of church to society. In one of the later parts of the *Ethics* to be written, he reflects on his experience:

> We begin ... by calling attention to one of the most astounding experiences we have had during the years of trial for all that was Christian. Whenever, in the face of the deification of the irrational powers of blood, of instinct, of the predator within human beings, there was an appeal to reason; whenever, in the face of arbitrariness, there was an appeal to the written law; whenever, in the face of barbarism, there was an appeal to culture and humanity; whenever, in the face of their violation there was an appeal to freedom, tolerance, and human rights; whenever, in the face of the politicization of science, art, and so on, attention was drawn to the autonomy of the various areas of life – then this was sufficient to evoke immediately awareness of some kind of alliance between the defenders of these threatened values and Christians. Reason, culture, humanity, tolerance, autonomy – all these concepts, which until recently had served as battle cries against the church, against Christianity, even against Jesus Christ, now surprisingly found themselves in very close proximity to the Christian domain.[5]

This reconciliation of civilized humanity and goodness with Christianity was not a matter of finding some compromise position, but rather a discovery that those dimensions of humane goodness have kinship with Jesus Christ. As Bonhoeffer noted, it was while some Christians were seeking to be more fully Christian that they found themselves in "some kind of alliance" with non-Christians on behalf of values and practices that both of them supported, though for different reasons.

Being fully Christian in society

But what is it to be "fully Christian"? This is often identified with radical forms of faith that emphasize the teaching, crucifixion, and/ or resurrection of Jesus Christ in counter-cultural or anti-cultural ways, stressing the discontinuity between faith and ordinary human goodness, wisdom and natural life. In other words, the relationship between church and society goes wrong not just when the church compromises with the norms and practices of society but also when it rejects them, failing to discern how they might be affirmed or how to criticize them with a view to possible transformation. Bonhoeffer, earlier in his *Ethics*, pointed up the contrasts between the two unsatisfactory options:

> Radicalism hates time. Compromise hates eternity.
> Radicalism hates patience. Compromise hates decision.
> Radicalism hates wisdom. Compromise hates simplicity.
> Radicalism hates measure. Compromise hates the immeasurable.
> Radicalism hates the real. Compromise hates the word.[6]

For Bonhoeffer, fully Christian faith simultaneously loves time, eternity, patience, decision, wisdom, simplicity, measure, the immeasurable, the real, and the word. How can the false dualisms be overcome? His theological solution is to appeal to the basic structure of the Gospel witness to Jesus Christ: his life, death, and resurrection:

> In Jesus Christ we believe in the God who became human, was crucified, and is risen. In the becoming human we recognize God's love towards God's creation, in the crucifixion God's judgment on all flesh, and in the resurrection God's purpose for a new world. Nothing could be more perverse than to tear these three apart, because the whole is contained in each of them... A Christian ethic built only on the incarnation would lead easily to the compromise solution; an ethic built only on the crucifixion or only on the resurrection of Jesus Christ would fall into radicalism and enthusiasm. The conflict is resolved only in their unity.[7]

These three core, inseparable dimensions of the Gospel suggest the essential ingredients in a balanced approach to how the church should relate to society.

Humanity and goodness

In line with the incarnation (Bonhoeffer prefers the term "becoming human" or "being human" – *Menschwerdung, Menschsein*) of Jesus, the church affirms the goodness and integrity of creation. Ordinary, natural life really matters to God and is to be nurtured, protected, and enhanced. Human rights are important. Marriage and family life, culture, politics, and economic life are good things, and the church has a responsibility to help them, and the institutions supporting them, to flourish.

In my terms, the cries of fellow human beings for the good things required for life, health, and sustainability need to be heard and responded to in the spirit of God's generous love for the world. For most Christians, most of the time this will be a matter of carrying out daily responsibilities in family, friendship, work, civil society, and church, and serving near and distant neighbors in whatever ways are possible. It will also involve much collaboration with those of other faiths and none.

All these areas call for continual discernment. Which responsibilities ought you to take on? How should time and energy be proportioned between responsibilities? Which organizations and causes deserve participation or support? How do you inform yourself adequately about the many relevant spheres? Should you collaborate or form alliances with people who agree with you on one issue but are opposed on many others? How should children be brought up? What about leisure, pleasure, entertainment, refreshment, and the need for retreat and withdrawal? These and a thousand other questions occur in the course of an average year. They cry out for wisdom and often involve discussion, argument, and deliberation. There are important decisions to be made even about how, and with whom, you might best come to decisions about them.

Churches vary enormously (even within one denomination or region) in the degree of advice, guidance, or instruction they give in such matters, and there are often glaring discrepancies in the amount of attention paid to different areas – why more on sex, less on money and possessions, when Jesus (and the Bible) has far more to say on the latter? They also vary in how they arrive at whatever teaching is given to members: following scripture; following tradition; the Pope's decision; deliberation among groups of bishops, elders or other leaders; democratic assemblies; working parties producing reports; formation of consensus; recognized teachers and educational institutions; individual conscience; or combinations of these.

As regards the future of theology, it is clear that this whole area of what is good for human life makes enormous demands: thinking about church and society has to be informed by scripture, tradition, and a wide range of contemporary people and sources. All spheres of life are constantly changing, and past judgments and decisions therefore need to be continually reviewed and revised. Some apparently simple solutions turn out to be problematic – for example, simply following the Bible, or a specific tradition, or a church leader, or one's own conscience. That "simply following" usually turns out to have great complexity, and even danger, in practice, and Bonhoeffer was extremely sharp in his exposure of this. The "packaged answers," argued against in chapter 4 above, are especially questionable here. Learning to think theologically in as wise a way as possible – including questioning, debating a range of possibilities, and being open to shifts in categories and to other surprises – is the only fully responsible option, and a church or a Christian avoids this route at their peril.

Bonhoeffer, whose approach I am broadly following, was especially sensitive to the range of "packaged" ethics that had proved inadequate in the face of Nazi totalitarianism. He discusses the specific failures of "reasonable people," "ethical fanaticism," "people of conscience," "the safe way of duty," those who "take their stand in the world in their very own freedom" and "private virtuousness."[8] His ethics is centered on faith in God who is in complete solidarity with the world. "In Christ the reality of God encounters the reality of the world and allows us to take part in this real encounter. It is an encounter beyond all radicalism and all compromise. Christian life is participation in Christ's encounter with the world."[9] This participation is as fully responsible people, with whatever resources are available to us – physical, spiritual, intellectual, social, imaginative, cultural, and practical. Bonhoeffer especially emphasizes taking free responsibility and the risks that this can entail.

He also stresses that each situation is different, so that taking full account of the reality of a situation is part of being responsible. In the course of writing his *Ethics*, he was surprised how congenial he found some Roman Catholic ethics that used "casuistry" – a word which has many bad connotations, but which basically means treating each case on its merits and taking into account its particularities in making moral judgments. The main reality in each situation remains for him, of course, Jesus Christ, but in this light justice needs to be done to the specificities that call for ever-fresh discernment.

The result is an ethics and politics that, under the heading of the human and the good, considers a wide range of topics, from reproduction and suicide to telling the truth and economic life, but not in such a way as to pretend to prescribe for all situations. Rather, this is preparatory teaching for the exercise of free responsibility within a community committed to the common good of humanity because of God's love for creation.

Crucifixion and judgment

In line with the crucifixion of Jesus, "God's judgment on all flesh," there can be utter realism about evil and everything else that can go wrong in church and world. God judges in love, for the sake of truth, forgiveness, and genuine peace. It is an ultimate verdict, a "No" to whatever is against love of God and neighbor, and at the same time offers "justification," a completely fresh start in faith by the grace of God. Jesus Christ takes responsibility before God for others to the point of death.[10] A church conforming to Jesus Christ accepts this verdict on itself, receives forgiveness, and also takes its share in responsibility toward the world.

For the church in relation to society, this means that it not only has a prophetic voice, crying out on behalf of those in suffering and in need, but also that it is willing to act and live in solidarity with them and with people in all walks of life. Bonhoeffer's sharpest prophetic words in his final years are for the church, culminating in a vision of a church that exists "for others" just as Jesus lived and died for others.[11]

The word of the cross is an ultimate word, relativizing other concerns and challenging any conception that worldly (even ethical) success is what matters most in history. It refuses any conception of smooth continuity in human progress toward fulfilling God's purposes or of human plans resulting in the Kingdom of God, and directs attention to the suffering, the marginalized, and the poor as those in whom Jesus Christ is to be encountered most surely. Bonhoeffer manages to emphasize this solidarity without idealizing victimhood or marginalizing responsibility toward all sorts of other people:

> Over against the successful, God sanctifies pain, lowliness, failure, poverty, loneliness, and despair in the cross of Christ. Not that all this has value in itself; it is made holy by the love of God, who takes it all and bears it as judgment. The Yes of God to the cross is judgment on the successful. But the unsuccessful must realize that it is not their lack of success, not their place as pariahs as such, that lets them stand before God, but only their acceptance of the judgment of divine love. It is a mystery of God's reign over the world that this very cross, the sign of Christ's failure in the world, can in turn lead to historical success; this cannot be made into a rule, though in the suffering of God's church-community it repeats itself here and there.[12]

Bonhoeffer was thinking about the cross and living its implications to the end of his life, exemplifying what is involved in taking the crucified Jesus Christ as his ultimate point of reference, and constantly trying to discern what this might mean in theology and practice.[13] He is himself a prophetic sign of what it means to take the cross seriously as reality, judgment, forgiveness, and responsibility.

Resurrection and New Life

In line with the resurrection of Jesus, there is the reality of new life and hope.

> The love of God became the death of death and the life of this human being. In Jesus Christ, the one who became human was crucified and is risen; humanity has become new ... Within the risen Christ the new humanity is borne, the final, sovereign Yes of God to the new human being. Humanity still lives, of course, in the old, but is already beyond the old.[14]

This confidence that evil, sin, and death do not have the last word, and that the reality now is that we can act and plan for the transformations that the resurrection life promises, led Bonhoeffer to be continually oriented to the future even in the darkest days of Nazi Germany and the Second World War, and in prison one of his main concerns was for how the coming generation was to live.

So his ethics and the letters, papers, poetry, and other works in his final years are full of thoughts about the shaping of life in church and society in the future. It is not so much the details of these that are important for us (and he was well aware how debatable many of his ideas and recommendations were) as the theological form they take: fresh, responsible thinking and living that seeks continually to be conformed to the life, death, and resurrection of Jesus Christ, and that therefore is dedicated to human flourishing (especially to those who are suffering), faces evil and death realistically, and works for the transformation of church and society. Two aspects of this theology deserve special note.

Ethics as formation; ultimate and penultimate

First is the importance of formation, or being conformed to the humanity, death, and resurrection of Jesus Christ.[15] This is obviously not a general ethics or politics that can be recommended to all, even though its implications are limitless and being faithful to it requires (as Bonhoeffer discovered in his opposition to Hitler) collaboration with many who do not share Christian faith. It is specifically and fully Christian, and its realization is inseparable from the community that undergoes formation in it, the church.

So Bonhoeffer has a good deal to say about "*being conformed to the unique form of the one who became human, was crucified and is risen*,"[16] and about the church as the body of Christ:

> The church is nothing but that piece of humanity where Christ really has taken form … The church's concern is not religion, but the form of Christ and its taking form among a band of people … The starting point of Christian ethics is the body of Christ, the form of Christ in the form of the church, the formation of the church according to the form of Christ. Only to the extent that what happens to the church really concerns all humanity is the conception of formation – indirectly – meaningful for all human beings.'[17]

This conception of the church as the place where people are formed for the sake of the good of all humanity is pivotal for his Christian ethics and will be considered further below.

Second, there is Bonhoeffer's crowning theological concept for integrating the life, death, and resurrection of Jesus with ongoing Christian living. How can you avoid compromise and radicalism? Bonhoeffer saw Christianity constantly setting up these and other dualisms – God and the world, sacred and secular, heaven and earth, inwardness and the public world. How to have appropriate distinctions without dualisms that contradict the reality of Jesus Christ who reconciles both sides? His answer is the distinction and dynamic interrelation of the ultimate and penultimate.

This partly grew out of his wrestling with characteristically Lutheran problems. The "ultimate" of justification by faith could be emphasized to such an extent that the "penultimate" of ordinary goodness and "the natural" was played down. It was possible to lump everyone together as sinners in need of the ultimate, salvation, and fail to discriminate among those who did and did not uphold justice, goodness, and the value of human life. In the face of the Nazi assault on common human values and rights, such failure to discriminate was disastrous. Similarly, Lutheranism had tended to distinguish between church and state in ways that made it especially hard to challenge state tyranny and injustice or to risk the sort of free, responsible decision that Bonhoeffer took in deciding to support the plot against Hitler. But the range of problems addressed goes far beyond Lutheranism: many are common to any Christian who wants to live responsibly in church and society in the light of the life, death, and resurrection of Jesus.

The penultimate is defined in relation to the ultimate but has its own integrity and must be valued and preserved for the sake of the ultimate. At its heart is "being human" and "being good."[18] It prepares for the ultimate without bringing it about or necessitating it. The ultimate is a matter of the free initiative and grace of God – Bonhoeffer especially focuses on justification through grace – and there is no way for human beings to cause or oblige this to happen. In the light of the ultimate, there is an "immeasurable responsibility" toward the penultimate:

> The hungry person needs bread, the homeless person needs shelter, the one deprived of rights needs justice, the lonely person needs community, the undisciplined one needs order, and the slave needs freedom. It would be blasphemy against God and our neighbour to leave the hungry unfed while saying that God is closest to those in deepest need. We break bread with the hungry and share our home with them for the sake of Christ's love, which belongs to the hungry as much as it does to us.[19]

Bonhoeffer's summary of the relationship again ties the concept back into overcoming the dualism of compromise and radicalism:

> Christian life is the dawn of the ultimate in me, the life of Jesus Christ in me. But it is also always life in the penultimate, waiting for the ultimate. The seriousness of Christian life lies only in the ultimate; but the penultimate also has its seriousness, which consists, to be sure, precisely in never confusing the penultimate with the ultimate and never making light of the penultimate over against

> the ultimate, so that the ultimate – and the penultimate – retain their seriousness. Once again it becomes clear that every radical Christianity and every compromise Christianity is impossible in view of the reality of Jesus Christ and Christ's coming into the world.[20]

Jesus Christ embodies both ultimate and penultimate and he is in person the reality of their right relationship.

Bonhoeffer here offers a creative theological concept that can help in thinking through many questions besides those of church and society, but the context in which he conceived it and wrote about it makes it especially relevant to this present topic.

A final lesson from Bonhoeffer: not direct application but free responsibility

There is one final lesson to learn from Bonhoeffer before looking to the future. The leading question for him is about "*how Christ may take form among us today and here*,"[21] but he insists that "this does not mean that the teachings of Christ or so-called Christian principles should be applied directly to the world in order to form the world according to them."[22] This is extremely important. The formation is of communities and people to act in each concrete situation in conformity with the humanity of the life of Jesus, the judgment, forgiveness and responsibility for others of his crucifixion, and the transfiguring newness of his resurrection, "united with Jesus in incomparable love and community."[23] Our action in a particular situation "today and here" is not according to some prior pattern, principle, or criterion, even if it has a biblical text in its support. Rather, taking seriously scripture, the realities of the situation, and anything else relevant, we will act in free responsibility for others before the living Jesus Christ.

There is, therefore, no attempt to identify what the good is for every possible eventuality, or to think up generalizations that stretch to all future cases, or to show how the Bible has direct guidance for each situation. This is not a quandary ethics; it is not problem-centered and act-centered. Rather, it is about the formation of people and communities in the Spirit of Jesus Christ so that through our prayer, our reading of scripture, our discernment of people and situations, our consideration of whatever else is relevant, and our deliberation with others, we can risk making judgments and decisions answerable to God – and even be willing, as was Bonhoeffer himself in his decision to take part in the plot against Hitler, to accept guilt for what we do.

This indirectness of ethical formation is strongly critical of authoritarian ethics, and it is no accident that Bonhoeffer worked it out while resisting a totalitarian system. But it has far wider implications. A great deal of Christian teaching in many traditions is of a direct, authoritarian, heteronomous sort. Whether the authority is the Bible or a church leadership or a rule book of some sort, Bonhoeffer's ethic of free responsibility in conformity with Jesus Christ refuses their apparently simple directness (though not their respect for authority). Instead, it invites into a different sort of simplicity, that of faith in Jesus Christ, who draws us into the messiness of real life, meeting the simplicities and complexities of actual human beings in free responsibility in community.

Continuing This Drama

Authoritarian directness, simplicity, and order might be seen, in terms explored in previous chapters, as one extreme with an "epic" character: there is one right way forward which is known to the authority whose orders are to be followed. At the other extreme is "lyric" freedom without accountability, "doing one's own thing." In between is responsible participation in the theodrama. Bonhoeffer's ethic of conformation to the humanity, death, and resurrection of Jesus Christ is his form of participation in the theodrama. His dialectic of ultimate and penultimate, avoiding compromise and radicalism, is a wisdom shaped by the drama and oriented toward its final act. A life of free responsibility within this drama is one of constant improvisation in the Spirit in the church for the good of humanity.

To continue the theodrama in line with Bonhoeffer, it is not necessary to agree with his specific ethical and political judgments even for his own time, let alone for ours. What is required is to seek "how Christ may take form among us today and here" and to be faithful to what is found. What might this mean for future theology on church and society?

Bonhoeffer's own example coheres in broad terms with an answer in terms of the pattern of theological creativity that has run through this manifesto: seeking wisdom on church and society from scripture, tradition, history, and many other disciplines; relating this, before God, to responsible participation in church and society today; and creatively thinking and communicating about all this.

But that is very general indeed. It can be made more specific through suggesting some major items for the twenty-first century agenda. I take it for granted that theological thinking is needed in relation to every sphere of life – family, marriage, sexuality, and gender; law, justice, and crime; the economy, employment, wealth, and poverty; housing; science and technology; agriculture and fishing; ecology, environment, and a sustainable lifestyle; medicine, hospitals, and health; security, the armed forces, war, and conflict prevention and resolution; education and training; culture, the arts, media, communications, and privacy; charities, voluntary organizations, and other NGOs; sport and leisure; democracy, politics and government; international relations, organizations, and networks; and the religions. Christians carry responsibilities within all those penultimate spheres and are therefore, in Bonhoeffer's terms, called to relate these to the "ultimate," discerning how, in the light of God's purposes for them, they are to be affirmed and inhabited, judged, challenged, and transformed.

That is a massive task for "ordinary" theology and "ordinary" theologians, those millions of lay Christians who think about their lives with whatever resources are available – which in terms of accessible taught or published theology are usually not great. Yet it is not a matter of regretting that somehow the church does not get round to equipping each of its members with answers to the questions they face about Christian responsibility at work and in the rest of their lives. The point is rather to form people in Christian faith, understanding, and practices so that they are prepared to think and take free responsibility wherever they live or work. They have to find answers; the main issue is about quality, which can always be improved. Theology, whether oral, written, or in some other form, can help, but it is often best sought in conversation with diverse partners. It may be that one of the most important theological roles is to facilitate and resource such conversation, aimed at responsibly shaping spheres, lives, and organizations before God.

There is also a massive task for more specialized and interdisciplinary thinking. It is rare that only one discipline is enough to tackle a significant question in the area of church and society, and the complexities in just one relevant discipline, social anthropology (as noted at the beginning of this chapter, and that with regard just to social anthropology of religion, not of other aspects of society), point to the scale of the challenge to engage seriously with more than one. There are serious efforts being made in some fields, but overall the level of engagement is very uneven and mostly quite low. So what ought to be high on the agenda for the immediate future? Arbitrarily limiting the list to seven items, I would suggest some of the most fruitful topics for the church in Western democracies are:

1. *Education.* This is a constant and fundamental concern of both church and society, there are recurrent bids to shape educational philosophies, priorities, institutions, and curricula, and everyone is affected by the outcomes. Closely linked to this is the need for theological wisdom on vocations, careers, and contributing responsibly to society.
2. *Disability.* This is the other side of education, with its emphasis on ability. Those with severe learning disabilities can stand for others who are marginalized and of low status. It may be that how church and society relate to incapacity and suffering is the single most illuminating sign of their spiritual health.

3. *Family*. This is another constant and fundamental concern full of issues that require public and private debate and judgments. It connects with marriage, reproduction, sexuality, and gender issues, which have been among the most controversial topics in recent decades in both church and society.
4. *Chaplaincy*. By this is meant the church relating its ministry directly and officially to spheres of life and their institutions. It is a large and under-recognized (because largely hidden) dimension of church activity and raises some of the toughest theological questions. At present the main involvements are with hospitals and health care, the armed forces, prisons, educational institutions, and businesses, but the practice of chaplaincy could with advantage spread far more widely.
5. *Money*. How to make, share, and spend money is vital to individuals, families, organizations, political debate, and religious life, and all the religious traditions have developed teaching on it. With a global economy and recent financial trauma having impacts on most people, discerning Christian responsibility on this is an extraordinarily complex and demanding task.
6. *Management*. Philosophies and practices of management and organizational leadership are formative far beyond business and affect most areas of organized life today, from churches and schools to health and the arts. At stake in forms of management are huge issues to do with human nature, values, and flourishing, as well as questions of power and authority.
7. *The Arts*. Culture is another critical sign of spiritual health. Intensity of expressive meaning is powerful for good and ill in church and society, and how it is cultivated, disseminated, and critiqued is a constant concern. This is an area in which both the convergence and divergence of church and society are evident, with abundant possibilities for richer religious and theological communication.

What, in those areas, does it mean to take on free responsibility before God?

Contemporary Case: Theological Tasks for the Church in Democratic Civil Societies

This second, shorter, case study aims to sketch in a little greater detail an agenda for theology in one area of the interaction of church and society, that of Christian responsibilities toward the public, political realm in Western democracies and their civil societies.

It is quite common in democracies (especially the United States) for Christians to assume that democracy is not only the best form of polity for a country but also the most Christian. Yet for the major part of Christian history, and for the church in many parts of the world today, that has not been the Christian consensus. The tendency to claim special religious warrant for a specific form of polity has indeed been common, but very different forms have been legitimated in this way, from the Roman Empire, theocracy and absolute monarchy to constitutional monarchy, anarchism, socialism, communism, and fascism. This historical flexibility of Christianity with regard to the political frameworks it inhabits warns against absolutizing or idolizing one contemporary form. In avoiding such idolatry, modern democracy has one advantage over some of the others in that it is hard to argue for it directly from the Bible. Scriptural support for it must therefore necessarily follow Bonhoeffer's indirect route (see above), and this helps to keep debate on the subject open and less tied into areas of theological controversy.

Nevertheless, a good deal is at stake in being able to argue for the Christian legitimacy of democracy in the face of other options. There is a theological task here that is of special significance in international relations and inter-faith relations. So that is the first item on the theological agenda, one that has recently generated a good deal of thinking. Within the democracies, there is little controversy about whether democracy is the best polity, but a good deal, not least among Christians, about which sort of democracy is preferable. There are Christian advocates of classic liberal democracy and its institutions,[24] of deliberative democracy,[25] and of radical or "fugitive" democracy.[26] One of the outstanding theological tasks is not only to continue this debate but also to draw into it large Christian constituencies that are only beginning to contribute to it – many American Evangelicals, for example, have been seriously rethinking their theology in the post-Bush era, and Pentecostals in many countries are developing theirs.

In what follows, three interrelated areas of church responsibility toward the public sphere in democracies are suggested as together forming a framework for balanced theological contributions.

The church as Body of Christ and school for Christian citizens

We start from the center of Bonhoeffer's theology of church and society: the formation of Christians in the church community. He sees Jesus Christ as in solidarity with all people in a threefold way through his humanity, crucifixion, and resurrection. For Christians, who are formed in correspondence with Jesus, this means that they too enter into a multifaceted solidarity, not just with fellow-Christians but with all others. How might the church help its members to realize this solidarity in responsible living with and for others? I would propose the following.

The primary way is through all-round Christian formation through catechesis and baptism, worship and prayer, preaching and teaching, Eucharist, studying scripture, pastoral care, community life and conversation, and the various disciplines and practices of Christian living. This is the main way in which Christians are shaped for free, thoughtful responsibility before God on behalf of other people.

There are also other ways more specific to Christian responsibility in the public sphere. The area of discernment of vocations and careers is one in which the church can make sure that its role is not just helping individuals match their talents to a job, but one of opening up possibilities of serving God in ways that might not have occurred to their members. How often is the career of a politician commended for consideration, and prayer offered for vocations in this sphere? Such commendation can have the effect not only of encouraging those called to be politicians but also of raising awareness among others of the importance before God of political activity. Likewise, the vocation of theologian might be commended with an emphasis on the importance of having public theology that consults with politicians and others in public life and seeks God's wisdom for one's own and other nations. Numerous other callings or part-time activities with public responsibilities are worth commending, and representatives of them worth hearing. Pervading all this, there needs to be theological thinking about vocations.

The demands of public life include the need to discern and balance commitments. A church that takes its members' participation in the public sphere seriously will from time to time address with theological understanding some of the major political and other public causes that elicit time, energy, and money. Such commitments are inseparable from the need to judge which parties, groups, and alliances are appropriate to join: some of the most anguished decisions are faced in this area where an ally is on your side on one issue but opposed on another, and any member of a political party with a broad platform routinely faces such tensions. Embracing these questions of commitment are those to do with basic loyalties. How are clashes of loyalties to be resolved? What are the limits of loyalty to state, party, locality, family, employer, church, or ideal when measured against loyalty to one's conscience before God?

The theology relevant to such matters of commitment overlaps with what is needed to encourage and inform the democratic responsibility to take part in public debate. Many churches guide their members on selected controversial issues, and many give platforms for them to be discussed. And there is no simple separation of internal church issues from political issues: some of the divisive secular issues of our time, especially in the areas of gender and sexuality, are also church-dividing.

The overall effect of such a combination of Christian formation with attention to vocations, commitments, and public debate could be for the church to be a school where some of the lessons of responsible Christian citizenship might be learned. But the horizon is broader than one's own locality and nation. The transnational character of the church gives it worldwide concerns, and such is the global scope of many careers, causes, loyalties, and issues that the fact that the church is local to every country gives it a unique potential as a school and network of global citizenship.

The church as people of God and a community among communities

From its earliest years, the church was not just a collection of individuals but had an organization, a community structure, a polity. So it has always been a community among communities, one organization among others in society. More fundamentally, it saw itself in continuity with Israel as "the people of God," and in taking over the scriptures of Israel as its Old Testament it inherited a social identity and a God inseparable from engagement in history and politics.

Chapter 3, above, discussed the history of religion in the Western democracies in recent centuries. It told how the European wars of religion, resulting from the attempts of particular denominations to dominate in an "epic" manner, has led to a range of settlements in different countries with different religious–secular balances. Essential to these are minimal secular rules, allowing for collaboration between those of different religious traditions and of none in the interests of the common good. Modern constitutional democracy, at its best, is the most thoroughly "dramatic" polity in this sense used here, because it creates this sort of minimal necessary framework for engaging deep differences in civil society and avoids the subsumation of the institutions of civil society under a single "epic" state or ideology.[27]

The church, as one of the corporate agencies in civil society, is a player in the drama with a strong interest in maintaining its dramatic character. It has given up its own epic ambitions, but it and others stand to lose a great deal if a different epic comes to dominate. All the main churches are therefore in favor of pluralist rather than secularist societies – secularist in this case meaning the imposition of a hegemonic secular identity on society (as described in chapter 3). The best hope for maintaining pluralist constitutional democracy, it is argued, is in the alliance of religious and secular people and groups who agree on the need to oppose both religious and secularist overarching epic solutions.

The first task of theology, therefore, is to think through and teach the Christian rationale (or, rather, rationales) for pluralism, democracy, and the importance of having healthy intermediate institutions constituting civil society, to argue for and contribute to the particular settlements and alliances that are needed to sustain pluralist democracy and civil society, and to enter into debate with the alternatives, both religious and secularist.[28] There is an added urgency due to the fact that, as chapter 3 suggested, none of the traditional settlements of religion in the public sphere (in Britain, France, Holland, Germany, Switzerland, United States, Canada, and elsewhere) is working well today. Hard thinking and debating, as well as tough negotiation and political confrontation, are needed if something as generally beneficial as the traditional settlements is to be created for the twenty-first century.

The second task is to resource the church's institutional involvement with both the state and intermediate institutions in many ways – contributing to such areas as parliamentary legislation, educational policy and curricula, ethical debate on many issues, chaplaincy training, and penal policy. Some of the most sensitive theological issues arise with the allies who might in some other ways be closest – other Christian denominations and other faith communities. Theology's wisdom can be challenged more by the need to work out with fellow Christians, Jews, Muslims, and Hindus a common platform on a controversial issue, such as the constitutional position of religions or religious education in schools, than it is by having to develop its own, purely Christian, position. Bonhoeffer's temptations of compromise and radicalism are never far away.

The third task is for the church in its own organizational conduct to be as good a sign as possible of what it stands for. This includes its polity and how that is run, its handling of power and authority, its financial priorities and ethics, its capacity for honesty and repentance, its record on gender, race, disability, and abuse, and much else.

Again, the horizon is broader than one country or region. The church is a global community, some denominations have global structures, and all the main ones have international involvements, often through missions, development agencies, and exchanges of many sorts. Western constitutional democracy is by no means the norm in the wider world, and questions of church and society can take very different forms. Theology of mission[29] has pioneered thinking on many of these matters, but the political and economic aspects of global Christian responsibility have not been prominent and cry out for theological engagement.[30]

It might be that the vision best suited to a Bonhoeffer-inspired theology of church and society (cf. the first quotation from him at the beginning of this chapter on the alliance of religious and secular around humane values) is of a global civil society in a complexly inter-faith and secular civilization, whose "settlement" finds means of sustaining minimal secular rules for the sake of peace and human flourishing. This moves on into the third, more prophetic, responsibility.

The church in the power of the Holy Spirit as witness to the Kingdom of God

Jesus came announcing: "The time is fulfilled, and the Kingdom of God has come near: repent, and believe in the good news" (Mark 1.14). He indicated the Kingdom of God by actions (such as healing, exorcising, feeding, forgiving, eating and drinking with those on the margins of society); by teaching (such as the Sermon on the Mount, with the Beatitudes, fulfilling the law and the prophets, peacemaking, not looking with lust, truth-telling, no vengeance, generosity in lending and secret giving, love of enemies, the Lord's Prayer, no anxiety about tomorrow, and the Golden Rule of doing to others as you would have them do to you); by parables (such as those comparing the Kingdom of God to an abundant harvest in those who respond to its message; to a surprise buried treasure or a long-sought pearl worth everything else one owns; to an abundant feast gathering guests, many unexpected, from all quarters but disastrously refused by some expected to be there; to finding a lost coin, sheep, or son; to a dishonest manager who shrewdly forgives debts; to a king who rewards those who have made good use of the money with which he has entrusted them; and to a judgment of people from all nations in favor of those who have fed the hungry, given drink to the thirsty, welcomed strangers, clothed the naked, taken care of the sick, and visited those in prison); by gathering and training a group of twelve disciples, symbolizing the twelve tribes of Israel, who were to become the nucleus of the church; and by prophetic symbolic acts, culminating in the Last Supper in which, with many echoes of Passover and in anticipation of his death, the bread and wine are identified with his body and blood shared with his disciples.

Above all, Jesus' own person and fate are inseparable from his message of the Kingdom of God. This identification is sealed by his death and resurrection. The content of the good news becomes the living Jesus Christ as the fulfillment and (because history still continues) ongoing realization and anticipation of the Kingdom of God. In Bonhoeffer's *Ethics* (which goes beyond an earlier work, *The Cost of Discipleship*, in which he connected the Sermon on the Mount's teaching on the Kingdom of God with the church) he integrates his contemporary working out of the Kingdom of God around the person of the crucified and risen Jesus. Above all, in his conception of the "ultimate," and in the reality of a new, transformed world given by the resurrection, he offers a vision in the light of which the church can offer penultimate hope to society. The Holy Spirit is given as the ongoing realization of the reality found in Jesus Christ.[31]

So the Holy Spirit empowers the church in witnessing to and acting responsibly toward the coming of the Kingdom of God, opening up society now to a better future, though without any epic ideology or program. It creates penultimate signs of hope that prepare for the ultimate without bringing it about. The signs point to an unimaginable fullness that continually inspires hope and imaginative, freely responsible action.

The Christian imagination, fed by Jesus' teachings and parables on the Kingdom of God, is intoxicated by the abundance of God's compassion, generosity, and love. Down the centuries, it has often been exemplified, as (just to take the Western tradition) in Augustine's sermons, Dante's poetry, Bach's music, Charles Wesley's hymns, and the overflowing, ecstatic prose of Thomas Traherne.[32] Long before them, as Paul's young churches worked out how to make the transition into the second generation in Asia Minor (today's Turkey), the Letter to the Ephesians opened with a burst of intense blessing, praise, and prayer, culminating in a daring evocation of fullness, recalling the note on which Jesus opened his ministry. The key, rich words and phrases accumulate: "the God and Father of our Lord Jesus Christ," "every spiritual blessing," "love," and "beloved," "his children', "glorious grace," and "riches of his grace," "redemption through his blood," "forgiveness of our trespasses," "all wisdom and insight," "mystery of his will," "plan for the fullness of time," "gather up all things in him," "hope in Christ," "the praise of his glory," "word of truth," "gospel of your salvation," "believed in him," "seal of the promised Holy Spirit," "pledge of our inheritance," "faith in the Lord Jesus," "love toward all the saints," "I do not cease to give thanks for you," "spirit of wisdom and revelation," "the eyes of your heart enlightened," "immeasurable greatness of his power," "he raised him from the dead," "far above all rule and authority and power and dominion," "above every name that can be named."

Then the final phrase describes the church as "his [Christ's] body, the fullness of him who fills all in all" (Ephesians 1:23). This is the final quotation in the programmatic opening section of Bonhoeffer's *Ethics*, and it suggests a Christian vision of church and society in which each is transformed beyond anything we can imagine. The letter later prays for its readers to

> have the power to comprehend, with all the saints, what is the breadth and length and height and depth, and to know the love of

> Christ that surpasses knowledge, so that you may be filled with all the fullness of God. (3.18–19)

As if asking to be filled with all the fullness of God is not enough, the prayer climaxes:

> Now to him who by the power at work within us is able to accomplish abundantly far more than all we can ask or imagine, to him be glory in the church and in Christ Jesus to all generations, forever and ever. Amen. (3.20–21)

What might be abundantly more than what has already been asked for?[33] This is a conception of fullness and abundance in the spirit of Jesus' vision of the Kingdom of God and of the corresponding conception in the Gospel of John, eternal life.[34] It allows an ultimate vision of church and society taken up into the fullness of love and of God. This in turn encourages modest, responsible, thankful, joyful, penultimate action in the present, creating with others in church and society signs of hope in the abundance of the Kingdom of God.[35]

7

Inter-Faith Blessing

> *Now the Lord said to Abram, "Go from your country and your father's house to the land that I will show you. I will make of you a great nation, and I will bless you, and make your name great, so that you will be a blessing. I will bless those who bless you, and the one who curses you I will curse; and in you all the families of the earth shall be blessed."* (Genesis 12:1–3)

The call of Abraham in the book of Genesis suggests "blessing" as a leading theological category for relating across differences, including those between the three faiths that look back to Abraham, Judaism, Christianity, and Islam.[1] In each of these, life understood through faith can be seen in terms of blessing: God blessing creation, people blessing God, each other and creation, creation blessing God and people. This God-centered "ecology of blessing" is understood and inhabited very differently by each, but there are deep analogies rooted in orientation toward God as the one who blesses and is blessed.

The significance of blessing is reinforced in Genesis by the story of Abraham receiving hospitality and blessing from Melchizedek, a religious leader of another tradition that acknowledges God as creator:

Inter-Faith Blessing

King Melchizedek of Salem brought out bread and wine; he was priest of God Most High. He blessed him and said:

"Blessed be Abram by God Most High,
Maker of heaven and earth;
And blessed be God Most High,
Who has delivered your enemies into your hand!"
(Genesis 14:18–20)

The best possibility for inter-faith relations between Muslims, Christians and Jews might be summed up as the giving and receiving of blessings, springing from each in their own way blessing God and sharing the blessings God has given them.

Yet Abraham's call also sounds a sobering note: "the one who curses you I will curse" (Genesis 12:3). Historically, and in many places today, relations between Jews, Christians, and Muslims (or pairs of them) include a great deal of cursing and enmity. One can take some comfort from the story's lack of symmetry between blessing and cursing. Abraham and his descendants are promised blessing, and all families are to be blessed in him; cursing is an activity reserved for God alone, and Abraham and his descendants are not encouraged to curse even those who curse them. Yet the reality of cursing and enmity as well as blessing is unavoidable, and inter-faith engagement must face its power and contemporary consequences.[2]

For Christianity, the biggest inter-faith story of the twentieth century related to a terrible strand in its history: its relations with Jews and Judaism. The main reason for this was the Holocaust (or Shoah) in which the Nazis killed about six million Jews between 1942 and 1945. The extent of responsibility for the Holocaust by Christians, their churches, and other organizations is a matter of considerable debate, but this much is undisputed: the Nazis had much popular support in Germany, a country with a long Christian (both Catholic and Protestant) tradition and high numbers of church members, and the Nazis drew strength from Christian persecution, prejudice, and polemic against Jews in many centuries and many places, especially in Europe; much Christian theology portrayed Judaism as a failed religion superseded by Christianity; and many members of churches collaborated with the genocide or failed to protest and oppose it.

There were, of course, other significant inter-faith stories involving Christianity during that century. Among these were remarkable engagements between Hindus and Christians in India and in the West; between Buddhists and Christians in Japan, South Asia, and the West; between Christians and what are sometimes called "primal religions" in North and South America, Africa, Asia, and Australasia; and between Christians and Muslims in the Middle East, South Asia, Africa, and the West. Yet within the twentieth century none of these involved such traumatic violence or raised such deep issues about the identity of Christianity as did relations between Christians and Jews. By the end of the century, relations with Muslims were coming strongly into the public sphere in the West and internationally, with origins in centuries of complex and often violent history in which Christians were deeply implicated.

In the light of such history, it is encouraging that two important inter-faith initiatives of the twenty-first century (or, for Jews, the fifty-eighth century; for Muslims, the fifteenth century), *Dabru Emet* and *A Common Word*, should have been taken by Jews and Muslims toward Christians. Each can be understood theologically as a remarkable blessing for Christians, with promise of more to come. Discerning how these blessings can best be understood and responded to, in the coming decades, is the main concern of this chapter.

A Jewish Blessing: *Dabru Emet*

In September 2000 the statement called *Dabru Emet* (*Speak the Truth*), "A Jewish Statement on Christians and Christianity" was signed by over 150 rabbis and Jewish scholars, philosophers, and theologians from the US, Canada, UK, and Israel.[3] It was issued as a press statement[4] and as part of a book *Christianity in Jewish Terms*,[5] that had essays on thirteen topics by Jewish signatories and by Christian respondents.

The statement opens:

> In recent years, there has been a dramatic and unprecedented shift in Jewish and Christian relations. Throughout the nearly two millennia of Jewish exile, Christians have tended to characterize Judaism as a failed religion or, at best, a religion that prepared the way for, and is completed in, Christianity. In the decades since the Holocaust, however, Christianity has changed dramatically. An increasing number of official Church bodies, both Roman Catholic and Protestant, have made public statements of their remorse about Christian mistreatment of Jews and Judaism. These statements have declared, furthermore, that Christian teaching and preaching can and must be reformed so that they acknowledge God's enduring covenant with the Jewish people and celebrate the contribution of Judaism to world civilization and to Christian faith itself.
>
> We believe these changes merit a thoughtful Jewish response. Speaking only for ourselves – an interdenominational group of Jewish scholars – we believe it is time for Jews to learn about the efforts of Christians to honor Judaism. We believe it is time for Jews to reflect on what Judaism may now say about Christianity. As a first step, we offer eight brief statements about how Jews and Christians may relate to one another.[6]

Dabru Emet does not claim to be representative, and is the outcome of discussion among a diverse Jewish group. Twenty of these, in the book accompanying the statement, engage in further discussion with eleven Christians, likewise diverse. So a mini-drama of dialogue and debate was created. The brief statements are:

Jews and Christians worship the same God.
Jews and Christians seek authority from the same book – the Bible (what Jews call "Tanakh" and Christians call the "Old Testament").
Christians can respect the claim of the Jewish people upon the land of Israel.
Jews and Christians accept the moral principles of Torah.
Nazism was not a Christian phenomenon.

The humanly irreconcilable difference between Jews and Christians will not be settled until God redeems the entire world as promised in Scripture.
A new relationship between Jews and Christians will not weaken Jewish practice.
Jews and Christians must work together for justice and peace.

Dabru Emet, with the accompanying book, is a fascinating blend of scholarship, theology, historical discernment, and some daring, provocative thinking that moves beyond any Jewish or Christian consensus. There has predictably been controversy about it, especially among Jews. The explanatory paragraphs accompanying each statement,[7] and even more the essays in *Christianity in Jewish Terms*, are realistic about the deep and "humanly irreconcilable" differences and the extent of disagreement within as well as between both traditions. They are exemplary in modeling a scholarly, faithful, and creative approach to issues central to the identities of Jews and Christians, and in drawing readers into the current drama of Jewish–Christian relations.

In the terms of the four elements of wise creativity discussed in previous chapters of this manifesto, *Dabru Emet* with *Christianity in Jewish Terms* is theologically creative in an inter-faith mode. It attends to the scholarly and creative retrieval of scriptures, traditions, and histories; it engages with God, communities of faith, and the contemporary world; it offers concepts and theological thinking that open up ways of avoiding some of the usual dead ends of Jewish–Christian relations; and its signatories have imaginatively used varied forms of communication (from newspaper advertisements to scholarly and media discussion). It also makes use of the range of "moods" – asserting, directing, questioning, experimenting, desiring (with some tension among the authors as regards which mood should take the lead). Above all, it sees itself as part of a drama that requires continuing engagement with living participants in one's own and the other tradition.

Before *Dabru Emet* there had been no such joint Jewish response to post-Holocaust developments among Christians; but it is more than a response to Christians. These Jewish voices are concerned simultaneously with the classic forms of their own faith, with the forms it might take in modernity for those living as Jews after the trauma of the Holocaust, and with inter-faith relations that include, but move beyond, toleration and respect. Its horizon therefore embraces the whole complex of the religious and the secular in the contemporary world, while sharply focusing on Judaism and Christianity. It therefore challenges Christian theology to engage with Jews and others on a range of religious and secular matters, without neglecting the specific Jewish–Christian issues that require continuing attention. The broader matters are dealt with elsewhere in this manifesto, but it is also important for the future of Christian theology to have on its agenda a set of tasks in relation to Judaism. These are in danger of neglect due to the more immediate, often political, urgency of relations with Islam.

There are four main tasks that emerge from *Dabru Emet* and its reception:

- Rereading scripture, both within the church and with Jews.
- Following through the rereading of scripture into every area of doctrine, ethics, politics, worship, and historical interpretation, alert for the pervasive effects of different ways of understanding how Christianity relates to Judaism, past and present.
- Embedding the results of such reassessment in current Christian catechesis, curricula, liturgies, church policies, and cultural expressions.
- Incorporating collegial engagement with Jews as part of normal Christian life in those places where the two live side by side, besides developing regional and international dimensions of conversation and collegiality.

The Christian theological development identified by the signatories of *Dabru Emet* as decisive in transforming relations with Jews was Christian acknowledgment of "God's enduring covenant with the Jewish people."[8] This has been a feature of many official Christian statements since the Holocaust,[9] and represents perhaps the most important shift in understanding Judaism among many Christians. In terms of the categories epic, lyric, and dramatic used in the previous two chapters, the Christian tendency has been to portray Jews as part of a Christian "supersessionist epic." Jews who did not become Christians were seen as having rejected Jesus as Messiah and the divine purpose for themselves. The church had superseded Israel in the sense of replacing it in the divine purpose, and the covenant with Israel was seen as obsolete and no longer valid. This was a triumphalist Christian epic, claiming an overview of God's purpose. For much of the past two thousand years, Christians were more numerous and more powerful than Jews in most places where they lived together, so this epic easily became a framework through which to justify marginalizing, demeaning, discriminating against, and persecuting Jews.

One effect of the Holocaust drawn attention to by *Dabru Emet* was that it served to question Christian supersessionism radically. Not only that, but it stimulated deep and continuing engagement between Jews and Christians on many levels and topics. In my terms, this has been genuinely dramatic. The outcome of engagement has not been epically predetermined, but allows for retrieving the past differently and for dialogue and collaboration that open up new ways forward together. The trust is that there are genuine Jewish and Christian resources for a better future and that these are best activated through engagement before God between living members of both communities.

If one were choosing just one such Christian resource it would probably have to be Paul's letter to the Romans, chapters 9–11. That is the only place in the New Testament where the problem of supersession is explicitly wrestled with at length. Paul juxtaposes the Christian theodrama, within which Jesus Christ is Messiah, with that of Israel, in which he is not acknowledged. He comes to the remarkable conclusion in Romans 11:29 about Israel: "the gifts and the call of God are irrevocable" (Romans 11:29). So God's covenant with Israel still stands. He goes on: "God has imprisoned all in disobedience so that he may be merciful to all" (Romans 11:32), confidently hoping in Israel's future – and, by the same logic, the future of all people.[10] But even more comprehensively – and of the greatest significance for inter-faith engagement – he refuses any epic overview, appealing to the unsearchability of God:

> O the depth of the riches and wisdom and knowledge of God!
> How unsearchable are his judgments and how inscrutable his ways!
> "For who has known the mind of the Lord?
> Or who has been his counsellor?"
>
> (Romans 11:33–4)

Paul is committed to going on wrestling with the questions, while simultaneously being faithful within his Christian theodrama and also open to the surprises of God. That is thoroughly dramatic theology, requiring ongoing, God-oriented engagement in the complexities of current history, and resisting the temptation to claim knowledge of just how God's purposes (in themselves mysterious) will be fulfilled. God's mercy on all, beyond our comprehension, is a theological basis for a Christian inter-faith theology of blessing.

A Muslim Blessing: *A Common Word*

In October, 2007, 138 Muslim scholars and leaders sent a letter called *A Common Word Between Us and You* (usually known as *A Common Word*) to the leaders of Christian churches on the subject of love of God and love of neighbor.

The summary included in the letter reads:

> *In the Name of God, the Compassionate, the Merciful*
> *A Common Word between Us and You*
> Muslims and Christians together make up well over half of the world's population. Without peace and justice between these two religious communities, there can be no meaningful peace in the world. The future of the world depends on peace between Muslims and Christians. The basis for this peace and understanding already exists. It is part of the very foundational principles of

both faiths: love of the One God, and love of the neighbour. These principles are found over and over again in the sacred texts of Islam and Christianity. The Unity of God, the necessity of love for Him, and the necessity of love of the neighbour is thus the common ground between Islam and Christianity. The following are only a few examples:

Of God's Unity, God says in the Holy Qur'an: *Say: He is God, the One! / God, the Self-Sufficient Besought of all!* (*Al-Ikhlas*, 112:1–2).
Of the necessity of love for God, God says in the Holy Qur'an: *So invoke the Name of thy Lord and devote thyself to Him with a complete devotion* (*Al-Muzzammil*, 73:8).
Of the necessity of love for the neighbour, the Prophet Muhammad said: "*None of you has faith until you love for your neighbour what you love for yourself.*"

In the New Testament, Jesus Christ said:

"*Hear, O Israel, the Lord our God, the Lord is One. / And you shall love the Lord your God with all your heart, with all your soul, with all your mind, and with all your strength." This is the first commandment. / And the second, like it, is this: "You shall love your neighbour as yourself." There is no other commandment greater than these.*" (Mark 12:29–31)[11]

As with *Dabru Emet*, the letter as a whole has the marks of theological creativity that this manifesto has identified. Its creative retrieval is seen in its use of the Bible and the Qur'an in interplay with each other and with traditions of interpretation of each (especially the Qur'an). It shows passionate devotion to God, and courageously and generously engages with Christians and with the current global situation. It has one big wise idea (whose treatment in the letter, as subsequent discussion has shown, is innovative and not uncontroversial): the centrality of love and compassion to both traditions. And it communicates clearly and in multiple directions, initially in letter form, and subsequently through many genres and media.

Yet theological creativity does not always carry with it historic significance. The reasons for *A Common Word*'s widespread, growing impact,[12] and its ringing true with many from both traditions and beyond them, are several.

It is unprecedented in bringing together so many of the leading religious authorities and scholars of Islam (the numbers of whom endorsing the letter has risen considerably since it was first sent) and uniting them in a positive, substantial affirmation. This is a remarkable achievement of solidarity that has enabled mainstream Islam to find a new voice which both stands for core teaching of the Qur'an and excludes violent, uncompassionate acts, programs, and language.

With regard to Christians, it is not only a friendly word that respectfully interprets Christian scriptures, but is also suitably modest. It does not claim to be the final word but to be "a common word," one that Muslims and Christians (and also, as subsequent responses have shown, Jews and many others) can share with integrity. This is mutual ground, where there is the possibility of working further on issues that unite and divide. It does not pretend that there are no differences between Muslims and Christians. Its modest step forward is taken by concentrating mainly on each tradition's scriptures, identifying them as the central resources for enabling deeper mutual understanding and trust. It therefore summons each to go deeper into their own faith, while also learning more of the other's. Its modesty therefore carries with it a radical vision of long-term, loving dialogue that might open up the richest resources of each faith.

Its central challenge to Muslims and Christians is to live up to their own teachings and seek political and educational as well as personal ways to do this for the common good. Therefore, its horizon is not limited to Muslims and Christians but acknowledges responsibility for the common good of all humanity, and the extreme dangers to this if Muslims and Christians do not follow their own teachings on what it calls "the all-embracing, constant and active love of God" and "the necessity and paramount importance of love for – and mercy towards – the neighbour."

Finally, among the signatories and in the subsequent reception of *A Common Word*, there have been fruitful alliances of leaders, thinkers, and communicators from many spheres: the professionally religious, academics, politicians, business leaders, cultural figures, media stars. Of special interest to theology is the extent to which reception of the letter has brought theologians and religious leaders together. This is a further aspect of the role of theology in the public sphere that was the subject of the previous chapter.

The most substantial response to *A Common Word* so far has been that of the Archbishop of Canterbury, Rowan Williams. In June, 2008, he convened a meeting of Christian scholars, who later joined about fifty church leaders from around the world.[13] All approved a draft of his eventual letter, *A Common Word for the Common Good*. It warmly welcomes *A Common Word*, celebrates points of resonance and convergence, faces sensitive issues (such as love in relation to God as Trinity, the problems of failure, defeat, and suffering, and the relation of religion to violence), and concludes by opening ways forward through proposing a range of forms of dialogue: of life, action, theology, and religious experience.[14] Together, these might be seen as a recipe for "dramatic" dialogue, drawing every aspect of the life of faith into ongoing encounter. It is a model of inter-faith dialogue that offers back to the other partner a positive response that also opens up new and challenging issues. At the time of writing, there has been no authoritative Muslim response to *A Common Word for the Common Good*.

It is still early to predict the long-term impact of *A Common Word*, but already it has led to more Muslim–Christian engagement than any other initiative and is beginning to stimulate the formation of networks, educational programs, and organizations. Within Christianity, a historical parallel is with the ecumenical movement. In a similar way to that, inter-faith engagement needs to be something of an ecology with many habitats. It requires realization at all levels: international, national, regional, and local, with networks and groups, large and small, together with accompanying institutional creativity in founding new organizations and transforming older ones. The vision at the end of *A Common Word for the Common Good* is on that scale, but it is likely that the energy, creativity, and courage needed in the inter-faith sphere will be even greater than what ecumenism has required among Christian churches.

Scriptural Reasoning as "First Inter-Faith Theology"

Perhaps the most striking theological feature of both *Dabru Emet* and *A Common Word* is their reliance on scriptures. Tanakh (Hebrew scriptures), the Bible, and the Qur'an are very different in relation to each other and in the ways in which they function as scriptures within Judaism, Christianity, and Islam. Yet each is part of the core identity of its faith; each is intrinsic to its ways of worshiping, believing, behaving, experiencing, and shaping life; and each has generated complex practices of reading and interpretation that continue to be essential to its community life and relations with others.

So it is fairly obvious common sense to consider it appropriate for Jews, Christians, and Muslims to engage with each other by studying their scriptures together, either bilaterally or trilaterally. This does not mean that any of the three accepts or reads the scriptures of the others in the ways in which they are accepted and read by those whose authoritative scriptures they are. Nor does it imply that members of one tradition will be able to agree on how to understand their own scripture – one of the frequently remarked results of inter-faith encounters is that they stimulate livelier intra-faith discussion. What it does mean is that the centrality of scriptures within each tradition leads sensibly to the centrality of scriptures in their engagements with each other. Negatively, inter-faith engagement (at least between Jews, Christians, and Muslims) that does not allow scriptures to be taken as seriously as they are within the traditions is in danger of failing to do justice to what matters most to each in their lives before God.

Reading scriptures together also has the huge advantage that they are inexhaustibly rich, endlessly generative of fresh thinking, imagining, and practice. They can therefore sustain conversation and collegiality among members of different faiths year after year.

Such long-term conversation and collegiality is one of the common lacks in inter-faith relations: there is a proliferation of one-off encounters, practical collaborations, and other short-term forms of relating, and many of these have the added limitation that they do not enable people to share with each other on the basis of their faith and religious practice. Within each faith community, there are many ways in which relationships are sustained over time, such as worship, learning and study, community activities, faith organizations, and family life. It is not desirable that inter-faith engagement compete with or substitute for any of these; but these can be complemented and enriched by periodic study of one's own scriptures with others. This usually has the effect of drawing one deeper into one's own scriptures and traditions at the same time as learning more about others.

In terms of this manifesto, the role of the Bible as the prime creative source of Christian theology (each chapter exemplifies this, and chapter 10 below sums it up) leads naturally into an affirmation of scripture study as the prime creative source for inter-faith understanding too. It is what one might call "first inter-faith theology." Just as commentary on, and interpretation of, the Bible can be called "first theology" among Christians,[15] so study of scriptures alongside each other can be first theology between faiths.

The most fully developed form of inter-faith scripture study between Jews, Christians, and Muslims is Scriptural Reasoning. This began in the early 1990s, when a group of Jewish text scholars (of Tanakh and Talmud), philosophers, and theologians formed a group called Textual Reasoning in order to bring together their concerns with both classic Jewish texts and traditional and contemporary Jewish philosophy, theology, and liturgy. Several members of this group then joined with some Christian academics (including myself), and later with Muslims, to form Scriptural Reasoning in order to study and discuss Tanakh, Bible, and Qur'an together. Scriptural Reasoning is now practiced in many academic settings, both universities and seminaries, and also in schools, local community settings, and between members of synagogues, churches, and mosques, as well as at regional, national, and international gatherings.[16]

Participants in Scriptural Reasoning have been involved with both *Dabru Emet* and *A Common Word*.[17] It is a practice that does not itself result in groups issuing such statements, but fosters some of the relationships and wisdom needed for bilateral and trilateral initiatives, and can also help to sustain them over time.[18] Scriptural Reasoning does not result in joint Jewish-Christian-Muslim theology. It is "first theology" for each in very different ways. This manifesto, and its companions on the future of Jewish and Muslim theology by Steven Kepnes and Aref Ali Nayed, are attempts to do theology within each of the three traditions, not to have a common theology. Scriptural Reasoning brought the three authors together and enabled their collegiality in the parallel projects. So mutual theological hospitality has been possible, nurtured by scriptures, traditions of interpretation, and contemporary debates. Deep differences could be faced without having to be resolved – Scriptural Reasoning has partly been about learning a wisdom of discussion and dispute concerning what *Dabru Emet* calls "humanly irreconcilable differences." Likewise, analogous wisdoms could be shared and assessed, for example, about how to interpret difficult or scandalous texts, how to cope with fundamentalists and extremists within one's own tradition, what in contemporary cultures to reject, welcome, and critically transform, and ways of relating prayer and worship to theology. The result is not a syncretistic theology but one that is Jewish, one that is Christian, and one that is Muslim – yet shaped in many ways by a wisdom-seeking collegiality that might be described as a setting for the exchange of blessings.

The task of a Christian inter-faith theology is therefore first of all to be a genuinely Christian theology that has attended to other faiths, and so is partly formed in the drama of mutual hospitality with them, learning from their ways of retrieving, their forms of engagement with God, community of faith and world, their thinking, and their communication and artistic expression. The effects of this attentiveness are often hard to identify, but it is also often evident when this dimension is lacking.

Explicitly inter-faith Christian theology, of course, needs to address the main tasks and questions between Christianity and other faiths. A four-point agenda in relation to Judaism was suggested above (p. 135), covering: scripture; doctrine, ethics, politics, worship, and history; integration into Christian teaching, policy, communication, and practice; and ongoing collegiality with Jews. There is a similar agenda in relation to Islam. The experience of Scriptural Reasoning suggests that such bilateral engagement is most fruitful when participants are also engaged trilaterally. Very often the "third party" opens up ways through bilateral dilemmas.

Is it possible to distill from all this a set of guidelines for best inter-faith practice? That is the next question to be addressed.

Seeking Wisdom for Inter-Faith Engagement: A Muscat Manifesto

In 2009, while writing this manifesto, the government of Oman invited me to lecture in the Sultan Qaboos Grand Mosque in Muscat on what I, as a Christian theologian, had learnt about engaging with other faiths and with Western modernity. The lecture included "A Muscat Manifesto," which in nine maxims proposes some basic guidelines for inter-faith engagement, especially between Muslims, Christians, and Jews. It might be seen as an Abrahamic program for mutual blessing, in line with the primacy of dramatic encounter (in the sense worked out in earlier chapters of this manifesto) and the need for theological creativity (in the sense developed above in chapter 1). It reads (with brief comments added):

Love of God and Neighbour

1. *Love God and each other, and have compassion for all God's creation*

This is essential to Judaism, Christianity, and Islam, and therefore to their relations with each other. The genius of *A Common Word* was to initiate a new phase of Muslim–Christian relations on this basis in a theologically creative way.

A Triple Dynamic

2. *Go deeper into our own faith, into each other's, and into commitment to the common good*

This is perhaps the central generative principle of inter-faith engagement. If any of the three is neglected, the health of the encounter is endangered.

Sources of Wisdom

3. *Seek wisdom through our own scripture, history, and theology, through each other's, and through engagement with the arts, sciences, philosophy, and other sources of wisdom*

This affirms a scripture-centered wisdom-seeking and extends it into other spheres.

Engaging with the Modern World

4. *Beware of assimilating to modernity and beware of rejecting it; seek to heal and transform it*

The religions may need each other most in discerning how to cope with the developments of Western modernity. Each has in different ways been challenged, compromised, and traumatized by the experience.

Partnerships of Difference

5. *Form personal relationships, groups, networks, and organizations dedicated to inter-faith conversation, collaboration, and education at all levels, from international to local*

One of the great challenges of the twenty-first century is the building between faiths of forms of collegiality able to cope with massive differences, fears, and enmities. Often the secret of such collegiality is the blessing of friendship.

Creative Communication

6. *Encourage the best communicators, artists, writers, and teachers to spread the message of love of God and neighbour, drawing on the richest sources*

It may be that some of the most fruitful inter-faith thought and action will flow from the efforts of gifted communicators and artists from different faiths to respond creatively to their problems and to each other.

An Ecology across Generations

7. *Cultivate a long-term vision of a habitable world, created and sustained by God for the good of all*

Communities of faith have the resources to take a long-term, trans-generational view of human life. The ecological crisis is only the most immediate of the problems that call for this perspective.

Signs of Hope

8. Create signs of hope within and between our faiths, inspired by the letter A Common Word between Us and You and the responses to it

The responsibility of Jews, Christians, and Muslims is not to play God and try to take control of the future, but modestly to offer signs that point to the future God promises. Central to these should be signs of love of God and neighbor.

God and God's Purposes

9. Do all this for the sake of God and God's good purposes

Inter-faith engagement suffers when it is only instrumental, even in the service of laudable aims such as understanding, collaboration, peace, or justice. In Scriptural Reasoning, for example, understanding and collegiality spring best from reading scriptures together for God's sake, "for the sake of the Name." This by no means excludes more practical aims, but the intention to please God above all is distinct and primary.

All the elements of theological creativity need to be activated if such a manifesto is to be realized, and each maxim can only be fulfilled through dialogues and collaborations being played out dramatically in many settings.

It should be evident that each maxim resists any tendency to pre-occupation with religions and their internal problems. The God who created all is concerned for the future of all, and, therefore, for all creation (1), the common good (2), philosophy, the arts, and the sciences (3), modernity in its secular as well as its religious aspects (4), institutions and relationships (5), communication in many modes (6), the whole ecosystem across generations (7), and all signs of hope, whether explicitly religious or not (8). The engagement of faiths with each other should not just be about mutual blessing but also about blessing all humanity and creation, and above all about blessing the name of God, however that may be conceived and expressed.

Civil Wisdom

For Jews, Christians, and Muslims there is, therefore, strong, God-centered motivation not only to engage with each other but also to serve the flourishing before God of the whole world. This has at times been taken up in an epic mode, with religion helping to inspire conquests, empires, and civilizing missions. Such hegemonic projects are still around, some with considerable potential for violence.

Yet within the mainstreams of the world's faiths, and also among those with little or no religious commitment, there is probably broad acknowledgment that imperial or hegemonic solutions are not an appropriate goal. The painful lessons of the past, exemplified by the religious and secular wars that have marked the European development of tolerant societies with a minimal secular framework (as discussed in earlier chapters), suggests the wisdom of having pluralist societies in which there is neither religious nor secular coercion. The previous chapter explored the sort of civil theological wisdom needed to resource Christians for their responsible participation in such a society. This chapter has offered a vision of inter-faith civil wisdom for the twenty-first century, has described signs of hope that it is possible, and has recommended some lines along which Christian and other theologians might proceed.

8

New Theology and Religious Studies

Shaping, Teaching, and Funding a Field

In which setting does the sort of theology advocated by this manifesto flourish best? A surprisingly definite answer to that important question will emerge in the course of this chapter: what I call *new theology and religious studies*. It is surprising, partly because, despite having already developed to a considerable extent in several countries in a variety of forms and types of institution, the fact that there is a family resemblance across all the variety has not yet been sufficiently recognized. There is an emergent paradigm in which theology, which seeks to answer questions of meaning, truth, goodness, and beauty that arise within and between specific religious traditions, is taught and researched in an interactive, collegial relationship with religious studies, which seeks to answer questions about specific religious traditions through a range of disciplines, but not normally with a view to producing constructive or normative religious positions. The institutional integration of the two has, so far in the twenty-first century, lacked clear articulation and advocacy.

Why is that opening question important? It matters in different ways for the various stakeholders in the field.

For most churches, the main burden of theological education will always be carried by their own institutions, or by those over which they have sufficient quality control for their own purposes, such as educating clergy and lay people, and resourcing the church's life and mission. Yet the vision of theology in this manifesto stretches across many more disciplines, engagements, and forms of communication than most church theological institutions can do justice to. So the crucial double question facing churches is: how can we best complement what our own institutions do so that the richest and broadest theology is available to our members, and also, at the same time (since churches are committed to the rest of humanity too), to others?

Pluralist societies (of the sort discussed in chapters 3, 6, and 7) are also stakeholders in the future of theology. The quality of education in and for churches and other religious communities affects not only the health of these institutions of civil society, but also the character of public debate, deliberation, and decision-making. There also need to be places where citizens can be educated, issues discussed, and subjects taught and researched across the boundaries of particular churches and religious communities, without any requirement that those researching, teaching, or being taught must pass a religious test. The crucial double question facing pluralist democracies is: how can we best help religious communities to serve the flourishing of civil society and also, at the same time, help all our citizens to become as well educated and thoughtful as possible about the questions raised within, between, and about religions?

Universities and schools in pluralist democracies have to take that question very seriously. So too do academic and professional disciplines, learned societies, and "guilds," many of which are international and also reach beyond the sphere of universities into many other sorts of institutions, professions, and media. For universities (with which this manifesto is most concerned) this means first recognizing the academic appropriateness of bringing all relevant disciplines to bear on the questions relating to religions (there is some resistance to this to be overcome, especially in secularist institutions). Then the crucial double question for universities is: how can we best do teaching and research on the questions raised within, between, and about religions to the highest standards, while also being academically and educationally responsible toward society – both its religious communities and the rest of civil society?

Stakeholders are not just institutional but also individual – especially students. Their motivation for entering the field varies enormously. Generalizing from my own experience of students (and of their teachers, all of whom were once students!), the main motives besides career considerations are: personal faith commitment; seeking answers to questions of meaning, truth, and goodness; fascination by one or more of the many academic disciplines in the field; and interest in the significance of religions for societies, civilizations, and human existence. Many combine two or more of those motives. I will make the assumption (which is, of course, arguable) that not only are all those motives to be respected but also that, whichever of them a particular student is moved by, they would be enriched if, in the course of their education, they were to engage not only with those similarly motivated but also with others. Then the crucial double question for a student in the field is: in which sort of setting will I be best educated, not only in line with my own core motivation but also so as to be able to respect and understand those of others?

This manifesto proposes that the answer to each of those stakeholder questions is the same: *new theology and religious studies*.

What is New Theology and Religious Studies?[1]

In 2000, representatives of British university departments of divinity, theology, religion, religious studies, biblical studies, and various combinations of those terms agreed on a "benchmarking statement" for the field. For some of us who took part in the process of consultation it felt like the "coming of age" of a new paradigm that had been slowly worked out over many years. The document that resulted showed the great variety in the field, but also the mutual recognition among different types of department and approach.[2] As one summary notes: "There is less tension between the disciplines in Britain than there is elsewhere."[3]

The field in Britain developed over centuries with successive waves of cultural, religious, and educational developments leaving their marks. No one template, no one ideology, no one definition has dominated. Participation in that benchmarking exercise was a vivid reminder of how many different strands of history, religion, and educational institution there are. Even in terms of paradigmatic departmental arrangements, one would need at the least to list Oxford, Edinburgh, Aberdeen, Birmingham, Durham, Lancaster, King's College London, Heythrop, Kent, Cambridge, and, to take just one of the younger universities that have learnt a great deal from the history and tried to incorporate its best elements from it, Chester. Even as I name these, I can think of others that do not fit easily with any of them, and distinctive features that may seem insignificant to outsiders might from inside a department be important results of hard-fought battles and tough negotiation. Yet, for all the many specific niches, the benchmarking statement also indicates that this is one ecosystem. In the absence of a better term, it can be named "theology and religious studies."[4]

The British paradigm has several distinctive features, which I would summarize as follows:

- Overall, the combination of theology and religious studies at its best allows for the pursuit, through a range of academic disciplines, of questions of meaning, truth, practice, and beauty raised by the religions, about the religions, and between the religions. There is no difficulty in arguing that pursuit of such a range of questions can be appropriately academic, but within the array of possible combinations of questions, disciplines, and categories there are many different possible configurations of department.
- This means that the particular phenomena of the field can be richly and rigorously described, analyzed, and explained in ways that are often not possible where theology is studied apart from the range of academic disciplines that come under the heading of religious studies.
- At the same time, it allows for issues of truth and practice, including normative practice, to be on the agenda in ways that

are often not possible in religious studies settings. It might be that the most serious academic objection to the separation of religious studies from theology is that, without theology, religious studies arbitrarily limits its inquiries and outcomes. This especially applies to questions raised by and between the religions: it might be possible for religious studies to explore answers that have been given to these questions, but not to come to conclusions about their truth or goodness, let alone offer constructive proposals in line with, or in critique of, particular traditions. On the other hand, theology, like other disciplines such as philosophy and economics, can be a broker among disciplines, stimulating interdisciplinary inquiries, being challenged by them, and in turn challenging them with theological questions, not least concerning purpose, truth, and practice.[5]

- The combination of theology and religious studies encourages the fulfillment and interrelation of three key transgenerational responsibilities: toward universities and their range of disciplines (a responsibility of excellence in the disciplines and toward the shaping of education and research, according to the best norms); toward religious communities and traditions (a responsibility of educational, critical, and constructive engagement); and toward societies and public understanding (especially the shaping of education, public policy, and public discourse). Crudely put, theology alone (and I include here Hindu, Buddhist, Jewish, Muslim, Christian, secular, and other tradition-specific bodies of thought, whether they call themselves "theology" or not, as well as forms of theology that try to engage critically and constructively across traditions) can find some difficulties in doing full justice to the range of academic disciplines and to the demands for public understanding adequate to a religiously diverse society; and religious studies alone can have difficulties with the normative side of some academic disciplines, with the constructive requirements of religious communities, and with the normative and public policy aspects of public debate.

- The combination of theology with religious studies allows for forms of collegiality in relation to each of those responsibilities – collegiality within departments and universities, between them, and within and between disciplines, religious communities, spheres of society, and different societies.
- The combination offers a more diverse curriculum to a wider range of students, which in turn affects the richness of collegiality among students.
- Finally, the combining of theology and religious studies gives a setting where the future of the field can be discussed and worked out in practice with the participation of the main interested parties. There can be benefits for more specialized environments (both theological – for example, seminaries or religion-specific universities; and religious studies – for example, departments in secular universities) in learning from places where both dimensions are present and engaged with each other.

So, at the very least, a case can be made that it is generally beneficial for theology to become more open to religious studies and vice versa. I would make a stronger claim. What has happened in Britain has been more than two different approaches to the field managing to get along or learning from each other in certain respects, recognizing that each has a contribution to make. That is certainly so in some universities, and it reflects the legacy of a difficult history in which religious studies had to fight for its existence in the face of theological (often church-led) domination, and later theology sometimes had to fight for its existence in the face of secularist domination. But, with the waning of church domination and the increasing recognition (at least within this field) of the unacceptability of an overall secularist framework, the issues, conflicts, negotiations, and power relations within the field are far less susceptible to a simplistic dichotomy (if, indeed, they ever were). What has happened is at its best something more than a compromise settlement: it is a new, unprecedented way of shaping the field.

What is new about it? It is not so much one element as the product of many that combine to form this new ecosystem. Each of the bullet points above contributes to the overall innovation: the range of questions the new field can cope with; the fuller opening of theology to descriptive, analytical, and explanatory disciplines, and of religious studies to normative and practical considerations; greater ability to deal with core responsibilities toward academy, religious communities, and society; fuller and more diverse collegiality around the core questions and responsibilities; a richer education for students; and a better setting for deliberating on the future of the field. The main stakeholders named above – churches (and other religious communities), pluralist democracies, universities (and other educational, scholarly, research, and professional bodies), and students – all stand to gain. And, from the standpoint of this manifesto, new theology and religious studies sets up a framework for Christian theological creativity unprecedented in its potential.

A Framework for Creativity

One point needs to be made clear before commenting further on the framework. No one department or institution could ever cover the whole of this vast field. In comparison with the full range of disciplines and subjects (which is constantly expanding further), even the largest institution is very limited in what it can research and teach. So alliances between institutions are important, and especially so for the sake of sustaining the integrity of a variety of traditions. One emerging pattern in Britain and elsewhere is for a university to have a close relationship with one or more Christian seminaries (for educating clergy and lay people) or seminaries of other faiths, or other types of institution (such as church-related teacher training colleges or youth work, counseling, or chaplaincy training centers). A student of a seminary can take courses in the university or in his or her own institution (validated by the university), and university students can likewise choose from what is on offer in both. Many staff teach in both types of course. This creates a larger, richer environment for undergraduates, postgraduates, teachers, and researchers. It particularly helps to make sure that the community and worship dimension of a faith tradition can be maintained in close relationship with its theology, while at the same time connecting it with the thinking of other traditions and a wide range of disciplines. The terms on which such institutional alliances and affiliations take place are various, but they flourish best in relation to universities that are themselves committed to the union of theology with religious studies.

Within such a setting, the sort of theology being advocated by this manifesto in previous chapters is far more likely to thrive. New theology and religious studies enables wiser creativity (chapter 1) in retrieval through all the relevant historically oriented disciplines. It is open to theological work springing both from engagement with God in tradition-specific ways within communities of faith, and from involvement in many spheres of life; it can also resource such thinking through the human and natural sciences and other disciplines. It can encourage theological conceptualizing and imagining to learn from, and be inspired by, what is going on a range of fields. And, especially through its inclusion of the literary, visual, performance, and other arts, it can help shape theological expression creatively.

The Bible can in this setting be studied through the whole array of relevant philological, historical, literary, and other methods without losing sight of its value for worship, preaching, catechesis, pastoral care, and the whole life of faith. Theology can be worked out within the church and also through academic collegial relationships, and there can be the added perspective of the human sciences on what goes on in both church and academy. As regards the "moods" of faith (chapter 4), a common perception is that the tendency of church-based theology is toward the indicative and imperative, while academic theology majors on the interrogative, subjunctive, and optative. That is not, in my experience, by any means a sound generalization, but it does seem to be the case that the diverse theology and religious studies environment helps to keep all five constantly in play. There is an extra dimension of drama (chapters 2 and 3), and an added resistance to epic theologies, in the pluralist environment of theology and religious studies. Each institution is an active player, and the field itself is constantly being renegotiated – often with deeply divisive issues at stake. The advantages for Christian theology on church and society (chapter 6) are also clear if it is being worked out in dialogue with both those of other faiths and university colleagues in history, the social sciences, politics, economics, and international relations. Inter-faith engagement (chapter 7) is one of the aspects of theology to gain most (study – and usually members – of many faiths being part of the ordinary life of the field), even more so if those of other faiths besides Christianity are among the allied institutions.

What about wisdom (chapter 1)? This is the most basic and encompassing question of all. In crude terms, the university's tendency is toward stressing education for understanding, knowledge, and know-how; the church is also concerned for those but emphasizes education for wisdom too. Yet, in fact (though not usually by name), wisdom is immensely important for universities too. They cannot flourish without it, and perhaps their core challenge in the twenty-first century is how to seek it, deliberate about its implications, and then embody it in shaping universities. I have written about this elsewhere;[6] here the main point is that such wisdom is likely at its best to be the outcome of the interplay between people nurtured by various traditions of wisdom, both religious and secular, and that new theology and religious studies is a good setting for that nurture and interplay.

No framework, of course, can guarantee wisdom or creativity in theology. The quality of collegiality and intensive conversation that is its vital condition (chapter 5) is the outcome of many other factors and it can happen in many other settings. I now turn to two of those.

Other Frameworks

Germany

Since the foundation of the University of Berlin in 1809, in which the great theologian Friedrich Schleiermacher played a leading role, German universities, and others influenced by them, have been among the most creative theological centers.

The University of Berlin was a historical surprise. At a time when universities were under great pressure for being old-fashioned, religiously dominated, educationally inadequate, and unable to keep up with, let alone pioneer, progress in academic disciplines, and when the fashionable "modern" way of the French Revolution and Napoleon was to have specialist higher education and research institutes, some of the seminal thinkers of modernity[7] generated the ideas upon which the University of Berlin was founded. Part of its daring was the extent to which it was a renewal of the medieval university, deeply indebted to its Christian roots while also being committed to thinking them through afresh in its modern context.[8] It was concerned with both the Hebraic and the Hellenic roots of Western civilization, it was sensitive to the needs of its society (and a leading factor in the remarkable nineteenth-century development of Prussia and later Germany), it championed intellectual and academic freedom against many religious and secular opponents, and it pioneered the modern research university as a place of research and of teaching shaped by research.

Not the least important of Berlin's surprises was its way of handling religion. Schleiermacher won his battle against Fichte to have theology included in the university, and, along with it, the education of clergy for the state Protestant Church. This was accompanied by a rigorous commitment to rational inquiry in all disciplines. So, during the coming centuries, the faculties of theology in Berlin and other German universities became places where some of the most significant dramatic engagements between Christian faith and modern understanding took place. A complexly secular and religious institutional space was created in which there could be fundamental debate and dispute about these issues. This contrasted with France, where a secularist ideology excluded theology from state educational institutions.

The Berlin paradigm, for all its benefits, has limitations that have proved increasingly serious. German universities themselves suffered the double trauma of Nazi and then, in the East, Communist takeover, but even in the context of constitutional democracy their almost complete dependence on the state and its bureaucracy has severely limited their capacity to respond to new circumstances and to innovate. The secular/religious tension that characterized the University of Berlin tended to relax over the years, especially in the twentieth century, in favor of the secularism that mostly dominated academic life. The limitation to officially recognized Protestant and Roman Catholic theology, and the influence of church authorities over many appointments has been a special handicap as Germany and the rest of Europe have become increasingly pluralist. Most acutely, there has so far been little institutional success in allowing for other types of Christian theology, let alone Muslim, Jewish, and others, to occupy professorial posts and to be otherwise fully and creatively part of the university world. The equivalent of religious studies in Anglo-American institutions has been the "science of religion" or "history of religions," but where this has been present in universities it has rarely been creatively involved with theology. There has been no parallel to the British process of ad hoc, diverse, experimental, locally negotiated settlements among stakeholders that led to the development of new theology and religious studies there. Ironically, the very strength and success of German theology has inhibited its capacity to undergo the transformations that I am advocating.

Yet there are signs of change in German theology and the universities that are its main institutional base. Some of these – I think especially of what has been happening in the Universities of Heidelberg, Tübingen, and Hamburg – retain the main strengths of classic German theology while opening up to other disciplines, other types of Christianity, other faiths, and other continents. German universities have been ahead of many others in global involvement. It may be that they are at present heading toward something analogous to the foundation of the University of Berlin. There is the opportunity for them to come up with another such surprise, conceptually sophisticated, state-supported initiative (which might typically contrast with the long-drawn out, pragmatically mediated British surprise of new theology and religious studies which only now is beginning to find an appropriate conceptuality). To judge from the Berlin precedent, the requirements for this are steep: intensive thinking and discussion to produce creative ideas and wisdom (where are the successors of Kant, Goethe, Schelling, Hegel, Fichte, and Schleiermacher, and, if they exist, are they talking to each other?), political and government recognition of the importance of the project, sufficient thoughtfulness and imagination on the part of the churches and other religious communities, and sufficient funding.

The United States

Theology in the United States has been institutionalized differently from either Britain or Germany, due partly to an Enlightenment-inspired separation of church and state. So there is a divide between private institutions, often with religious roots, where theology may be taught, and state-supported institutions with departments of religious studies from which it is excluded. The American scene is in fact far more complex than that, especially in private universities that have divinity schools as well as religious studies, and a few state universities, such as the University of Virginia, that engage with tradition-specific theologies. There is no combining of theology and religious studies on the British scale, and far more debate, tension, suspicion, and even polemics, between them.

Yet in the US, as in Britain, the very labels "theology" and "religious studies," as used to characterize whole institutions or departments, have become increasingly problematic. Surveying the actual settings, the most obvious feature is the diversity, reflecting as in Britain a complex history of power struggles and negotiation, and resisting a resolution of the debates in favor of one conception or the other. Rather, there is an emergence of many types that combine theology and religious studies in ways analogous to those found in Britain. Given the strength and large number of denominational or ecumenically Christian institutions in the US, and the tiny number of state universities that seem likely ever to welcome the teaching of theology in any form, the prospects for developing further something analogous to the British model of new theology and religious studies are likely to lie with seminaries, with the divinity schools of private universities, and with alliances of institutions. There are more signs of such opening up of seminaries and private universities than there are in Germany. There is much scope for individual institutions to respond to the needs of their complexly religious and secular society, and they are in fact doing so.

The main weakness, in contrast with Britain and Germany, is that so few universities (especially those high in the international rankings) see theology as an academic subject worth seriously developing. Even fewer are eager to become affiliated with a range of tradition-specific theological institutions. The result is that theological discourse is very fragmented, even within Christianity, and there are few settings with flourishing collegiality across the boundaries of theology and religious studies. Where that collegiality is being developed it is of potentially global importance, but at present the major voices in the field advocate either theology or religious studies, with little vision for their union.

There is an irony somewhat like that remarked upon in relation to Germany. In the US, the very success and wealth of Christian educational institutions, together with the eighteenth-century ideology of separation of church from state, make it especially difficult to transcend the binary opposition and respond to the attraction of the new theology and religious studies paradigm. Like Germany's nineteenth-century success, the American pattern was sustainable in the twentieth century but is now in need of further transformation.

New theology and religious studies offers both the US and Germany, and many other countries that have not been mentioned, a creative alternative upon which to improvise within their situations for the twenty-first century. Such improvisation, guided by the paradigm proposed here, can be very effective at the level of curriculum and individual courses without needing systemic change. Indeed, it was through an accumulation of such micro-changes that it developed in Britain in the first place. One of the key questions for theology in the twenty-first century is how far universities around the world can begin to do justice to the profound questions that are raised not only about the religions, but also within and between them. This global perspective will be addressed below.

Curriculum and Teachers

What is the ideal curriculum for twenty-first century Christian theology? Clearly, it should try to enable what is advocated in the chapters of this manifesto: those sorts of retrieval of the past; engagements with God, church, and society; imaginative, thorough, and wise thinking; and quality of expression; and all in conversation with religious studies and other fields. To go much further than that is to be drawn into the sort of detail that has to take into account a particular institution's aims, resources, traditions, balance of subjects and teachers, student preferences, and so on. Working out a curriculum draws into dramatic engagement an institution's teachers, students, administrators, funders, and other stakeholders.

Perhaps the main practical objection to new theology and religious studies is that, by expanding the cast in the drama, it makes such engagements more complex and difficult. I would argue that the advantages of facing the difficulties outweigh the disadvantages of constricting the field. Yet, even when the cast is more restricted, the ideal of new theology and religious studies can be influential and beneficial.

Far more important than the details of curriculum are the teachers. The future of Christian theology is above all in the hands of those who teach it. At the heart of good teaching is face-to-face communication and conversation. Randall Collins's study of the sociology of philosophies over many centuries and cultures, referred to in chapter 5 above, is clear about the central role of face-to-face conversation between colleagues and between teachers and students in the most influential philosophical traditions.[9] This has been so regardless of the availability of other forms of communication, whether print or electronic. So teachers who sustain good face-to-face relations with students are central to this subject, as to others.

But who is the teacher? Students can be willing to put up with all sorts of apparent inadequacies, difficulties, or idiosyncrasies in face-to-face communication if they are convinced the teacher has something worthwhile to share. What that is can vary enormously – deep knowledge of a text or historical period, an authoritative survey of what is going on in a field, clarity about what is needed by way of introduction to a subject, interdisciplinary expertise, long wrestling with intractable theological questions, adventurous ideas, a significant research topic, practical experience, or wise judgment – and hopefully more than one. Yet, especially the nearer one comes to those theological questions that challenge students regarding their own engagements with God, church, society, and the kind of wisdom that cries out for personal response, the more the person of the teacher is also at issue. How far does a teacher embody his or her theology and communicate it by character and way of life?

That is an extraordinarily sensitive matter. The question of character is often raised in the limit cases of teachers who are accused of abusing their roles and violating a code of ethics. But all religious and educational traditions recognize the immense potential influence for good on students of teachers who do more than "just teach," and who in some way act as examples, role models, or embodiments of what they stand for. In Christian theology, especially when taught by Christians,[10] the question is intensified.

Nor is it only an individual matter: there are teaching traditions, theological lineages that may cross many generations. These can be associated with a church, a religious order, a school of thought, a person, a university, a place, a text, a practice, a vision. They can have several key teachers, and the character of the whole tradition is an issue.

The dangers associated with exemplary teachers and formative traditions are almost as great as their potential for good. It is another area that cries out for discernment and wisdom: there are few more momentous events in one's life as a student than when one recognizes someone as "my" teacher, or when one takes steps to participate in a particular theological lineage. The future of theology is shaped by such commitments.

Funding

Funding is an aspect of stakeholding in theology that has not yet been directly considered. Educational and research institutions are expensive. Who pays for them? The main funders at present are the church, the state, students, sponsors of teaching and research, and benefactors. Why should each of them go on doing so? And on what conditions?

Churches are the most obvious supporters of the field. They need theological institutions to help educate their members, their clergy and other workers, and anyone else interested in the field. How much they give, and toward which sort of student and institution, is always a matter for debate. The thrust of this chapter is that there is a strong case for funding their own institutions, for contributing to universities that teach theology and religious studies, and for sponsoring alliances of their own institutions with universities and with those of other denominations and faiths. The conditions on which they give support include, of course, the need to ensure that their members and clergy are well educated in their own theology; but they need not be limited to that. They will also be concerned, if they share a commitment to the sort of theological inquiry advocated by this manifesto, that the theologies of other denominations and other faiths be well taught, and that theology be established as a lively subject in as many universities as possible.

The state (or bodies supported by the state) in pluralist countries needs theology for the sake of the health of the religious communities that are such an important part of civil society, and also because of its contributions to the education of all its citizens (whatever their allegiance) and to informed public debate on many issues. I suggest that it gets best value for its money if it invests primarily in helping theology and religious studies to flourish in universities and other settings. The conditions on which it does so appropriately include criteria of academic and teaching quality, transferable skills, access to all its citizens, and the fulfillment by universities of responsibilities toward the public good.

The four main motives, found in various combinations, of students who study theology are, as mentioned above: personal faith; a search for meaning, truth, and goodness; interest in the field's academic disciplines; and desire to explore the role of religion in human life and societies. Their (or their parents' or other funders') main conditions for paying fees include academic and teaching quality, transferable skills, a congenial learning community, and better career prospects.

Sponsors of teaching and research are increasingly important in the funding of university departments of theology and religious studies. A range of religious and other organizations sponsor students or whole courses in various types of tailor-made theology – for example, for hospital, military, prison or educational chaplaincy, or Muslim youth work, or pastoral care, or inter-faith engagement. It is an advantage if such courses can draw on a wide range of disciplines in theology and religious studies, as well as other university departments. Research in the field, which is expanding rapidly worldwide, is sponsored both by the bodies that support such courses and also by research bodies, both state-funded and private. Their motives and conditions vary widely, but most of them can best be met within a diverse theology and religious studies environment rather than one that is exclusively dedicated either to theology or to religious studies.

Finally, there are benefactors. Cultures of benefaction in relation to theology vary, from the United States, with its tax system favoring charitable giving, and its massively endowed private universities, seminaries, and charitable foundations, to the almost total dependence of German university and church theology on state support from taxation. Around the world, religion is one of the main motives for benefaction, and theological education has been a major beneficiary of this – above all, of course, through churches deciding to use the money donated to them for this purpose.

There can be no generalizing about the motives of benefactors or the conditions on which they give, but it is worth concluding this section with a hymn to the wise ideal benefactor: the one who gives a permanent endowment for the good of the field. What a joy to find someone who takes the trouble to discern what is needed for the long-term flourishing of the field and its responsibilities, and then gives an endowment to enable that! What even greater joy when that benefactor appreciates the need not only for teaching posts, student support, and research projects, but also for public education, outreach and impact, libraries, travel, exchanges and collaborations with other institutions, international networks, buildings, and high-quality management and administration! And perhaps the greatest joy of all is to see a benefactor of one faith support the study of other faiths as well as their own, alongside the engagement of all faiths together for the common good! Such endowment liberates academics from the endless round of gathering short-term funding, it establishes something that lasts across generations, and it ensures the flourishing of new theology and religious studies for the sake of a better world.

The Global Potential of New Theology and Religious Studies

I have argued that the mixed British ecology of theology and religious studies has a great deal to recommend it. It is good for the field academically; and it creates a place of collegial study and conversation that brings benefits to both the religious communities and the society as a whole. Within it (though, of course, not only within it), the sort of theology advocated by this manifesto can flourish. Even in those places where it is more difficult to realize within institutions, new theology and religious studies can act as a paradigm encouraging improvisations that enrich theology, together with other disciplines concerned with religion and the contemporary world.

The field has been considered specifically only in Britain, Germany, and the US (in each of which I happen to have been a student), and further discussion would need to look at other countries and continents. Yet, from my own limited knowledge (including time at relevant institutions in Ireland, Holland, Sweden,

Canada, Israel, Jordan, Egypt, Oman, Kenya, China, and India), the paradigm of new theology and religious studies is also relevant to many other parts of the world. It has, of course, to be thought through, taking full account of local circumstances. It can come as a liberating possibility to those who only have available the past paradigms of various forms of theology or religious studies. It is sad, for example, to see a new university department in the field conceived in a narrow way, constricted by a secularist religious studies ideology, for want of anyone who appreciates the alternatives. It is equally sad to see a church institution so protective of its distinctive identity that it fails to see the advantages for its students and staff of alliances with other institutions and of conversation and collaboration with the disciplines of religious studies. Positively, there is the opportunity in many countries to transform current departments and institutions and found new ones. Worldwide, the field is expanding considerably (see chapter 1 above) and it matters greatly whether or not the main model becomes that of new religious and theological studies.

In conclusion, it might be helpful for those with institutional responsibility for the field in the coming decades to bear in mind the mind the following tasks and maxims:

- Develop rich descriptions of the field, both historical and contemporary, using the field's academic disciplines to do so.
- Develop rationales for the field, not just in the fairly general terms I have used, but also in Jewish, Christian, Muslim, Hindu, secular, and other terms. Then bring the rationales into dialogue with each other and build departments and institutions that can be justified and nourished by more than one tradition.
- Whatever the nature of the settlement in one's own department, make the case for it being open in both directions, toward both theology and religious studies, and being supportive of the overall diverse ecology of new theology and religious studies.
- Hold together the three transgenerational responsibilities toward universities, religious communities, and societies, and build forms of collegiality around each responsibility.

- Seek the good of the whole field of theology and religious studies, and put intellectual and political energy into debates about its future in order to help it become "mutual ground" (rather than "neutral ground") for those of many religions and none.
- Seek funding for the field, and especially endowments, as the best material way to ensure long-term flourishing.
- Have a global vision for the field, commensurate with the global presence of the religions, and embody this not only in the curriculum but also, whenever possible, in the teaching and student body, in institutional alliances, and in responsibilities undertaken.

9

Becoming a Theologian
The Apprentice

You can study or teach Christian theology from a wide range of personal positions, Christian, non-Christian, or somewhere in between or hard to categorize. It is a strength that the subject can be engaged in from many angles, including being treated as an academic subject like any other: it demands intelligent study but not a particular religious commitment in the student or teacher. A university context of theology and religious studies is especially suited to embrace a variety of commitments among students and teachers, encouraging discussion about those commitments as part of what the field is about. It is not helpful to the field to insist on a sharp division between Christian "insider" and non-Christian "outsider." Both those terms include a huge variety of positions that may differ sharply from each other or be held in complex interrelationship; and many people are on a journey between positions, studying Christian theology in order to help make up their minds.

Yet it is clearly essential to the field of Christian theology that there are those who are committed to it as Christians. This chapter asks about those whose vocation as Christians might be to study and produce the sort of theology advocated in the manifesto. What formation might be appropriate to becoming such a theologian? What sort of core self-understanding might be desirable, which "practices of self" should be nurtured?

Disciple and Apprentice

Jesus taught his closest followers by living with them, leading them, conversing with them, praying with them, instructing, correcting, and serving them. He let them learn by participating in what he was doing and by going out to do it themselves. They were called "disciples" (*mathetai*), meaning "learners," underlining how central being schooled and formed was for what they were called to say, do, and be. It was what we might call an apprenticeship, in which speaking and hearing is set in the context of learning within a relationship by imitation and by doing.

The sort of Christian theology this manifesto is about requires in its authors a comparable all-round formation. In this chapter, I take for granted that the student theologian is a disciple of Jesus Christ, one who desires to follow him, learn from him, imitate him, and shape his or her life in conformity with him. The manifesto's most concentrated expression of what is involved in such theological discipleship is given in the "dramatic code" in chapter 3, which culminates with the "Here I am!" of accepting a vocation.

I am using "apprentice" rather than "disciple" for two reasons. First, I want to reserve Christian discipleship for the relationship with Jesus. It is, of course, possible to extend it to other relationships, but I prefer not to do so in the learning of theology. Discipleship tends to be exclusive – it does not easily extend to being a disciple of more than one teacher. If Jesus is the unique teacher for Christian theologians, it safeguards that role if others are not seen as having disciples. Ideally, the apprentice theologian learns from many teachers, both contemporary and from previous centuries, in person and through study. Second, for all the vital importance of teachers, it helps keep theology in perspective if pursuit of it is seen as like being apprenticed to a trade or craft. All Christians are disciples and learners; trained theologians are those disciples who have undergone a particular apprenticeship, gaining knowledge and skills that can be acquired in many ways – for example, through books, radio, television, or computers.

So what might that involve? Chapter 5 above focused on the sorts of belonging that can be involved, including being part of the church, and that is assumed in what follows. But it is also necessary to consider the individual person, the self of the theologian.[1] The reflections will focus on three particular selves. The first is Jesus, as both learner and teacher. The second is the author of the Fourth Gospel, John, as a model for any disciple-theologian. The third is the twenty-first century apprentice. The framework consists in the four elements of the quest for wise and creative theology, first introduced in chapter 1.

Retrieval – A Receptive, Reading Self

Jesus

Luke's Gospel opens with the author claiming to have read other accounts, based on receiving the testimonies of eyewitness, of "the events that have been fulfilled among us," and to have investigated them carefully before writing down his own account for his first reader, Theophilus. In Luke's first chapter, Zechariah receives the message of the birth to his wife Elizabeth of John the Baptist, who even before his birth is to receive the Holy Spirit. Then Mary receives the message of the birth of Jesus and the promise of the Holy Spirit coming upon her. Mary meets with Elizabeth, who is filled with the Holy Spirit and gives a loud cry of blessing, while Mary responds with the Magnificat (Luke 1:46–55). After the birth of John the Baptist, Zechariah is filled with the Holy Spirit and speaks a prophecy, the Benedictus (1:68–79). Both the Magnificat and Benedictus (and indeed the whole of Luke's Gospel) are shot through with the language of the Septuagint (the Greek translation of the Hebrew scriptures), showing a tradition steeped in Bible-reading.

In Luke's second chapter, Jesus is brought as a baby to the temple in Jerusalem where Simeon, on whom "the Holy Spirit was" (2:25), praises God over him, as does the aged prophet Anna. When Jesus is twelve, he goes to Jerusalem and is found in the temple "sitting among the teachers, listening to them and asking them questions" (2:46). The final verse of the chapter says that "Jesus increased in wisdom" (2:52). In the third chapter, John the Baptist opens his ministry by quoting the words of Isaiah. When Jesus is baptized, the Holy Spirit descends on him and there is a voice from heaven. In the next chapter, Jesus is led by the Holy Spirit into the wilderness and responds to each of the temptations he meets there with words of scripture. Then he begins to teach in Nazareth in the synagogue, reads from the book of Isaiah, and says: "Today this scripture has been fulfilled in your hearing" (Luke 4:21).

What has been happening? Jesus himself is described as receptive – a listener, a questioner, a learner of wisdom, and, above all, a receiver of the Holy Spirit – and also as a speaker and reader of scripture. Others too are receivers of the Holy Spirit and are immersed in the language of scripture. And Luke is offering all this to Theophilus – and us – to be read. Luke's chapter 24 gives a final intensity to the emphasis on reception and scripture. Jesus leads his disciples through "the law of Moses, the prophets and the Psalms" (24:44) and then concludes by promising the Holy Spirit, "power from on high" (24:49). The genesis of Christianity, here and throughout the New Testament and in the early church, is inseparable from receiving the Holy Spirit and paying attention to oral and written testimonies and teachings, all within a culture pervaded by the speaking and reading of scripture. Theology in line with this needs to be continually alert in the Spirit to the words of scripture, testimony, and teaching. The theologian who follows Jesus is someone who is receptive to God and to past and present teachers and witnesses, is filled with the Holy Spirit, is saturated in scripture, and is growing in wisdom. Creative theological retrieval of Jesus and the Gospel requires a receptive, reading self.

John

John's Gospel also shows Jesus as a receptive and reading self. The Holy Spirit comes and rests on him (John 1:32) and is given "without measure" (3:34), and this is above all exemplified in his relationship with his Father. Jesus is constantly referring to scripture, directly or indirectly, and engages his disciples, conversation partners, and opponents in questions of interpretation. John's Jesus opens up a theological vocation for disciples in distinctive ways. They are challenged to think further through surprising, ironic, or paradoxical statements, rich symbols and images, scriptural statements that are only understood retrospectively, dramatic scenes, dense discourses, apparently simple statements that invite endless meditation – above all, those beginning "I am …," and the extravagant promise that the Spirit would lead them into all the truth (16:13).

John's Jesus is, of course, the product of John the theologian, and scholars endlessly discuss how the two are related. A specially fascinating issue is how the fourth Gospel relates to the other three, both historically and theologically. Yet there are moments in the Gospel when the author takes direct responsibility for his theology. This is so above all in the Prologue, which has featured more than once in this manifesto as a prototype for Christian theology.[2] It shows John as a reader of scripture who interweaves texts and daringly interprets them. It portrays Christian existence as radically receptive: receiving witness (John 1:7), receiving Jesus ("To all who received him …" 1:12), and receiving abundance ("From his fullness we have all received, grace upon grace" 1:16). It sets an unsurpassable horizon of God and "all things," within which theological thinking might operate, while also giving a central reference point: the Word made flesh and living among us (1:14). And in that concept of the Word, already identified with God (whom "no one has ever seen" – 1:18), becoming visible flesh ("we have seen his glory" – 1:14), John does in his own name what his Jesus also does: he sets up a paradox that can generate puzzlement and debate century after century. It is hard to avoid being drawn deeper into theology if one takes this Prologue seriously.

Then there is John's ending – or, rather, endings (20:30–31; 21:24–5). Both refer to the writing of his book. The movement has been from the Word in the beginning with God to the words written by John that the reader is reading. There could be few more direct ways of placing receptivity and reading at the center of living. The purpose is to transform the reader: "But these are written that you may come to believe that Jesus is the Messiah, the Son of God, and that through believing you may have life in his name" (20:31). The second ending also identifies the author as the disciple who is referred to in his final story, and draws in the receivers of testimony in the contemporary community as guarantors of authenticity: "We know that his testimony is true" (21:24). But it also recognizes the impossibility of doing justice to the subject matter – if everything Jesus did were written down the world could not contain the books – and implicitly opens the way for the writing and reading of all those other theological books that have been written since by those who desire to be led by the Spirit into all the truth.

The apprentice

The apprentice Christian theologian today is faced with the resulting abundance of theology and related material. That comes in many meaning-laden forms, from archaeological sites to art, music, and architecture, but above all in texts. If you want to become good at retrieval you have to become a good student of texts. How might that best happen?

There are some basic requirements. You need if possible to learn some of the main languages in which the classic texts and the most influential commentaries and reflection on them are written, or at least to learn how to consult trustworthy translations and scholarship that will alert you to the questions at issue in the original languages. There is the wider world of scholarship, historical inquiry, and interpretation of texts that is mentioned in connection with the Bible in chapter 10 below. These fields are immense, but good teaching can help the apprentice to become sure-footed within them, able to consult relevant material while concentrating on the central question: what is the theological understanding to be gained from this text? You do have to be taught such things competently. To attempt to proceed in Christian theology without a grounding in the Bible and the two thousand years of Christian history and thought is foolish. It is possible to argue over how extensive the grounding should be, but it is hard to dispute that it is necessary for good theology.

There are also the requirements that the following sections on engagement, thought, and communication will discuss, embracing the apprentice's expression, intellectual life, and personal involvements with God, church, and world. Those have profound effects on receptivity and reading, just as the quality of retrieval in its turn shapes them. But here the focus is specifically on what some of the main "practices of self" might be for whoever wants to become a wiser reader. I would suggest three maxims.

- *Read and reread slowly*. Rich texts take time to read – indeed, the best are inexhaustible, and go on yielding fresh meaning century after century. Long hours and slow exploring and savoring are the reader's practical recognition of their abundance. The obvious practice of self is the dedication of prime time to study, year after year. Given the character of the most important texts for Christian theology, this is a way to wisdom that involves much soul-searching, patience, and delight.
- *Be apprenticed to wise readers*. Good readers are formed mainly through learning from other good readers, and hours spent with texts together are among the most fruitful in a theological education. Joint reading and interpretation of texts is at the heart of theological collegiality. It is a place of learning and testing for apprentices, as they slowly find that, drawing on the long hours of study, their contributions and judgments begin to carry more weight.
- *Reflect on yourself as a reader*. It is a commonplace of hermeneutics that the self of the interpreter is very important – each one brings presuppositions, prejudices, interests, disabilities, gifts, previous learning, and blind spots to reading a text. Reflexivity is essential to developing into a wiser reader, one who can unlearn as well as learn, and who is open to radical challenge, suspicion, doubt, and change for the better. For the Christian, this will involve self-examination before God, resulting in confession and

> repentance. Of the classic sins, perhaps those most common among theological readers are pride (how hard it is to give up a favorite interpretation!), anger (theological polemics are rightly notorious), envy or jealousy (competitive readings abound, and "success" invites resentment and detraction), and sloth (how easy to avoid making those long detours of study and research required for a really reliable judgment!), but the most devastating temptations are to do with subtle falsehood and dangerous foolishness, many of which combine more than one deadly sin. The other side of such self-critical reflexivity is cultivation of the desire and capacity for holiness in intention and generosity in interpretation.

Such studious, collegial, and reflexive reading is fundamental in the making of a theologian who is a disciple of Jesus and a companion of John.

Engagement – A Loved and Loving Self

Jesus: prayer, community, and service in love

"You are my Son, the Beloved; with you I am well pleased" (Luke 3:22). At Jesus' baptism, after receiving the Holy Spirit while praying, and before plunging into the intensive engagement of his ministry, he is unconditionally affirmed by God as loved. Jesus practiced prayer, alone and with others, and he taught prayer. At the heart of prayer is entering more fully into the love of God and following what Jesus called "the greatest and first commandment" – to "love the Lord your God with all your heart, and with all your soul, and with all your mind" (Matthew 22:17–18).

Inseparable from Jesus' ministry were his twelve disciples or "learners," chosen after a night of prayer. His engagement was with and through them. He is radically social, sharing his life with others, and being for them. Who he is and his significance are especially revealed to those with whom he is closest: love and understanding go together. A pivotal event in each of the Synoptic

Gospels is the Transfiguration. As Luke tells it, he took his closest disciples, Peter, James, and John, up a mountain to pray, and while praying was transfigured, his face and clothes shining. Then Moses and Elijah (representing the law and the prophets, and the wider, long-term community) appear, talking with him about his forthcoming "exodus" in Jerusalem. The story ends with a cloud overshadowing them and a voice saying: "This is my Son, my Chosen [some manuscripts: my Beloved]; listen to him" (Luke 9:35). Here he intensively engages not only with God but also with key figures of his tradition and with his closest followers, all looking ahead to the public engagement in Jerusalem that culminated his life.

At the Last Supper, the night before his death, he gathered his disciples for Passover, rehearsing the Exodus from Egypt. He prepared them for his death, initiating what has become the central celebration for most of the world's Christians. Luke includes in the story a dispute among the disciples about who is greatest. Jesus' response at this climactic moment gives an insight into his self-understanding:

> "The kings of the Gentiles lord it over them; and those in authority over them are called benefactors. But not so with you: rather, the greatest among you must become like the youngest, and the leader like one who serves. For who is greater, the one who is at the table or the one who serves? Is it not the one at table? But I am among you as one who serves." (Luke 22:25–7)

The loved and loving self of Jesus was utterly involved with God, his disciples, and slave-like service.

John: foot-washing, friendship, and prayer

John does not, unlike the Synoptic Gospels, give an account of Jesus sharing bread and wine, as symbols of his body and blood, on the night before his death. Instead, he intensifies Luke's theme of service with the story of Jesus washing his disciples' feet, and connects it with Jesus as teacher. John is a theologian whose feet have been washed by Jesus, his teacher. Jesus interprets this:

> "Do you know what I have done to you? You call me Teacher and Lord – and you are right, for that is what I am. So if I, your Lord and Teacher, have washed your feet, you also ought to wash one another's feet. For I have set you an example, that you also should do as I have done to you. Very truly, I tell you, servants are not greater than their master, nor are messengers greater than the one who sent them. If you know these things, you are blessed if you do them." (John 13:12–17)

This begins the Farewell Discourses in chapters 13–17, one of the most distinctive elements in John's Gospel, where the significance of what the disciples are taking part in becomes clear: it embraces the intention that "the world may know that I love the Father" (14:31), being led into "all the truth" (16:12), and "I have sent them into the world" (17:18). That is the scope of service in love.

John, in the Farewell Discourses, also intensifies the bond of discipleship. Jesus and the disciples mutually indwell each other in love and joy, as summed up in the organic image of the vine:

> "I am the vine, you are the branches. Those who abide in me and I in them bear much fruit, because apart from me you can do nothing ... As the Father has loved me, so I have loved you; abide in my love. If you keep my commandments, you will abide in my love, just as I have kept my Father's commandments and abide in his love. I have said these things to you so that my joy may be in you, and that your joy may be complete." (John 15:5–11)

This is immediately followed by another distinctive Johannine image: discipleship as friendship. "I do not call you servants any longer ... but I have called you friends" (15:15). Loving and being loved are the dynamic core of both friendship and the vine. The author's distinctive self-description at significant moments in the Gospel as "the one whom Jesus loved" (13:23; 20:2; 21:7; etc.), the beloved disciple, is uniquely individual; but, given the nature of friendship, and of this friend, it is also the calling of all disciples. Perhaps the most moving moment is John's account (exclusive to his Gospel) of the creation of a new family at the foot of the cross:

> When Jesus saw his mother and the disciple whom he loved standing beside her, he said to his mother, "Woman, here is your son." Then he said to the disciple, "Here is your mother." And from that hour the disciple took her into his own home. (John 19:26–7)

The Discourses culminate with Jesus praying at greater length than anywhere else in the Gospels. The prayer (see also below on thinking) brings many of the richest Johannine themes intensively together: the hour, glory, Father and Son, authority, eternal life, the divine name and word, truth, the world, scripture, joy, the evil one, holiness, believing, mutual indwelling, unity, knowing, and love. It also takes up many of the themes in the Lord's Prayer of the Synoptic Gospels.[3] John is showing Jesus performing what he taught and, as often, is complementing the other Gospels with a further theological dimension, above all, that of love:

> "I made your name known to them, and I will make it known, so that the love with which you have loved me may be in them, and I in them." (17:26)

In John's Gospel engagement with the God of love, the community of love, and loving service are most obviously and intensely central to the life of discipleship.

The apprentice: prayer, collegial friendship, and service

How might the apprentice theologian today, learning from Jesus, John, and others, grow into fruitful engagement with God, church, and world?

The relationship with God in love and prayer is utterly and unconditionally vital. The basic simplicity for a theologian or any other Christian is trust in being loved by God. As the meaning of Jesus' baptism is summed up in his Father's affirmation of him as beloved, so too is the Christian's baptism. Each tradition within Christianity has its own ways of learning to pray, and there are often many paths within one tradition. Engagement with the actuality and implications of being loved by God is the main purpose of prayer. John's Gospel may be read as a guide to living, dwelling, abiding (*menein*) in this reality.

A theologian does not know any shortcuts to living in intimacy with God – indeed, often needs to go on detours. Granted the innumerable faithful paths to mature prayer that are possible, here are just three guidelines that an apprentice might find worth following whichever path he or she is on.

- The essential starting point is the prayer: Come, Holy Spirit! The discussion of this prayer in chapter 3, above, called it "a basic, comprehensive Christian prayer." It is so for the apprentice theologian too. The single most important reality for the theologian, as for other Christians, is the love and generosity of God in pouring out the Holy Spirit in abundance, and the astonishing promise that if we ask we will receive. "If you then, who are evil, know how to give good gifts to your children, how much more will the heavenly Father give the Holy Spirit to those who ask him!" (Luke 11:13). We also have to be aware of what we are asking: this is the Spirit that draws us irrevocably into the drama of God's loving purposes for the world, the Spirit that led Jesus the way of the cross.
- The classic forms of prayer and praise are immense theological treasuries, distilling centuries of engagement with God. There are first of all the psalms and prayers of the Bible; then the liturgies, hymns, and written prayers of all the traditions, together with oral forms handed on across generations; and a library of devotional books. To take just one example from my own Anglican and some other traditions: the short prayers called "collects," a different one for each Sunday of the year, with others for feasts and special occasions, are dense with theological wisdom. To pray these meditatively and with theological alertness for a year would lead you through the major events and people of the Bible, together with the main Christian doctrines and practices, integrating mind, heart, and will, all taken up into relationship with the Trinitarian God of love.

- Then there is *parrhesia*. Part of its definition is: "in relation to God, *confidence, boldness, joyful sense of freedom*." "We have access to God in boldness and confidence through faith in him [Jesus Christ]" (Eph 3:12). "And this is the boldness we have in him, that if we ask anything according to his will, he hears us" (1 John 5:14). *Parrhesia* is also used in the Septuagint of Wisdom crying out openly in the street and the squares (Proverbs 1:20), and in the New Testament it describes the free, overflowing speech in public that shares the Gospel (e.g., Acts 28:31). It combines the free intimacy within a family or in friendship with freespokenness in public, including situations of danger. In prayer, it is about trust in the God "to whom all hearts are open, all desires known, and from whom no secrets are hidden," willingness to let the conversation of prayer go in new directions, improvisation on classic forms, and entering into the inexhaustibility of the mystery of God and of what God can inspire in prayer – including silence and speaking in tongues. New theology is an overflow of *parrhesia*, connecting its intimacy with God to its free communication.

As regards apprenticeship in community, studying theology often raises problems about the church. I am assuming that being Christian means being a church member (it is possible to argue otherwise, though not if you take the New Testament as a guide), but that leaves many further matters for discernment. Which church should you be in? Is it right to continue where you are? What is the appropriate role for you as a theologian? Should you, if it is possible, be ordained? What do you do and say about problems with your church's theology, practice, or leadership? There can, obviously, be no general answer to such questions. They go to the heart of your vocation as a Christian theologian, and need to be wrestled with in prayer and in conversation with wise counselors. Granted, as with prayer, the innumerable faithful paths possible for a theologian within the church, here are three guidelines that an apprentice might find worth following whichever path he or she is on.

- Understanding the actual church, as well as theology about it, is vital for Christian wisdom. This is partly about retrieving with discernment the centuries of history of the church in different periods, places, and traditions. It is also about the church today around the world at all levels. You can only ever appreciate a little of the diverse community of two billion or so people of which you are a member, but continually expanding and deepening appreciation of it is vital for Christian living as well as thinking. The ecology of levels is especially important – the church is local, regional, national, and international. Today, the pervasiveness of rapid communication and travel brings all these levels into new dynamic interplay. It is possible for the prayer practices of the Urapmin, a tribe of less than 400 people in Papua New Guinea, to affect my prayer and theology.[4]
- An apprentice Christian theologian is a learner and potential teacher in the church as a school of wisdom and love, so the quality of that schooling is of special concern. It involves becoming fluent in a Christian "language" – the idiom developed over many years by a particular tradition; becoming practiced in the wider Christian "culture" of which that language is part – habits of action, relating, instinctive responses, and so on; and becoming to some extent multilingual, able to be an understanding host and guest in relation to other Christian traditions. You need to seek out best practice among the various modes of schooling, above all finding the wisest teachers in person, in writing, or in other media. The goal is to be so fluent as to be able to improvise well.
- You should especially value and seek out collegial friends. These are friends who share something of your theological vocation or analogous vocations in other disciplines. It is worth setting a very high priority on long-term, intensive conversation with a few fellow-theologians whom you trust and love as friends, one to one and in small groups. A great deal of the creativity and wisdom in any discipline or sphere of life can be traced to collegial friendships. The capacity for creativity multiplies when such friendships in different spheres interrelate. The triple

> dynamic (as seen in inter-faith relations, in chapter 7 of this volume) is enriched, enabling movement deeper into Christian theology, deeper into the thought of others, and deeper into engagement with the common good. Collegial friendship is where loved and loving selves are formed together in wisdom. It is the deep secret of theological engagement across churches, religions, disciplines, and spheres of life.

What of apprenticeship in service? This is the daily matter of attending to the needs of near and distant neighbors. "I am among you as one who serves" and "Whoever wants to be first must be last of all and servant of all" (Mark 9:35) are the watchwords of everyday life in the spirit of Jesus and John. A job in church or society is often the main sphere of practical service for theologians who are not full-time students or teachers, but the main thing is habitual attention to others through prayer and action. Apprenticeship is doing this under the guidance and inspiration of those whose greatness lies in the quality of their service. These are "the saints" in the broadest sense, found in all traditions and spheres of life. Blessed is the apprentice who finds such saints!

Thinking – An Imaginative, Discerning Self

Jesus

The receptive, reading self of Jesus, evoked above through the Gospel of Luke, was steeped in scripture and grew in wisdom. Filled with the Spirit, he announced the coming of the Kingdom of God, the sphere where God's will is done, and focused his energies on realizing it. The quality of his mind is seen as he fulfills his vocation. It emerges in the debates with his opponents, his responses to trick questions, how he teaches and deals with his disciples, how he interprets scripture and responds to encounters and events. On the one hand, his thinking imaginatively envisions the Kingdom of God, above all in vivid parables. On the other hand, he is constantly discerning how best to speak and act – responding to temptations, choosing disciples, interacting with a wide range of people, challenging leaders, taking initiatives in preaching, healing, and symbolic acts, and making judgments about what his vocation requires.

This is above all a mind drawn toward God and God's Kingdom. He is led to the Garden of Gethsemane and to crucifixion. His "crucified mind" (Kitamori) is a mind in the service of the God of love within the drama of history. It imagines and discerns the way of God's love and follows it. The most radical challenge to the disciple's imagination is the cross and resurrection, as vividly seen in Peter's response to the attempt by Jesus to teach him to face it:

> Then he began to teach them that the Son of Man must undergo great suffering, and be rejected by the elders, the chief priests, and the scribes, and be killed, and after three days rise again. He said all this quite openly. And Peter took him aside and began to rebuke him. But turning and looking at his disciples, he rebuked Peter and said, "Get behind me, Satan! For you are setting your mind not on divine things but on human things."
>
> He called the crowd with his disciples, and said to them, "If any want to become my followers, let them deny themselves and take up their cross and follow me. For those who want to save their life will lose it, and those who lose their life for my sake, and for the sake of the gospel, will save it. For what will it profit them to gain the whole world and forfeit their life?" (Mark 8:31ff.)

The most radical challenge to the disciple's discernment is in the denial of self and in following the way of the cross. This is about "Christ the power of God and the wisdom of God. God's foolishness is wiser than human wisdom, and God's weakness is stronger than human strength" (1 Cors. 1:24–5). Paul also says: "Therefore we have been buried with him by baptism into death, so that, just as Christ was raised from the dead by the glory of the Father, so we too might walk in newness of life" (Roms. 6:4). To think "in Christ," to "have the mind of Christ" (1 Cors. 2:16b), is to be taught by the teaching and example of Jesus in his parables, interpretation of scripture, debates, and actions; but above all it is to be conformed to his incarnation, death, and resurrection. This shapes a transformed mind in the Spirit, as explored above in chapter 6 on Bonhoeffer's ethics of affirmation, judgment, and transformation. Bonhoeffer is a model of integrating theology and life, according to this pattern, through a lifetime of seeking to discern thoughtfully in complex situations how to follow Jesus.

John

The Gospel of John can be seen as a pedagogy, leading readers into the fathomless meaning of the incarnation, death, and resurrection of Jesus – as is suggested by the title of Jean Vanier's extraordinary commentary: *Drawn into the Mystery of Jesus through the Gospel of John.*[5] John imaginatively uses one story and symbol after another to open readers up to the paradox of the crucifixion as the glorification of Jesus, before telling his carefully crafted climactic narrative of the passion, death, and resurrection. In between the "signs" and the culminating story of death and resurrection comes the mind-stretching teaching of the Farewell Discourses (chapters 13–17). John's strongly dramatic imagination has already been commented upon in previous chapters; its theological power is enhanced by the daring and scope of his thinking. His Prologue has been a recurring theme in this manifesto.

The distinctively theological character of John's mind is exemplified by his account of the prayer of Jesus in John, chapter 17, before he goes to his arrest and death. There, one core theological idea after another is drawn upon (cf. above on prayer). It is a *tour de force* of theological concentration. The mind that tries to fathom John's meaning in a passage such as this finds itself drawn beyond its previous boundaries, sounding the depths of single terms and terms in various combinations (just consider the meaning of "one" and "in" in the following: "that they may be one, as we are one" – v.11, cf. 22; "As you, Father, are in me and I am in you, may they also be in us" – v.21; "I in them and you in me, that they may become completely one" – v.23; "so that the love with which you have loved me may be in them, and I in them" – v.26). Thinking is invited into the reality of what is thought about. In order to take up the invitation, it is drawn simultaneously to imagine, meditate, and pray in order to have any hope of following where John leads. The goal is discernment of something of the life and love of God.

The apprentice

The apprentice who reads and rereads, worships, converses, and serves others is, of course, already thinking while doing all that. Those practices are themselves conceptually formed and contribute to shaping the apprentice's thinking. Indeed, thinking is better developed through such nourishing practices than by thinking about thinking. Guidelines for developing this primary theological thinking (taking for granted the elements mentioned above – receptivity and reading, prayer, collegial friendship, and service) include the following.

- Nurture your theological imagination, above all through the poetry, symbols, and imagery of scripture, but also through the riches of Christian and other traditions, and through literature and the arts, including music and architecture.
- Practice the disciplines of thought, such as description, logic, conceptualization and categorization, assessment of evidence, appropriate forms of argument, the formation of judgments, meditation and contemplation.
- Above all, value wise discernment that unites vision, judgment, and love, and seek out those who have it.

A further point needs adding to this list, namely, a capacity for reflexivity and self-criticism. As soon as one enters into topics where there are differences and disputes, one needs to reflect on one's own thinking in relation to others and be prepared to be reflexive and self-critical. The interpretation of the Gospel of John is a good example. Why is it that Bultmann's interpretation is more convincing than Raymond Brown's, or vice versa? Why does Bach's

St John Passion move me more or less than that of James MacMillan? The answers might say much about what my teachers taught me, about having been formed as a Protestant or a Catholic, and about all sorts of other personal, cultural, academic, and spiritual influences. But if I am not simply to reflect passively all those influences, then I need to be able to exercise self-reflexive discernment.

The same capacity needs to be exercised communally by whole traditions as they reflect on their Christian identity, and it is vital for theologians to be contributors to this. Prophets, saints, sages, and reformers have constantly done this. But there is a task that only theologians can do, the sort of criticism that can show conceptually how a widely accepted theological method, position, doctrine, or tradition might be inadequate, and then propose how it might be repaired. It is the achievement of Origen, Augustine, Aquinas, Luther, Calvin, and Barth. Most recently, it is seen in David Kelsey's *Eccentric Existence* which comprehensively critiques traditional doctrines of creation and offers an alternative. Twenty-first century apprentices need to internalize such models of critical and constructive thinking in preparation for analogous theological tasks facing those who seek to be wise and creative in their current theological engagements with God, church, and world.

In academic theology the classic culmination of apprenticeship is still modeled on the medieval craft guilds: you have to produce your "master-work" and submit it for examination, including a face-to-face *viva voce* with those senior in the guild. The work is usually a dissertation or thesis, prepared for over years through smaller essays, examinations, and research projects. It is no accident that this pattern of a training completed by a major piece of your own work has endured so long, since it makes very good sense. It tests your capacity, in writing and discussion, to perform disciplines of thought and expression, to think for yourself, to be self-critical, and to take full responsibility for what you say. It usually involves a good deal of what I have been calling retrieval, as the basis without which fresh theological thinking does not ring true. It is a test of wisdom in a limited sense – few people produce a good thesis without learning more about themselves and their limitations, or being able to make sound judgments in their specialty. Examiners are not directly assessing your wisdom, yet completing a dissertation that passes rigorous scrutiny can mark the achievement of a certain maturity in disciplined, original, and responsible thinking. This is an essential foundation for seeking theological wisdom in the years to come. The attitude that, appropriately, often accompanies this achievement is one of modest confidence: you can do something, but you are aware how very much more there is to learn.

Communication – A Witnessing, Poetic Self

Jesus

Jesus had years of quiet preparation for his public ministry, to which only the Gospel of Luke refers (Luke 1–2). Luke and the other Gospels set his entry onto the public scene in the context of a long tradition of witness to God and God's purposes, above all by the prophet Isaiah, and the witness of John the Baptist immediately prepares the way for Jesus (Matthew 3; Mark 1; Luke 3; John 1). Witness is perhaps the most distinctive form of biblical communication. It takes many forms – the stories of patriarchs, kings, judges, prophets, Jesus, and others; testimony to God and God's ways with the world in psalms, prophecies, law, wisdom, and apocalyptic; letters, prayers, and cries. In terms of earlier chapters, witness might be seen as a specially dramatic form of speech and action, a public communication that is itself an event in the ongoing drama.

Jesus as a witness is first of all concerned with the Kingdom of God: "Now after John was arrested, Jesus came to Galilee, proclaiming the good news of God, and saying, 'The time is fulfilled, and the kingdom of God has come near; repent, and believe in the good news'" (Mark 1:14). The accounts are full of the impact he made: amazement at his teaching with authority (Mark 1:27; Luke 4:31; etc.), praised by everyone for his teaching (Luke 4:15). The people in his home town wondered how he could have learned to be such a gifted speaker: "All spoke well of him [literally, 'witnessed to him,' *emarturoun*] and were amazed at the gracious words that came from his mouth. They said, 'Is not this Joseph's son?'" (Luke 4:22). Those "words of grace" come through the Gospels in many forms, from riddling responses and vivid epigrams to extended teachings and brilliantly told parables. They are poetic (at least in the Greek of the New Testament – there is interesting scholarly discussion about the form of the original Aramaic) not in the sense of being in the genre of poetry (like the psalms or much wisdom and prophetic literature), but in their crafting of language, use of imagery, and pointed rhetoric. Jesus models poetics in the service of witness.

But witness suggests pointing beyond oneself. Jesus does, of course, point to God and the Kingdom of God, but his own person becomes identified with this message. He is so bound up with his witness that the fate of his mission converges with the fate of his person. The effect of the climactic events of the drama, Jesus' passion, death, and resurrection, is to seal this identification, and Jesus the witness becomes the content of his disciples' witnessing; the proclaimer becomes the proclaimed. The effect of this is to make witnessing essential to Christian life, with poetics of many sorts as welcome aids; but at the same time both the verbal witnessing and its poetic quality are relativized by the priority of following the way of the cross, testifying to Jesus Christ in costly and, if necessary, suffering love.

John

Witnessing (*marturia*) is explicitly highlighted right from the start of the Gospel of John: "There was a man sent from God whose name was John. He came as a witness to testify to the light, so that all might believe through him" (John 1:6–7). The Gospel is triply one of witness.

First, it makes a special point of telling of many testimonies to Jesus, beginning with John and moving through the first disciples (in the first chapter Jesus is called Rabbi, Messiah, Son of God, King of Israel, and Son of Man), the woman at the well (John 4 – Jesus as prophet, Messiah, Savior of the world), and so on until the climactic testimony of Thomas face to face with the risen Jesus: "My Lord and my God!" (John 20:28).

Second, Jesus' testimony to himself is more explicit in John, above all in his "I am" sayings, echoing the divine name (6:35; 8:12; 10:7; 10:11; 15:1). The identification of person and message is intensified and made more fully explicit in this Gospel.

Third, the author of the fourth Gospel adds his own voice to the testimonies he describes, both by setting up the framework of the Prologue and by "signing" his work at the end: "This is the disciple who is testifying [*marturōn*] to these things and has written them, and we know that his testimony is true" (John 21:24).

John's sense of his vocation as a witness inspired by the Spirit (he is one who receives, along with the Holy Spirit, the commission, "As the Father has sent me, so I send you" – John 20:21) is matched by the care he gives to his writing. It is richly imaginative, subtly resonant with other scriptures (including the Synoptic Gospels), multi-leveled, and above all, as chapter 2 of this volume has shown, dramatic.

So John exemplifies the witnessing and poetic self of a Christian theologian.

The apprentice

So, the apprentice Christian theologian is one who, "in the Spirit," seeks for God's sake to read, pray, love, converse, serve, imagine, think, and have the mind of Christ; and also, like Jesus and John, seeks to be a witness who communicates with poetic care and creativity. Granted all that, what might some helpful guidelines be for developing the quality of that communication?

- Your communication is first of all centered in God: from God, to God, before God, and for God's sake. The constant inhabiting and renewal of a God-centered communicative ecology across the centuries and continents is the basic wisdom of theological communication, requiring daily practices of prayer, study, conversation, and new learning.

- Let your theology serve teaching and preaching. This, of course, means being alert to the possibilities of many media, but the most important Christian communication day by day still happens face to face. It is guided by a passion to communicate in love and truth, which should energize painstaking apprenticeship in the arts of teaching and preaching (or, for those theologians who do not preach, the resourcing of preaching), and accountability before those who have mastered these arts. It means crossing many boundaries of world-views, languages, cultures, personalities, and prejudices, and in all of this the art of listening comes first.
- Risk it! To be a witness is to be vulnerable. It is unlikely that the twenty-first century will in this regard be any less dangerous than the first.

10

The Bible
Creative Source of Theology

The single most important spring for the thinking in this manifesto has been the Bible. It has entered into each chapter, directly and indirectly, so it is an appropriate focus through which to offer a concluding review of the whole vision that has been offered. There has, of course, been much besides biblical interpretation in the manifesto, but the best way to grasp its main thrust is to understand how the Bible has been used throughout the book. And, finally, the Bible can also suggest grounds for hope in the future of theology.

How the Bible Has Shaped This Manifesto

The biblical manifesto within this theological manifesto was given at the start of chapter 1: the cry of Wisdom to desire her more than anything else. The cries of the Bible in desire, joy, affirmation, judgment, anguish, bewilderment, invitation, questioning, trust, and adoration have echoed through the chapters, and discernment of their meanings and how to respond to them has been the central concern. Such discernment is at the heart of theological wisdom, and its greatest tests come in engagement with the cries of our time.

The code of cries in chapter 3 has been their most concentrated expression, combining cries with another of this manifesto's key categories, drama. Chapter 2 argued for the primacy of the dramatic, complemented by the epic and the lyric, in doing justice to the Bible and to life. In biblical and theological engagement with the ongoing drama, a double wisdom was found: on the one hand, a wisdom of intensity and reserve; on the other hand, a complementary wisdom of extensity and ramification. Both the figural interpretation of scripture and the development of doctrines exemplify this wisdom, which in its second form reaches out to relate to the whole of reality as created through God's Word. So the Bible urges theological exploration beyond the Bible, and later chapters seek to show the generativity of the dramatic code in many engagements: with the formation of a public sphere that can cope with a plurality of religious and secular forces; with Charles Taylor's account of Western modernity; with the complex forms of belonging to church, academy, and a range of other relationships that are part of theological existence; with contemporary society; with other faiths; and with the university and its many disciplines.

The widest range of biblical reference is in chapter 4, "Desire Above All," whose attempt to work out a balanced dynamic of theological "moods" covers indicative testimonies and promises, imperative law and teaching, interrogative prophecy and lament, subjunctive wisdom and parable, and optative praise and apocalyptic. The most extended example is in chapter 6, "Church and Society," through Bonhoeffer's approach to a Christian social ethic with reference to Jesus Christ as incarnate, crucified, and resurrected. Perhaps the most innovative use of scripture is outlined in chapter 7's account of inter-faith relations between Jews, Muslims, and Christians. An institutional setting where, in the twenty-first century, there might be a flourishing, not only of such inter-faith engagement, but also of specifically Jewish, Muslim, Christian, and other thinking within, between, and about the religions, is suggested in chapter 8's proposal of "New Theology and Religious Studies."

Finally, chapter 9 is a biblical approach, through Jesus and the author of the fourth Gospel, to the formation of apprentice theologians. Each of the desirable elements in the shaping of a theologian is important in the theological interpretation of scripture: receptivity (first of all to the Holy Spirit), reading wisely and self-critically, prayer, collegial friendship, involvement in service, a well-nourished imagination, disciplined thinking, mature discernment, care and creativity in communication, and risky witnessing.

What Sort of Bible Reading is This?

Previous chapters, therefore, have been steeped in biblical interpretation; but there has been little reflection on how this approach to the Bible might be characterized overall. It is worth trying to articulate this now as a suggested guideline for future theology.

First, it reads the Bible as the canonical Christian scripture. There are many ways of reading the Bible, and all of them can be relevant to Christian theological interpretation of it. These include reading it as a work of literature; as a source for history, or itself as a historical text with its contexts and history of reception; and as a text of interest to linguists, sociologists, ethnographers, political scientists, economists, psychologists, gender students, comparative religionists, and phenomenologists of religion. To read it as a Christian is by definition also to read it as a collection of texts that testifies authoritatively to God and God's ways with the world.[1]

Second, the "also" in the previous sentence means that there is no necessary conflict or tension between theological interpretation and good scholarship. Attention must be paid to those who can best help us read the Bible as an ancient text in context. While most scholarship has to be fairly routine, it is essential if reading is to be as true as possible. The obvious first tasks are deciding on the text (there are many variations among ancient manuscripts, and thousands of decisions to be made about what the most reliable text is) and then translating it. Many words in Hebrew or Greek simply do not correlate with those in English or other modern languages, and there are numerous other difficulties in translation. Translation is also interpretation, as the simple exercise of reading several Bible translations side by side will demonstrate. Reading the Bible is greatly helped by knowing the original languages, and it is an impoverishment if a Christian community does not have some members with this capacity. Reading texts is also affected by understanding their contexts, so theological reading must embrace whatever can be learnt of the centuries about which the Bible writes. Scholarship is essential to the future of Christian theology, though in theological discourse it is often hidden – as, for example, the scholarly literature on the Prologue of John is taken for granted but not referred to in the various theological interpretations of it offered in previous chapters.

Third, that "also" means too that there is no necessary conflict or tension between theological interpretation and hermeneutics. If scholarship mostly examines the text and its archaeology, looking backwards to its authors, contexts, genres, and what it meant to its original readers, hermeneutics (the art and theory of interpretation) looks forward from the text at how it has been received since it was written and how it might best be read now. The Bible has continually generated fresh interpretations, and they have multiplied more than ever in modernity. From historicism, postcolonialism, and feminism to existentialism, structuralism, and psychoanalysis, one approach after another has offered its readings. So too has a range of academic disciplines, each scholarly "school" and each Christian tradition. Add to this the interpretations that every reader and every study group generates, and the ways iconographers, hymn and song writers, musicians, poets, dramatists, novelists, film-makers, painters, sculptors, and others draw on the Bible. If theology is not to lose its way in this forest of meanings it has to try to understand them and make wise hermeneutical judgments. Hermeneutics too is essential to the future of Christian theology, though, as with scholarship, it is often hidden, and is most effective in the background of theological discourse.

Fourth, there is the core activity: thinking through the theological wisdom of scripture. This is, of course, inseparable from and interwoven with the first three. Central to it is constant rereading of the Bible with a concern for God and God's purposes. It is possible to discern some of the guidelines that those who have done this have found most fruitful over the centuries.[2] My suggested maxims for Christian theological reading, all within the encompassing principle of *reading for the sake of God and God's purposes*, would include the following (each might take a chapter to introduce adequately):

- Listen to the Bible as the loving God's cry to humanity.
- Figure yourself and your period into the Bible as playing a role in this "theodrama," the ongoing dramatic narrative of God's involvement with the world.
- Read the Old Testament with the New Testament for their mutual theological illumination.
- Give priority to the plain sense of scripture, in all its literal and metaphorical richness, and be open also to other senses.
- Learn from the many witnesses to Jesus Christ within and beyond the Bible.
- Learn as part of the church, the Bible's primary community of interpretation.
- Learn especially from wise readers of scripture, past and present, and from saints, those who interpret scripture through how they live their lives.
- Learn through study with others, within and beyond the church.
- Read in the Spirit, desiring God and God's future.

There is a second encompassing principle, which is another way of stating the first: *read in love for God and all God's creatures*. Augustine saw the twofold command to love God and our neighbor as the unsurpassable rule for reading scripture, the rule of love – *regula caritatis*.[3] Anything that goes against love of God and love of neighbor is, for Christian theology, unsound biblical interpretation.

The Four Elements of Wise and Creative Theology in the Bible

Such maxims can fulfill many functions, but the main one intended here is one that provides pointers to the classic ingredients in wise theological interpretation of scripture for those who want to practice it. Creative Christian theology will be enhanced the better one learns to follow such guidelines. In this regard, it is no accident that the Bible itself exemplifies the elements of wise and creative theology discussed in chapter 1 and recurring through later chapters.

Retrieving the past

The Bible is full of retrieval of the past. Remembering is one of its main concerns. It writes down things that have been passed on orally for many years. It has many stories and histories. It prescribes practices of memorizing and reciting. Those who edited its books often shaped them from diverse sources they had inherited, and made far-reaching judgments as to what should be included. Its prophets and other authors often quote and interpret scriptural material. Indeed, this "intertextuality" of the Bible, with one text taking up another, is one of the main ways in which it does its theological thinking. Christian theology, especially, pivots around the interplay between the Old and New Testaments. In short, retrieval of the past pervades the Bible. As it does this, it introduces an array of ways to grasp and express the past. Its main genres – narrative, law, prophecy, psalms, and wisdom – all have some element of remembering, and their authority is inseparable from their past orientation. The prophets, who are the most present- and future-oriented, are passionately concerned about Israel's faithfulness to its covenant with God, reaching back to the Exodus and to creation.

Perhaps the most pervasively influential way in which the Bible retrieves past events is through festivals and worship. Most of the festivals of Israel commemorated historical events, above all the Exodus at Passover, still celebrated by Jews; and the New Testament in turn took this as a type of Jesus' Last Supper, still celebrated by most Christians as the Lord's Supper, Eucharist, Holy Communion, or Mass. In worship, it is the Psalms that have especially taken up past events and people into the poetry of praise and thanks to God, and they still today are key elements in much Jewish and Christian liturgy. Such ongoing performance transcends "retrieval" by taking it up into current "engagement."

Engaging with God, community, world

Within scripture, there are numerous records of engagements in the present that are resourced by the past. The Bible is clear that new situations cannot simply be responded to by repeating the past, but require fresh discernment. The Bible is deeply concerned with faithfulness, but this is not seen as identical repetition of past understanding and behavior. The book of Job teaches this lesson (among many others). In the face of Job's suffering, his friends repeat their tradition's maxims about God punishing the wicked and rewarding the good, leading to the conclusion that Job must be suffering because he has done wrong in God's eyes. Job resists this interpretation and wrestles in anguish with the meaning of his suffering, all the time crying out to God. It is he, rather than the friends with their packaged answers, who searches out the depths of what is happening (see chapter 1 of this volume)[4] and is vindicated by God at the end of the story. Job has engaged wholeheartedly and simultaneously with both God and the disturbing, unprecedented reality of his situation; his theological wisdom, to which he comes so painfully, expands and transforms the tradition rather than just repeating it.

The prophetic books give perhaps the most vivid and profound insights into an engagement resourced by the tradition and grappling with new developments. This is true supremely of the book of Isaiah. It was written (probably by at least three authors, linked through a "school" or tradition of prophecy, beginning with First Isaiah) before, during, and after the destruction of the Jerusalem Temple in 586 BCE and the exile of many of her people to Babylon for seventy years. This was the event that, after the Exodus, was probably the most traumatic and transformative of all that happened to Israel during the period in which its scriptures were conceived. We can follow First Isaiah (Isaiah 1–39), his vocation as a prophet beginning with a dramatic vision of God (Isaiah 6), his prophecies against foreign nations, and his judgment against Israel because the rich exploit the poor and there is corruption among priests, prophets, political, and military leaders. On the eve of the exile he foretells disaster but yet sustains hope in God. Then, during the exile, Second Isaiah (Isaiah 40–55) sounds the depths of suffering but also retrieves in a new way the theology of God as both creator and redeemer, offering radical comfort and hope. After the return from exile, around 538 BCE, Third Isaiah (Isaiah 56–66) offers both judgment and hope in the context of national restoration. The overall result is one of the most influential theological texts in Judaism and also in Christianity – Isaiah was so important for the early church that it was called "the fifth Gospel."[5] The exile and return catalyzed a massive effort of renewal through retrieval and reinterpretation, including writing, gathering together, and editing many biblical writings. In conjunction with the prophecies of Isaiah, Jeremiah, and Ezekiel, this makes the period surrounding the exile the most formative in the Old Testament for both retrieval and engagement, and a resource for future centuries in times of change and trauma.

The New Testament testifies above all to engagement with Jesus Christ – through the Gospel accounts of his teaching, action, suffering, death, and resurrection, and through the young church's living and preaching in his name. Jesus is a new, intensive focus for engagement with God and the world together, generating a community that, in his Spirit, continues and improvises upon his engagement.

Luke's account of the Transfiguration sums up the key dynamics (Luke 9:28–36). There is the primary relationship with God – Jesus is praying, and the voice of God affirms him. There is retrieval of the scriptures in the persons of Moses and Elijah, united with the climactic engagement of his life – his forthcoming death that they are talking about under the type of the "departure [literally, 'exodus'] which he was about to accomplish in Jerusalem" (v.31). The church involvement and witness is represented by the participation of his three closest disciples, who are given the fundamental message: "This is my Son, my chosen, listen to him!" (v.35). And the intensity of focus on Jesus himself is shown in his transfiguration: "And while he was praying, the appearance of his face changed, and his clothes became dazzling white" (v.29). This is in line with the Gospel of John's fundamental summary statement: "The Word became flesh and lived among us, and we have seen his glory, the glory as of a father's only son, full of grace and truth" (John 1:14). Incarnation, the utter, unqualified involvement of God with humanity, is at the root of the Christian theology of engagement.

Paul's letters are the most immediate evidence of early Christian engagement in church and world; Luke's account in the Acts of the Apostles witnesses to this in narrative form. Both are pervaded by reference to their scriptures, the Old Testament; both are also involved in a radical break with that tradition: the opening of the church to Gentiles without them having to fulfill the entry requirements to Judaism or some of its ritual practices. This break was a condition for the church's global engagement and spread in the centuries to follow. Luke's way of telling it underlines (as in Peter's three times repeated dream and much of the story being narrated twice) what a significant development this was, not least in requiring Peter to go against his scriptures and in generating dispute that threatened the church (Acts 10, 11, 15). Here the church was going beyond what Jesus did or taught, shifting the boundaries of the community in a way that transformed its identity. This was innovation without a precedent, and controversial in its reading of scripture. It has been a paradigm for many later disputes that have threatened to divide the church as it tried to decide between its habitual reading of the Bible and some innovative engagement – for example, on the abolition of slavery, the role of women in the church, democracy, contraception, or homosexuality.

Thinking

Fresh theology calls for creative thinking. Philosophical and systematic theology, or practical and pastoral theology, or ethics and spirituality, are perhaps what first spring to mind at the mention of constructive thinking in theology; but it is vital also to recognize Paul,

Luke, John, the three Isaiahs, the author of the book of Job, and other biblical writers as creative thinkers. The forms in which they write may not be argumentative or theoretical in the ways that later developed, especially in the scholastic and academic traditions of Western theology, but their biblical genres embody intensive thinking.

The author of the book of Job, whose adventurous thinking has already been commented upon,[6] sets up a complex and subtle debate about one of the perennial human problems, and century after century this thought has proved to be gripping, provocative, and profound. The school of Isaiah faced a massive national and religious trauma and offered an array of ways of understanding what was happening. This is perhaps most generative in stretching the previous conceptions of God as "I am," the creator and redeemer, who is utterly involved with us and who also utterly transcends us and continually does new things. It is a receptive, responsive thinking whose first rule is:

> Incline your ear, and come to me;
> Listen, so that you may live.
> (Isaiah 55:3)

Its horizon and center is a God who also thinks, but in ways that our prior conceptions cannot grasp; as we are attentive, our thought and all our capacities participate in being stretched in response to his thoughts and ways:

> For as the heavens are higher than the earth,
> So are my ways higher than your ways
> And my thoughts than your thoughts.
> (Isaiah 55:9)

We do not reach or possess the stars, but we may orient our ways by them.

Both Job and Isaiah are mostly poetry. Their "maximal speech" poses the deepest questions and opens new intellectual paths for a theology that is willing to read and reread their inexhaustible poetry.

Paul's genre is the letter. Like Job and Isaiah, he has repeatedly generated theological inquiry and debate, sometimes amounting to revolutionary transformation. He wrote in passionate engagement with a variety of young church communities, many of which he had helped to found. These were the settings in relation to which he worked out some ideas (most of them heavily indebted to his Jewish scriptures) that were to prove extraordinarily productive in the following two millennia. Just to take his Letter to the Romans, these include: grace (chapters 1–6, 11–16); justification by faith (chapter 4); the "how much more ..." of chapter 5; baptism into the death of Jesus (chapter 6); the whole creation groaning and longing (chapter 8); the agony of relations between his own people, the Jews, and Christians (chapter 9–11); the church as the body of Christ (chapter 12).[7]

Perhaps the supreme theological achievement of the New Testament is the Gospel of John, who for that reason has in previous chapters been taken alongside Job as a principal biblical reference point.

These and many other examples show the ground-breaking thought that went into writing the Bible. These authors challenge us both to try to grasp what they meant and also to do something analogous in thoughtful response to God and, in the light of God, to the cries and opportunities of our time.

Communicating

The Bible is a rich collection of expressive forms – narratives of various types, laws, prophecies and visions, psalms and songs, proverbs, letters, sayings, parables, and more. It represents an immense achievement of authorial craft, often the product of long traditions, both oral and written. In literary terms, some books are recognized as classics by most standards – the stories of the Abraham, Isaac, Jacob, Joseph, Moses, Saul, or David; prophecies of Isaiah and Jeremiah; Job; the Song of Solomon; Proverbs; and the Psalms. Yet some of the books that are less attractive as literature are still powerful communications; the overall criterion for their inclusion has properly not been literary but, in a broad sense, theological.

This suggests a reasonable conclusion about the relation of expression to theological creativity: it can be very important, but aesthetic judgment is not the leading criterion. Whether within or outside the Bible, alertness to language, genre, form, style, and other aspects of expression can be vital to right understanding. At the crudest level, to read Genesis 1–2 as being in the same category as a modern scientific cosmology, or the Gospels as newspaper reports written immediately after the events they narrate, is to misread them. Their actual achievements, especially as theology, will be missed or distorted. Failure to appreciate the interplay of their form and content will seriously impair the reception of their message. It is also likely, in turn, to affect the sort of theology one might write in line with the Bible. Those who, for example, take the Bible as a set of propositions, that can be grasped without attending to their literary forms and contexts, are likely to think and write theology very differently from those who do not. The whole mindset of theologians who take the Bible seriously will be affected by their level of sensitivity to its forms of expression. One aspect of this has been explored in chapter 4 of this volume as the "moods" of theology – the balance between questioning, asserting, commanding, exploring, and desiring. Theologians who read scripture mainly as a source for assertions and commands, missing its direct and indirect encouragement of questioning, exploring, and, above all, desiring God's as yet unrealized future, are unlikely to write in ways that encourage their readers to question, explore, or desire.

Narrative and poetry (which often overlap) are perhaps the two basic literary forms for Christian theology. In this manifesto, narratives of various types have largely been treated under the categories of drama and epic, with priority given to the dramatic in order to undermine tendencies to integrate all theology within some grand single metanarrative. Large sections of the Old Testament are poetry (which can be dramatic, epic, or lyric), and for Christians it is especially important that many of the texts that have been most formative for the New Testament and for Christian worship and theology are in poetry – prophets, Psalms, and much wisdom writing. Some narratives are closely akin to poetry in their imaginative density and imagery. Appreciation of this will profoundly affect their use in theological prose. Poetry is notoriously difficult to translate and is likely to require more commentary in order to enable as much understanding as possible of its semantic fields and resonances. Beyond theological prose it also raises the question of theological poetry: might Dante be one of the greatest of Christian theologians? Might there be a twenty-first century Dante?[8]

The fruitfulness of the Bible and of later Christian theology is inseparable from their expressive creativity. For theology to do what the Bible did, as well as to interpret what the Bible said, means that it should pursue creativity in expression and performance in many modes. And this in turn means openness to the whole range of artistic and cultural forms and media.

A Biblical Hope for Twenty-first Century Theology

I conclude with three biblical texts from which this century's theology might, in line with previous chapters, draw inspiration.

The first picks up the wisdom manifesto of chapter 1, this time through Proverbs, chapter 8. There, Wisdom promises:

> I love those who love me,
> and those who seek me diligently find me.
> (Proverbs 8:17)

The climax of the chapter is Wisdom telling how God created her before everything else. She is not divine but is fundamental to creation, related to everything, and utterly intimate with God. Her testimony to this primordial intimacy is:

> I was daily his delight,
> rejoicing before him always,
> rejoicing in his inhabited world
> and delighting in the human race.
> (Proverbs 8:30–31)

The calling of theology is into the joy and love of a wisdom that is intimate with God and delights in whatever God delights in.

The second text is the promise that has occurred more than once in previous chapters:

> When the Spirit of truth comes, he will guide you into all the truth. (John 16:13)

That encourages theologians to be open to the Spirit and to desire more and more theological truth, whether that is through fuller understanding of what has come from the past or through innovations, improvisations, and surprises.

The third text, in the appropriate form of a prayer, both suggests something of the dimensions of the understanding, knowledge, truth, and wisdom that are waiting to be entered into, and also recognizes that even these are not everything:

> I pray that you may have the power to comprehend, with all the saints, what is the breadth and length and height and depth, and to know the love of Christ that surpasses knowledge, so that you may be filled with all the fullness of God. (Ephesians 3:18–19)

The answer to that prayer is the fulfillment of our wisest and wildest desires. But it is an answer that, given the infinite life, love, and wisdom of God, is likely to go on being fulfilled inexhaustibly; and the conclusion of the prayer seems to acknowledge an unimaginable abundance beyond even what has just been asked for:

> Now to him who by the power at work within us is able to accomplish abundantly far more than all we can ask or imagine, to him be glory in the church and in Christ Jesus to all generations, forever and ever. Amen. (Ephesians 3:20–21)

Notes and References

Chapter 1. A Cry for Wisdom: Theology for the Twenty-first Century

1 Cf. David F. Ford, *Christian Wisdom: Desiring God and Learning in Love* (Cambridge University Press, Cambridge 2007).

2 For a lengthier engagement with Job, see Ford, *Christian Wisdom*, op. cit., chapters 3 and 4, as well as Susannah Ticciati, *Job and the Disruption of Identity: Reading beyond Barth* (T&T Clark, London 2005).

3 John 1:1–18: [1]In the beginning was the Word, and the Word was with God, and the Word was God.[2]He was in the beginning with God.[3]All things came into being through him, and without him not one thing came into being. What has come into being [4]in him was life, and the life was the light of all people.[5]The light shines in the darkness, and the darkness did not overcome it.[6]There was a man sent from God, whose name was John.[7]He came as a witness to testify to the light, so that all might believe through him.[8]He himself was not the light, but he came to testify to the light.[9]The true light, which enlightens everyone, was coming into the world.[10]He was in the world, and the world came into being through him; yet the world did not know him.[11]He came to what was his own, and his own people did not accept him.[12]But to all who received him, who believed in his name, he gave power to become children of God, [13]who were born, not of blood or of the will of the flesh or of the will of man, but of God.[14]And the Word became flesh and lived among us, and we have seen his

glory, the glory as of a father's only son, full of grace and truth.[15](John testified to him and cried out, "This was he of whom I said, 'He who comes after me ranks ahead of me because he was before me.'") [16]From his fullness we have all received, grace upon grace.[17]The law indeed was given through Moses; grace and truth came through Jesus Christ.[18]No one has ever seen God. It is God the only Son, who is close to the Father's heart, who has made him known.

4 First and second editions: David F. Ford (ed.), *The Modern Theologians: An Introduction to Christian Theology in the Twentieth Century* (Blackwell, Oxford, 1989 and 1997); third edition: David F. Ford with Rachel Muers (eds.), *The Modern Theologians: An Introduction to Christian Theology since 1918* (Blackwell, Oxford, 2005).

5 For accounts of this development, see Sheridan Gilley (ed.), *Cambridge History of Christianity*, vol. 8: World Christianities *c.*1815–1914 (Cambridge University Press, Cambridge, 2005), and Hugh McLeod (ed.), *Cambridge History of Christianity*, vol. 9: World Christianities *c.*1914–2000 (Cambridge University Press, Cambridge, 2006).

6 Karl Barth, Dietrich Bonhoeffer, Paul Tillich, Karl Rahner, and Hans Urs von Balthasar, with the sixth being French theologian Henri de Lubac.

7 For example, German universities required theology students to learn Hebrew, Greek, and Latin in order to have first-hand access to scripture and the traditions of Eastern and Western Christianity.

8 See Paul Murray (ed.), *Receptive Ecumenism and the Call to Catholic Learning: Exploring a Way for Contemporary Ecumenism* (Oxford University Press, Oxford, 2008).

9 I owe this felicitous phrase to Dr Nicholas Adams.

10 These are the classics selected for special discussion in the third edition of *The Modern Theologians*. See note 4 of chapter 1, above.

11 Karl Barth, *Church Dogmatics*, revised study edition, 31 vols. (T&T Clark International, London, 2009).

12 Seventeen in the German edition (*Dietrich Bonhoeffer Werke*, ed. Eberhard Bethge et al. (Chr. Kaiser Verlag, Gütersloh, 1993–2005)), sixteen in the English (*Dietrich Bonhoeffer Works*, ed. Wayne Whitson Floyd Jr. (Fortress Press, Minneapolis, 1995–)).

13 Dietrich Bonhoeffer, *Ethics*, ed. Clifford J. Green et al., trans. Reinhard Krauss et al., vol. 6, *Dietrich Bonhoeffer Works* (Fortress Press, Minneapolis, 2005).

14 Dietrich Bonhoeffer, *Letters and Papers from Prison. The Enlarged Edition*, ed. Eberhard Bethge (SCM Press, London, 1971).

15 In logic, this is a third form of reasoning beyond deduction and induction that thinks up explanations and resolutions of questions and problems. I describe it in line with Coleridge's use of the term, on which see Daniel W. Hardy, "Harmony and Mutual Implication in the Opus Maximum," in Jeffrey W. Barbeau (ed.), *Coleridge's Assertion of Religion* (Peeters, Leuven, Paris, Dudley, MA, 2006), especially pp. 50ff. The later, better-known, use of the term by C. S. Peirce and other pragmatist philosophers is also borne in mind (for a theological appropriation of Peirce on abduction, see Peter Ochs, Peirce, *Pragmatism and the Logic of Scripture* (Cambridge University Press, Cambridge, 1998)).

16 For references and discussion, see Hardy, op.cit., p. 50f.

17 Hardy (ibid., p. 52) concludes: "In that 'being drawn', human beings are most truly enabled to affirm themselves and the order of all things, as they are illuminated in Reason and directed in love toward 'all things both great and small, for the dear God who loveth us, He made and loveth all.' [from Coleridge's poem, "The Rime of the Ancient Mariner"] This 'abduction' is indeed a maximal insight, a fitting conclusion, both methodological and realistic, to Coleridge's lifelong pursuit of the mutual implication of all things in the Logos and the Spirit."

18 Karl Barth, *Church Dogmatics II: The Doctrine of God, Part 2*, trans. G. W. Bromiley et al. (T&T Clark International, London, 2004), pp. 94–194.

19 Hans Urs von Balthasar, *Mysterium Paschale: The Mystery of Easter*, trans. Aidan Nichols (Ignatius Press, San Francisco, 2000).

20 Paul Tillich, *Systematic Theology I* (SCM Press, London, 1978), pp. 85, 147–50.

21 Karl Rahner, *Foundations of Christian Faith: An Introduction to the Idea of Christianity*, trans. William V. Dych (Crossroad, New York, 1978), p. 79.

22 Bonhoeffer, *Ethics*, op.cit., pp. 146–70.

23 His most felicitous translator is Sr Gemma Simmonds – cf. Henri de Lubac, *Corpus Mysticum: The Church and the Eucharist in the Middle Ages*, ed. Laurence Paul Hemming and Susan Frank Parsons, trans. Gemma Simmonds with Richard Price and Christopher Stephens (SCM Press, London, 2006).

24 Dietrich Bonhoeffer, *Act and Being: Transcendental Philosophy and Ontology in Systematic Theology*, ed. Wayne Whitson Floyd Jr. and Hans-Richard Reuter, trans. H. Martin Rumscheidt, vol. 2, *Dietrich Bonhoeffer Works* (Fortress Press, Minneapolis, 1996).

25 Dietrich Bonhoeffer, *Life Together and Prayerbook of the Bible*, ed. Geffrey B. Kelley et al., trans. Daniel W. Bloesch and James H. Burtness, vol. 5, *Dietrich Bonhoeffer Works* (Fortress Press, Minneapolis, 1996).

26 Dietrich Bonhoeffer, *Discipleship*, ed. Geffrey B. Kelly et al., trans. Barbara Green and Reinhard Krauss, vol. 4, *Dietrich Bonhoeffer Works* (Fortress Press, Minneapolis, 2001).

27 Bonhoeffer, *Ethics*, op.cit.

28 Bonhoeffer, *Letters and Papers*, op.cit.

Chapter 2. Drama in Bible, Theology, and Life

1 Cf. Hans Urs von Balthasar, *Theo-Drama*, 5 vols. (Ignatius Press, San Francisco, 1988–98). The English usage that appears to be most common is "theodrama."

2 Ben Quash, *Theology and the Drama of History* (Cambridge University Press, Cambridge, 2005), especially chapters 1, 3, 4, and 5, offers a superb theological discussion of drama, epic, and lyric in both Hegel and von Balthasar, to which the present discussion is indebted.

3 Rudolf Bultmann, *The Gospel of John: A Commentary*, trans. G. R. Beasley-Murray (Blackwell, Oxford, 1971), pp. 13–83.

4 Ibid., p. 62.

5 Cf. Ford, *Christian Wisdom*, op. cit., pp. 12–13, 67–8.

6 Cf. ibid., pp. 12–13, 67–8.

7 John David Dawson, in *Christian Figural Reading and the Fashioning of Identity* (University of California Press, London, 2001), gives a wonderfully perceptive account of figural reading and his conception of it lies behind the present discussion. His account is all the more helpful because he shows clearly its relevance to ongoing Christian life and political action (he begins with the teaching of a German bishop in Nazi Germany) and engages with both ancient and contemporary theology. His two main exemplars of figural reading are Origen of Alexandria (*c.*185–254), who might be said in my terms to practice

a Spirit-led wisdom of ramification, centrally concerned with the creative transformation of Christian living in the ongoing drama, and Hans Frei (1922–88), whose main concern might be described as a wisdom of reserve centered on the identity of Jesus Christ.

8 Cf. Ingolf U. Dalferth, *Theology and Philosophy* (Blackwell, Oxford, 1988).

9 Hans Frei, *Types of Christian Theology*, ed. George Hunsinger and William C. Placher (Yale University Press, New Haven, 1992). For further discussion of Frei's typology, see David F. Ford, *Theology: A Very Short Introduction* (Oxford University Press, Oxford, 1999), pp. 21–31, and David F. Ford, *Shaping Theology: Engagements in a Religious and Secular World* (Blackwell, Oxford, 2007), pp. 14–17.

10 Frei proposes five types on a continuum. At one end, a particular philosophy (his main example is that of Kant) is the criterion for judging Christianity, and those aspects not judged rational according to this system are rejected. At the other extreme are theologies that allow for no philosophical critique at all. Next to this are the two that together approximate to the position of this manifesto. First of these is theology that gives priority to the narrative testimony to Jesus Christ and engages with philosophies or world-views in an ad hoc manner, open to their contributions and critiques but not allowing them to dictate the framework and criteria. The other, central type, is more equally balanced, and allows neither the narrative testimony nor the philosophy to assume priority – they engage in mutually critical correlations and each case has to be argued about on its merits. I would accept that this is an appropriate approach on some theological questions, but on a core matter such as the main lines of the Gospel rendering of who Jesus Christ is there must be a Christian theological presumption in favor of reliability. The remaining type (nearest to Kant) chooses a particular philosophy as a way in to the Gospel, as Bultmann uses existentialism, interpreting Jesus Christ in those terms. This can give profound insights; but, apart from the fundamental theological problem of whether any philosophy should be given this privilege, one weakness, as in Bultmann's interpretation of John discussed briefly above, is in failing to do justice to the dramatic character of the testimony.

11 David H. Kelsey, *Eccentric Existence: A Theological Anthropology*, 2 vols. (Westminster John Knox Press, Louisville, Kentucky, 2009.

12 Ibid., vol. 1, p. 39.

13 An interesting question is whether Kelsey overemphasizes the distinctiveness of each strand, and even whether there are in fact three narrative logics – his wisdom-centered approach to creation struggles to achieve narrative status, and I am still pondering the strength of his case for the distinctiveness of the two plotlines of consummation and reconciliation in relation to the story of Jesus. Many of the theological advantages of his three narrative logics are also gained by drama as understood in this manifesto. I wonder whether John's Gospel could help here. It plays little constructive role in Kelsey's theology, but if read as simultaneously epic, lyric, and above all dramatic, and as centered on the question of Jesus' identity which believers indwell, then it may offer a stable integration of creation, consummation, and reconciliation that takes up the Synoptic gospels into the sort of theology that Kelsey is aiming at.

14 Ibid., vol. 1, p. 45.

15 Charles Taylor, *A Secular Age* (Belknap Press of Harvard University Press, Cambridge, Mass., and London, 2007).

Chapter 3. A Dramatic Code for Twenty-first Century Theology

1 Grace Davie, *Europe: The Exceptional Case. Parameters of Faith in the Modern World* (Darton, Longman and Todd, London, 2002).

2 Philip Jenkins, *God's Continent: Christianity, Islam, and Europe's Religious Crisis* (Oxford University Press, Oxford and New York, 2007).

3 There are several current positions rooted in different traditions that approximate to the position I am sketching here. From the secular side, one of the most insightful and persuasive proposals is that of Jeffrey Stout in *Democracy and Tradition* (Princeton University Press, Princeton, NJ, 2004). Among Christian thinkers, see especially Luke Bretherton, *Christianity and Contemporary Politics: The Conditions and Possibilities of Faithful Witness* (Wiley-Blackwell, Oxford, 2010).

4 Cf. Ford, *Shaping Theology*, op. cit., pp. 129–34.

5 Taylor, *A Secular Age*, op. cit.

6 Ibid., p. 3.

7 This is a self that is not "porous" to the influences of spirits, demons, magic, and other aspects of the "enchanted world," but is bounded, with a strong sense of self and non-self, self-possession and self-control, and has the capacity to disengage, to distance itself from tradition and social authority, and to see things objectively (often with an implication of superiority). See ibid., pp. 37–42, 134–42, 300–7.

8 The disembedding is from immersion in social ritual, cosmos, and a received conception of the human good – see ibid., pp. 151–8.

9 See ibid., pp. 473ff.

10 The book concludes in its Epilogue with an apparent yearning for a more epic account, as he suggests a marriage of his own Reform Master Narrative with the problematic (and distinctly epic) narrative he labels "Intellectual Deviation" – ibid., pp. 773ff.

11 Cf. ibid., p. 61.

12 Ibid., p. 56.

13 Ibid., pp. 712ff.

14 This is especially clear in his sharp analysis of the opposite tendency as "excarnation" – see ibid., pp. 288, 554, 613ff., chapter 20.

15 Ibid., p. 636.

16 Ibid., p. 668.

17 Ibid., p. 671.

18 Ibid., p. 637.

19 Cf. chapter 1 of this volume, and Ford, *Christian Wisdom*, op. cit., pp. 14–51.

20 For an attempt to do this, see David F. Ford and Daniel W. Hardy, *Living in Praise: Worshipping and Knowing God* (Darton, Longman and Todd, London, 2005).

21 For two excellent examples, see Rowan Williams, *The Wound of Knowledge: Christian Spirituality from the New Testament to St John of the Cross* (Darton, Longman and Todd, London, 1990), and Mark A. McIntosh, *Mystical Theology: The Integrity of Spirituality and Theology* (Blackwell, Oxford, 1998).

22 "And all of us, with unveiled faces, seeing the glory of the Lord as though reflected in a mirror, are being transformed into the same image from one degree of glory to another; for this comes from the Lord, the Spirit … For it is the God who said, 'Let light shine out of darkness,' who has shone in our hearts to give the light of

the knowledge of the glory of God in the face of Jesus Christ" (2 Cors. 3:18, 4:6). On this passage, see Richard B. Hays, *Echoes of Scripture in the Letters of Paul* (Yale University Press, New Haven and London, 1989), pp. 122–53. See also Paul Ricoeur on the "christomorphic self" in *Figuring the Sacred: Religion, Narrative, and Imagination*, ed. Mark I. Wallace, trans. David Pellauer (Fortress Press, Minneapolis, 1995), pp. 267–8. For a theology of Christian subjectivity that centers on these verses from 2 Corinthians, see David F. Ford, *Self and Salvation: Being Transformed* (Cambridge University Press, Cambridge, 1999).

23 Perhaps the richest (and most architectonically impressive) attempt to do this in the past century is by Karl Barth, in Parts 1, 2, and 3 of *Church Dogmatics IV: The Doctrine of Reconciliation* (T&T Clark International, London, 2004).

24 One of the most remarkable achievements of the ecumenical movement is the Lima Document of 1982 on Baptism, Eucharist and Ministry. See *Baptism, Eucharist and Ministry: The Agreed Text* (CCBI Publications, London, 1982).

25 Peter's international audience is emphasized: "Parthians, Medes, Elamites, and residents of Meopotamia, Judea and Cappadocia, Pontus and Asia, Phrygia and Pamphylia, Egypt and the parts of Libya belonging to Cyrene, and visitors from Rome both Jews and proselytes, Cretans and Arabs – in our own languages we hear them speaking about God's deeds of power" (Acts 2:9–11).

26 *Intimior intimo meo* (Augustine, *Confessions* III.6.11).

27 The Hebrew can mean simply "wind" but also "spirit" as in Holy Spirit.

28 Revelation 22:17:
The Spirit and the bride say, "Come."
And let everyone who hears say, "Come."

29 See 1 Cors. 12–14, especially 12:4–11.

30 See Galatians 5:22–3.

31 For some further thoughts on this theme, see Ford and Hardy, *Living in Praise*, op. cit., pp. 187–92.

32 Again, as with previous cries, these require thinking through all the major doctrinal loci, in this case with a focus on sociality.

33 See Emmanuel Levinas, *Totality and Infinity: An Essay on Exteriority*, trans. Alphonso Lingis (Duquesne University Press, Pittsburgh, 1969),

p. 50; cf. *Self and Salvation*, op. cit., chapter 2. For a powerful poetic testimony to the primacy of responsibility before the other, see Micheal O'Siadhail, *A Fragile City* (Bloodaxe Books, Newcastle upon Tyne, 1995).

34 On Job 28, see Ford, *Christian Wisdom*, op. cit., pp. 134–8; cf. Ticciati, *Job and the Disprruption of Identity*, op. cit., pp. 183–90.

35 I owe the phrase to Nicholas Wolterstorff in conversation regarding an appointment in theology.

36 For example, the calling of Samuel in 1 Samuel 3 and Paul's encounter on the Road to Damascus in Acts 9.

Chapter 4. Desire Above All

1 Søren Kierkegaard, *The Sickness Unto Death: A Christian Psychological Exposition for Upbuilding and Awakening*, ed. and trans. Howard V. Hong and Edna H. Hong (Princeton University Press, Princeton, 1980), p. 35.

2 In this chapter, the meaning of "mood" is rooted in the literal grammatical use of the term for the indicative, imperative, interrogative, subjunctive, and optative moods, but is used theologically in a more extended, metaphorical sense. So, for example, many desires (even in Greek, which has a distinct optative mood) are expressed in indicative mood (e.g. "My soul longs for you"); many questions are not in the interrogative mood ("I wonder whether …"); and commands can just as well be indicative ("I require you to do this") or interrogative ("Will you do this?") as imperative ("Do this!").

3 See chapter 1 of this volume, pp. 3–4.

4 Søren Kierkegaard, *Fear and Trembling* (Cambridge University Press, Cambridge, 2006).

5 David Kelsey, *Eccentric Existence*, op. cit., p. 9.

6 *In Joan. Evang.* LXIII, 1 (quoted in Erich Przywara, *An Augustine Synthesis* (Sheed and Ward, London, 1936), pp. 75–6).

7 Ibid., p. 76 (from *In Ps.* CIV, 3).

8 Ibid., p. 77 (from *De Trin.* XV, ii, 2).

9 See Rachel Muers, *Keeping God's Silence: Towards a Theological Ethics of Communication* (Wiley-Blackwell, Oxford, 2004).

Chapter 5. Belonging: Church, Collegiality, Conversation

1 Randall Collins, *The Sociology of Philosophies: A Global Theory of Intellectual Change* (Harvard University Press, Cambridge, MA, 1998).

2 *The Methodist Worship Book* (Methodist Publishing, Peterborough, 1999) pp. 281–96.

3 The full response is: "I am no longer my own but yours. Put me to what you will, rank me with whom you will; put me to doing, put me to suffering; let me be employed for you or laid aside for you, exalted for you or brought low for you; let me be full, let me be empty; let me have all things, let me have nothing; I freely and wholeheartedly yield all things to your pleasure and disposal. And now, glorious and blessed God, Father Son, and Holy Spirit, you are mine and I am yours. So be it. And the covenant now made on earth, let it be ratified in heaven. Amen." (Ibid.)

4 See Hays, *Echoes of Scripture in the Letters of Paul*, op. cit., chapter 2, on Romans 9–11.

5 I find the most convincing interpretation of it in Hays, ibid., chapter 4.

6 For my own attempt to develop it, see Ford, *Self and Salvation*, especially its treatment of "facing" and "transformation."

7 Though note the severe exclusion to follow in 4:3–4: "And even if our gospel is veiled, it is veiled to those who are perishing. In their case the god of this world has blinded the minds of the unbelievers, to keep them from seeing the light of the gospel of the glory of Christ, who is the image of God."

8 For more on the theology of this extraordinary letter, see Frances M. Young and David F. Ford, *Meaning and Truth in 2 Corinthians* (Wipf and Stock, Eugene, OR, reprinted 2008).

9 One critical factor was the church becoming majority non-Jewish, and, later, becoming larger and more powerful than Judaism. When statements originating in a situation where Christianity was largely Jewish (so that its debates were internal to Judaism, with all the bitterness of a family quarrel), and sometimes persecuted by the Jewish authorities, were transferred directly and aggressively to the later situation, the results were often disastrous.

10 In what follows, I especially have in mind the worship in Catholic, Orthodox, and mainstream Protestant churches, but most of what is said could also with little change be adapted to Pentecostal and independent Evangelical and other churches. It is not only worship according to a written form that is traditional, ritualized, and the outcome of communal theological thinking and debate.

11 See Ford, *Christian Wisdom*, op. cit., pp. 252–64.

12 For further discussion of this theme, see "Faith and Universities in a Religious and Secular World," in Ford, *Shaping Theology*, op. cit., pp. 115–42.

13 For my account of this, see ibid., and "Theology and Religious Studies for a Multifaith and Secular Society," in *Theology and Religious Studies in Higher Education: Global Perspectives*, ed. Darlene L. Bird and Simon G. Smith (Continuum, London, 2009), pp. 31–43.

14 Collins, *The Sociology of Philosophies*, op. cit.

15 For my own attempt, see David F. Ford, *The Shape of Living: Spiritual Directions for Everyday Life* (Zondervan, Grand Rapids, MI, 2002).

16 He concludes his book: "Christianity is surviving amid European secularism and often achieving far more than mere survival ... (T)actics and movements that originate here are likely to spread to other parts of the world ... Death and resurrection are not just fundamental doctrines of Christianity; they represent a historical model of the religion's structure and development" (Jenkins, *God's Continent*, op. cit., pp. 288–9).

17 For an account of them, see *The Modern Theologians*, 3rd edn, op. cit.

18 On the latter, see Ford, *Christian Wisdom*, op. cit., chapter 10.

Chapter 6. Church and Society

1 Fenella Cannell tackles the issue in her introduction to *The Anthropology of Christianity*, ed. Fenella Cannell (Duke University Press, Durham and London, 2006), pp. 1ff.

2 Cf. Michael Lambek (ed.), *A Reader in the Anthropology of Religion Second Edition* (Blackwell, Oxford, 2008), General Introduction, pp. 2–3: "An anthropological approach comprehends arguments that are variously holistic, universalistic, ethnographic, comparative, contextual, historical, dialogical, and critical ... Anthropologists have also,

over time, variously emphasized evolutionist, rationalist, functionalist, social structural, structuralist, symbolic, interpretive, political, Marxist, social constructionist, phenomenological, psychoanalytic, poststructuralist, cognitive, aesthetic, and ethical approaches or modes of understanding."

3 Cf. ibid. p.4: "Indeed, these are among anthropology's hardest and most enduring questions – questions about difference, rationality, community, modernity, symbolization, meaning, relativism, mimesis, projection, mediation, power, order, hierarchy, harmony, conflict, alienation, love, well-being, dignity, aesthetic coherence, creativity, playfulness, reproduction, fertility, maturation, death, tedium, excitement, motivation, suffering, and redemption. The anthropology of religion points to the unique conjunctions of morality, desire, and power, of subjection and freedom, of worldliness and asceticism, of ideal and violence, of imagination and embodiment, immanence and transcendence, inwardness and outwardness, origins and ends, order and chaos, structure and practice, cosmos and history, that have constituted distinct human worlds."

4 Ibid., p. 13.

5 Dietrich Bonhoeffer, *Ethics*, op. cit., pp. 339f.

6 Ibid., p. 156.

7 Ibid., p. 157.

8 Ibid., pp. 78–80.

9 Ibid., p. 159.

10 The concept of God taking responsibility for the world and its evil and of us being "conformed" to this responsibility in the church is one of the key teachings of Bonhoeffer's *Ethics* – cf. ibid., "Ethics as Formation," pp. 76ff., especially p. 83.

11 See especially "Outline for a Book," in Bonhoeffer, *Letters and Papers from Prison*, op. cit., pp. 380ff.

12 Bonhoeffer, *Ethics*, op. cit., pp. 90–1.

13 See, for example, the many references to the cross and to death in Bonhoeffer, *Letters and Papers from Prison*, op. cit.

14 Dietrich Bonhoeffer, *Ethics*, op. cit., pp. 91–2.

15 Cf. his summary statement when he begins his discussion of formation: "The human being, accepted, judged, and awakened to new life by God – this is Jesus Christ, this is the whole of humanity in Christ, this is us. The form of Jesus Christ alone victoriously encounters the

world. From this form proceeds all the formation of a world reconciled with God" (ibid., p. 92).

16 Ibid., p. 93.

17 Ibid., pp. 97–8.

18 Ibid., p. 159.

19 Ibid., p. 163.

20 Ibid., p. 168.

21 Ibid., p. 99.

22 Ibid., p. 93.

23 Ibid., p. 95.

24 See Ronald F. Thiemann, *Religion in Public Life: A Dilemma for Democracy* (Georgetown University Press, Washington, DC, 1996).

25 See Jeffrey Stout, *Democracy and Tradition*, op. cit.

26 See Romand Coles and Stanley Hauerwas, *Christianity, Democracy, and the Radical Ordinary: Conversations between a Radical Democrat and a Christian* (Lutterworth Press, Cambridge, 2010).

27 See the more extended discussion of these themes in chapter 3 of this volume, pp. 45–50.

28 The new *International Journal of Public Theology* is a sign of growing interest in this area.

29 See Lamin Sanneh, "Theology of Mission," in *The Modern Theologians*, 2nd edn, op. cit., pp. 555–74, as well as journals such as *International Review of Mission* and *Missiology: An International Review*.

30 For two recent examples of this kind of engagement, see Stephen Plant, "International Development and Belief in Progress," in *Journal of International Development* 21 (2009): 844–55, and Max L. Stackhouse, *Globalization and Grace: God and Globalization*, vol. 4 (Continuum, New York and London, 2007).

31 In an extremely important summary statement, early in his *Ethics*, he wrote: "The subject matter of a Christian ethic is God's reality revealed in Christ becoming real [*Wirklichwerden*] among God's creatures, just as the subject matter of doctrinal theology is the truth of God's reality revealed in Christ. The place that in all other ethics is marked by the antithesis between ought and is, idea and realization, motive and work, is occupied in Christian ethics by the relation between reality and becoming real, between past and present, between history and event (faith) or, to replace the many concepts

by the simple name of the thing itself, the relation between Jesus Christ and the Holy Spirit" (Bonhoeffer, *Ethics*, op. cit., pp. 49–50).

32 For an excellent example of the latter, see Traherne's *The Kingdom of God*, which can be found in *The Works of Thomas Traherne*, vol. 1, ed. Jan Ross (D. S. Brewer, Cambridge, 2005).

33 For an attempt to respond to this question, see Ford, *Self and Salvation*, op. cit., chapter 5.

34 John brings "Kingdom of God" and "eternal life" together in the story of Nicodemus (John 3) and after that only uses the latter term.

35 One of the very best accounts of this is in the work of Daniel W. Hardy. See Daniel W. Hardy with Deborah Hardy Ford, David F. Ford, and Peter Ochs, *Wording a Radiance: Parting Conversations on God and the Church* (SCM Press, London, 2010), and Daniel W. Hardy, "Receptive Ecumenism – Learning by Engagement," in *Receptive Ecumenism*, ed. Paul Murray, op. cit., pp. 428–42.

Chapter 7. Inter-Faith Blessing

1 This chapter will concentrate on the three Abrahamic faiths, without any implication that Christian relations with others are less important. It is therefore more of a case study in inter-faith theology than a complete presentation. If justice were to be done to the relationship of Christianity with non-Abrahamic faiths, this would have to be explored by taking full account of the particularities and the very different histories between Christianity and these faiths. Yet it is likely that a set of guidelines analogous to the Muscat Manifesto with which this chapter concludes would be appropriate in their cases too. The main areas of difference requiring special attention in engagement with Hinduism and Buddhism, for example, would probably be reference to God, the character and role of scriptures, and the nature of signs of hope. But there might also be more fundamental questioning of the whole approach to engagement.

2 The mention of enmity in the Melichezedek story ("who has delivered your enemies into your hand") suggests a similar conclusion. This and other passages in the three scriptures and their traditions are open to interpretations in support of enmity and violence. In many

situations the trust, present in each, that God's main way of delivering enemies into our hands is through bringing about reconciliation, has not prevailed.

3 The title, *Dabru Emet* (*Speak the Truth*), is taken from Zechariah 8:16.

4 It was published in the *New York Times* and *Baltimore Sun* during September 2000, and received coverage on radio, television, and in other media. For the full statement, see the website of the Institute for Christian and Jewish Studies (<http://www.icjs.org/programs/ongoing/njsp/dabruemet.php>).

5 *Christianity in Jewish Terms*, ed. Tikva Frymer-Kensky, David Novak, Peter Ochs, David Fox Sandmel, and Michael A. Signer (Westview Press, Boulder, CO, 2000).

6 *Christianity in Jewish Terms*, op. cit., p. xvii.

7 See *Christianity in Jewish Terms*, op. cit. pp. xvii–xx.

8 *Christianity in Jewish Terms*, op. cit., p. xvii.

9 Three of the most important such statements have been the 1947 Seelisberg Statement, the 1961 World Council of Churches "Resolution on Antisemitism," and the Vatican II declaration *Nostra Aetate*.

10 The logic is that of the "how much more" of Romans 11:12: "Now if their stumbling means riches for the world, and if their defeat means riches for Gentiles, how much more will their full inclusion mean!" Cf. Romans, chapter 5, and Paul Ricoeur on this, in *Figuring the Sacred: Religion, Narrative, and Imagination*, trans. David Pellauer, ed. Mark I. Wallace (Fortress Press, Minneapolis, 1995), pp. 281–3.

11 For the full text of the letter and responses to it, see the website: <http://www.acommonword.com>.

12 In early 2009, HRH Prince Ghazi of Jordan summed up the responses to date to the letter, including many international conferences, over 600 articles in English alone, a series of formal written responses by leading Christian figures, and a great deal else. For his full summary, see Prince Ghazi of Jordan, "Concept of Dialogue: On 'A Common Word Between Us and You'," in *Annual Dialogue Report on Religion and Values of the C-1 World Dialogue 2009*, ed. Alistair Macdonald-Radcliff and Roland Schatz (Innovation Publishing, Boston, Beirut, Pretoria, Tianjin, and Zurich, 2009), pp. 17–19.

13 Bodies represented included: World Council of Churches, Roman Catholic, several Orthodox (including leaders from the Middle East), Methodist, Anglican, Lutheran, Reformed, and Evangelical.

14 "We suggest an approach drawing on *Dialogue and Proclamation*, a 1991 Vatican document whose four categories of inter-religious dialogue have been found widely helpful. They are:

a) *the dialogue of life*, 'where people strive to live in an open and neighbourly spirit';
b) *the dialogue of action*, 'in which Christians and others collaborate for the integral development and liberation of people';
c) *the dialogue of theological exchange*, 'where specialists seek to deepen their understanding of their respective religious heritages'; and
d) *the dialogue of religious experience*, 'where persons rooted in their own religious traditions share their spiritual riches'.

This typology can be applied more generally to the whole pattern of encounter between Christians and Muslims …

Three imperatives are suggested by this:

a) to strengthen grass-roots partnerships and programmes between our communities that will work for justice, peace and the common good of human society the world over;
b) to intensify the shared theological discussions and researches of religious leaders and scholars who are seeking clearer insight into divine truth, and to realize this through building and sustaining of groups marked by a sense of collegiality, mutual esteem, and trust;
c) to deepen the appreciation of Christian and Muslim believers for each other's religious practice and experience, as they come to recognize one another as people whose lives are oriented towards God in love.

… The approach of your letter shows the importance of shared and attentive study of Biblical and Qur'anic texts as a way of ensuring both that all dimensions of encounter are present and also that Christians and Muslims are held accountable to, and draw on the riches of, their respective traditions of faith whilst recognizing the limitations – at least initially – in our ability to comment authoritatively on the others' scriptures."

The full text of the Archbishop of Canterbury's response, *A Common Word for the Common Good*, can be found on: <http://www.acommonword.com>.

15 See Kevin Vanhoozer, *First Theology: God, Scripture & Hermeneutics* (Inter-Varsity Press, Downer's Grove, IL, 2002).

16 For further information about Scriptural Reasoning, see the website of the Society for Scriptural Reasoning, available at: <http://etext.lib.virginia.edu/journals/jsrforum/>. For print resources on Scriptural Reasoning, see chapter 8 in Ford, *Christian Wisdom*, op. cit., pp. 273–303; David F. Ford and C. C. Pecknold, *The Promise of Scriptural Reasoning* (Blackwell, Oxford, 2006); Peter Ochs, "Reading Scripture Together in Sight of Our Open Doors," in *The Princeton Seminary Bulletin* 26(1), new series (2005): 36–47; and Steven Kepnes and Basit Bilal Koshul (eds.), *Studying the "Other", Understanding the "Self": Scripture, Reason and the Contemporary Islam–West Encounter* (Fordham University Press, New York, 2007). Scriptural Reasoning can be practiced bilaterally too. One example of this is provided by some meetings of the ongoing Christian-Muslim "Building Bridges Seminar," hosted annually by the Archbishop of Canterbury. Some of the proceedings from the second meeting of the seminar, in Doha in 2003, can be found in Michael Ipgrave (ed.), *Scriptures in Dialogue: Christians and Muslims Studying the Bible and the Qur'an Together* (Church House Publishing, London, 2004).

17 Among the leading signatories of *Dabru Emet* who also contributed to *Christianity in Jewish Terms* were members of the Textual Reasoning group who became core members of the Scriptural Reasoning movement, Peter Ochs, Robert Gibbs, Randi Rashkover, Steven Kepnes, and Laurie Zoloth; and Peter Ochs was one of the first Jewish respondents to *A Common Word*. Among the leading signatories of *A Common Word* who have been members of the small group coordinating strategy in its aftermath have been participants in Scriptural Reasoning – Aref Nayed and Tim Winter (Abdal Hakim Murad). See Tim Winter's chapter "Qur'anic Reasoning as an Academic Practice," in *The Promise of Scriptural Reasoning*, op. cit., pp. 105–19.

18 The follow-up to *A Common Word* has included some Scriptural Reasoning, as in the October 2008 conference in Cambridge and Lambeth Palace, "A Common Word and Future Muslim-Christian Engagement." The communiqué from that conference, signed by the Grand Mufti of Egypt, Dr Ali Gomaa, and the Archbishop of Canterbury, Dr Rowan Williams, said: "One of the most moving elements of our encounter has been the opportunity to study together passages from our scriptures. We have felt ourselves to have been together before God and this has given us each a greater appreciation for the richness of the other's heritage as well as an awareness of the potential value in being joined by Jewish believers in a journey of mutual discovery and attentiveness to the texts we hold sacred. We wish to repeat the experience of a shared study of scriptural texts as one of the ways in which we can come, concretely, to develop our understanding of how the other understands and lives their own faith. We commend this experience to others." See: <http:// www.archbishopofcanterbury.org/2818>, and the website of the Cambridge Inter-Faith Programme: <http://www.interfaith.cam.ac.uk>.

Chapter 8. New Theology and Religious Studies: Shaping, Teaching, and Funding a Field

1 Some of what follows is taken with little amendment from my chapter, "Theology and Religious Studies for a Multifaith and Secular Society," in *Theology and Religious Studies in Higher Education*, op. cit., chapter 2. It was originally delivered as a paper to a conference at St Anne's College, Oxford, 6–7 July, 2006, on the theme: "Theology *and* Religious Studies or Theology *vs* Religious Studies," organized by the national subject center for the field within the Higher Education Academy. I was struck by how little contention there was about its main point that Britain had succeeded in developing a new paradigm.

2 For the full Theology and Religious Studies benchmark statement in its present form (2007), see: <http://www.qaa.ac.uk/academicinfrastructure/benchmark/statements/Theology.asp>.

3 Available at: <http://www.prs.heacademy.ac.uk/view.html/prsdocuments/384>.

4 The national association for university academics in the field is called the Association of University Teachers in Theology and Religious Studies. For more on this, see David F. Ford, Ben Quash, and Janet Martin Soskice (eds.), *Fields of Faith: Theology and Religious Studies for the Twenty-first Century* (Cambridge University Press, Cambridge, 2005).

5 Economics is an especially apt comparison. Many parts of people's lives are involved with and shaped by money and by economic systems, practices, and understandings. When economics is studied academically there is no suggestion that staff or students should not be involved personally with money or other aspects of the economy. It is also common for universities not only to have economics departments that study (in ways analogous to a religious studies mode) the history, theory, statistical analysis, and contemporary workings of economic systems, but also to have departments (in some ways analogous to theology that engages with living religious traditions) of applied economics that are closely connected with governments and business, and to prepare students in business or management schools directly for careers in business. In the course of pursuing applied economics and business studies many normative and practical questions must be not only raised but also answered, in ways similar to theology's critical and constructive contribution to contemporary religious communities. The career-oriented aspect is paralleled by the training of religious ministers in some university departments of theology and religious studies, or by the now widespread arrangements whereby universities validate qualifications taught by theological institutions run by particular religious communities.

6 See especially: "An interdisciplinary wisdom: knowledge, formation and collegiality in the negotiable university," in Ford, *Christian Wisdom*, op. cit., chapter 9; and "Faith and Universities in a Religious and Secular World," in Ford, *Shaping Theology*, op. cit., chapter 7.

7 Including Kant, Hamann, Herder, Goethe, Schiller, Schelling, Hegel, Fichte, and Schleiermacher.

8 In the magisterial opening chapter of the four-volume *A History of the University in Europe* of which he is the General Editor, Walter Rüegg sums up what he calls "the essential outlines of an academic ethic in the process of formation" distilled into "seven values which in the Middle Ages legitimated, in religious terms, the amor sciendi and

the university which was its institutional form" (Walter Rüegg, "Themes in Universities in the Middle Ages," in *A History of the University in Europe*, vol. 1, ed. H. De Ridder-Symoens, general editor Walter Rüegg (Cambridge 1992–2004), p. 32.

9 Collins, *The Sociology of Philosophies*, op. cit.

10 Christian theology does not have to be taught by Christians, but clearly there are aspects of doing constructive theology for which apprenticeship to a Christian practitioner is important.

Chapter 9. Becoming a Theologian: The Apprentice

1 For a philosophical and theological exploration of selfhood, see Ford, *Self and Salvation*, op. cit.

2 See chapters 1 and 2 of this volume, pp. 4–7, 27–31.

3 I owe this perception, and many others, to Richard Hays and Richard Bauckham in the course of reading the Gospel of John together over a six-month period in 2008.

4 See Joel Robbins, " God is Nothing but Talk: Modernity, Language, and Prayer in a Papua New Guinea Society," *American Anthropologist New Series*, 103(4) (December 2001): 901–12. Robbins is the leading figure in a new group of anthropologists developing the "anthropology of Christianity," which holds great promise for richer understanding of both global and local Christianities around the world today.

5 Darton, Longman and Todd, London, 2004.

Chapter 10. The Bible: Creative Source of Theology

1 This is a vast and highly controversial topic. I find the most perceptive and congenial recent discussion of it in Kelsey, *Eccentric Existence*, op. cit., vol. 1, chapter 3B, "The Concept of Christian Canonical Holy Scripture," pp. 132–56.

2 For more on this, see Ford, *Christian Wisdom*, chapter 2.

3 See Augustine, *Teaching Christianity* (*De Doctrina Christiana*), trans. Edmund Hill, ed. John E. Rotelle (New City Press, New York, 1996), I.39–44 (pp. 123–6).

4 For a fuller discussion, see Ford, *Christian Wisdom*, op. cit., chapters 3 and 4.

5 See John F.A. Sawyer, *The Fifth Gospel: Isaiah in the History of Christianity* (Cambridge University Press, Cambridge, 1996).

6 For more on this, see Ticciati, *Job and the Disruption of Identity*, op. cit.

7 Grace became one of the most discussed themes in Christian theology, especially in the West. Justification by faith was at the heart of the Protestant Reformation and its explosion of theological thought. "How much more" has been taken by Paul Ricoeur as a way of conceiving the incarnation. Romans 6 has inspired much thought about Christian initiation in relation to the death and resurrection of Jesus. Romans 8 has been a key text for both trinitarian and ecological theologies of the past century. In the aftermath of the Holocaust, Romans 9–11 has been the focus of unprecedented discussion. Paul's idea of "the body of Christ" (in Romans and even more in 1 Corinthians) has been formative in many ecclesiologies, and in the twentieth century the Pentecostal and Charismatic movements have given rise to a vast literature on gifts of the Spirit within the church as the body of Christ.

8 For an excellent collection of recent work on Dante as theologian, see Vittorio Montemaggi and Matthew Treherne (eds.), *Dante's Commedia: Theology as Poetry* (University of Notre Dame Press, Notre Dame, 2010).

Index